# Sport and the American Dream

A publication of
Leisure Press
597 Fifth Avenue: New York, N.Y. 10017

Library of Congress Catalog Card Number: 82-83943

ISBN: 0-88011-112-7

Cover illustration: Caroline Arien

# Sport and the American Dream

## Howard L. Nixon II, Ph.D.

**LEISURE PRESS**

NEW YORK

DEDICATION TO MOM, DAD, SARA, MATTHEW, LUKE, AND DANIEL
who have encouraged and allowed me to pursue my own American
dreams and who are the biggest part of those dreams.

# Contents

# *Preface*

Sport and the American Dream are two salient dimensions of American consciousness. Sport occupies a prominent place in American popular culture and its imprint is seen in the sports talk, images, and personalities found in diverse realms of American life from business and politics to religion. The pursuit of the American Dream of achievement, mobility, and success continues to be a major driving force in the lives of the majority of Americans. This book is an effort to connect sport and the American Dream and examine the extent to which elements of the American Dream influence participants in the assorted realms of American sport, from Little League to professional and Olympic sports.

It is hoped that by looking at the connection between the American Dream and sport, it will be possible to see more clearly the extent to which the American Dream is a reality or a myth for those in sport as well as in American society in general. It should be evident from this book that sport mirrors many of the real and mythical elements of American society—including especially the competitive striving and success syndromes—even as it exists as a romanticized fantasyland in the minds of many fans. Both the mirror image and the fantasyland can be found in this treatment of sport and the American Dream.

The book is written for readers with sociological interest in American sport, but it also is written for a larger audience interested in sport but without any background in sociology. For this larger audience, discovery of the sociological perspectives and insights to be found in this book should open up new ways of looking at and understanding sport and its relationship to American society. For those unaccustomed to reading about sport from critical or sociological perspectives that penetrate the public masks and myths of sport and society to their reality, this book may seem to be jarring, disillusioning, unduly harsh, or even erroneous. Sport, however, like all human creations and despite our romantic myths, has real problems, shortcomings, and disappointments as well as real virtues. Reading about sport and the American Dream in these pages should help clarify both sides of sport and American society.

In an effort to make the book readable to as many people as possible, technical social science jargon has been avoided as much as possible. The author has attempted to translate the theoretical ideas and research findings that constituted the basis for this analysis of sport and the American Dream into language that is precise, clear and interesting. There is extensive use of concrete illustrations from the popular—usually journalistic—literature of sport. Many good sociological insights and some good evidence can be found on the pages of popular magazines such as *Sports Illustrated* and *Inside Sports*. It is hoped that by writing as clearly and simply as possible, the complexities of sport, the American Dream, and American society and their interconnections have not been oversimplified or misrepresented. It might be noted, parenthetically, that readers wishing to pursue topics in the text at greater length or in more technical terms can consult the relevant end notes for each chapter for either more extended comments or further reading references.

As always in an extensive writing project of this sort, there are many people to thank. First, I must thank Frank Manchel, who not only contributed a film commentary to this project but also helped inspire my original interest in it in our discussions about his book concerning "Great Sports Movies." Early support of this project also came from the Graduate College of the University of Vermont, which gave me a summer fellowship to begin work on it, and from my colleagues Jan Folta, Gordon Lewis, and Frank Sampson, who wrote letters of recommendation for my fellowship application. Gordon deserves additional mention for his help in securing photos for the book. Also worthy of thanks for their special help are Keith Scott Morton, Steve Pastner, Karlo Salminen, Dick Whittier, Roger Clow, Don Fillion, Bill DiLillo and the University of Vermont Photo Service, and Bill Cummings of GROUP II PHOTOGRAPHERS, who either contributed pictures, processed them, or made suggestions of how to obtain them. In fact, I found the collection and use of suitable photos almost as demanding as writing a chapter for this project. In regard to the cover, I would like to thank Chris and Fred Fengler for suggesting a contest among student artists at the University of Vermont , and I would like to thank Lynda McIntyre and her graphic arts students for accepting and responding to the challenge of my contest proposal. I am proud to have the work of one of those students, Caroline Arlen, on display on my cover. Through her artistic talents, she was able to create a striking and imaginative representation of central elements of the theme of "Sport and the American Dream." At Leisure Press, I want to make special mention of the assistance I received from the Publisher, Dr. James Peterson, and from the Managing Editor, Miriam Lamb. Finally, but not last in importance, I want to thank my wife, Sara, who probably is my toughest and best critic.

Howard L. Nixon II
Burlington, Vermont

# 1

# Sport, Society, and the American Dream

# Introduction

Even when Americans experience hard times, they seem to hang on to a vision or hope of a better life for themselves or their children. Studies of American values over the past few decades[1] have shown that Americans tend to care a great deal about achievement, success, material comfort, and "getting ahead." The combination of these values with others concerning equality of opportunity, ambitiousness, and hard work forms a complex of values regarding success and the means of attaining it that might be referred to as the "American Dream." This concept of the American Dream implies that the United States is a land of boundless opportunity in which upward social and economic mobility and "success" are regularly achieved by the ambitious and hard working, regardless of their social origins.

The concept, or "ideology," of the American Dream has been accepted as a matter of faith by believers in the American way of life. It reflects what many Americans in this century have believed to be central truths or real and universal possibilities of life in American society. In fact, all of us probably are familiar with some dramatic story of a self-made Horatio Alger type who was able to rise above his humble origins to achieve great riches, power, or fame. The avenues to success may vary in these stories: business, military, law, medicine, politics, entertainment, sports. However, a common theme in these stories is that seemingly insurmountable obstacles to success are overcome by relentless dedication and hard work.

Unfortunately, despite the many individual instances of "rags to riches" stories or even of "self-made" millionaires, the American Dream has been an overly romanticized myth, or perhaps a cruel hoax, for many segments of society including ethnic and racial minorities, women, the poor, and the less talented. There are many vantage points from which to examine how the American Dream *actually* is played out in the lives of American people. The purpose of this study is to explore the reality and myth of the American Dream through a sociologically oriented examination of the meaning and implications of opportunity, mobility, and success in sport.

Sport seems an ideal vehicle for understanding the pursuit of the American Dream both because achievement and success are so openly and explicitly emphasized in sport, and because the rags to riches story so often seems to be told by the contemporary mass media with sports figures as the main characters. It now seems part of the popular imagination that young men from humble social origins are regularly propelled into lives of instant celebrity and permanent financial security through the use of their physical gifts and hard work in professional athletic careers. The sociological perspective will enable us to penetrate beyond social myths and illusions about sport and the American Dream to the underlying social realities in sport and American society. By examining through the eyes of a sociologist how and how much "success" is pursued and achieved in various realms of sport, this study should reveal much about the actual social structure and dynamics of American society in general as well as sport in particular.

# Sport and Society through a Sociologist's Eyes

Sociological questions are motivated by an interest in looking critically at the commonly accepted, or officially defined, descriptions and explanations of social behavior. Sociologists do not accept beliefs about society or social interaction merely because they are widely accepted. Peter Berger has said there is a prominent "debunking motif" inherent in sociological consciousness? A sociologist believes assumptions about how and why people interact in various ways because these assumptions have been systematically tested and supported with concrete evidence. This critical or skeptical orientation might give sociologists a reputation for being "radical" or "cynical," especially as they appear to challenge traditionally accepted beliefs about society such as the American Dream. In fact, sociologists merely reserve judgment until they have gathered enough convincing facts.

What may make the critical or debunking tendency of sociologists seem annoying, offensive, or threatening is that the beliefs they challenge or want to test often are taken for granted by certain segments of society as basic premises underlying how they see their society and organize their actions in it. For example, many proponents of sport in America have taken for granted that sports involvement builds character, teaches discipline, and nurtures a sense of loyalty to the group. People who are committed to sport believe these assumptions and want others to believe them because they help give meaning and legitimacy to the institution of sport and their own involvement in it. Especially among those most committed to sport, failure to accept these beliefs or worse, the willingness to challenge or test their validity, may represent "troublemaking" or heresy.

Since people are not inclined to like those who seem to threaten the meaning or importance of what they do, it is little wonder that the work of sociologists is not always enthusiastically anticipated or warmly received. Nevertheless, if we are to understand the real meaning of social interaction and the causes and consequences of our actions in society, it is necessary to probe beneath the surface of social rules, roles, and relationships to determine whether tranditional, intuitive, or official interpretations of social reality are based on fact. It is through the eyes of the sociologist that we can search for the facts about sport, American society, and the American Dream.

Social organization is what sociologists study to uncover social facts. When people interact over time through verbal or nonverbal language, they exchange ideas and expectations about each other and the society around them. Through such exchanges, they learn or create a shared sense of what is important to them and how they should act toward each other and other members of society. When values, norms or rules, roles, and relationships that emerge from social interaction form patterns and persist over time in generally the same form, they become the core of social organization. The application of the sociological perspective to sport allows us to identify and explain patterns of social organization in sport that might reveal the extent to which the American Dream is a reality in sport.

Social organization is not static; it has a dynamic dimension. The dynamic element of society that can reinforce existing patterns of values, norms, roles, and relationships or transform them into new ones is a social process. A variety of social processes characterize the modes of interaction in sport and influence the character of the sports institution and its relationship to the rest of society. Competition is, of course, a fundamental mode of interaction in sport, but cooperation and conflict also are important social processes in sport. There are a number of other elementary and societal social processes that are important for understanding the changing character and implications of sport in American society. These other processes include socialization, deviance, social control, inequality and stratification in the allocation of social and economic rewards, status striving and social mobility, social discrimination, organizational growth and bureaucratization, professionalization, commercialization, urbanizations, demographic change, power, and organized challenges to authority and to established institutions and values.

By looking at the effects of elementary and societal social processes on the social organization of sport from the debunking perspective of the sociologist, it should be possible to separate myth from reality in regard to sport and the American Dream and to understand both better. However, the sociologist's ostensibly systematic and objective search for social facts should not delude us into believing that a sociologically oriented examination of sport and the American Dream will be free of value biases, misinterpretations of fact, and wrong conclusions. At times, sociologists seem to delude themselves by a myth of their own objectivity or value neutrality[3] Nevertheless, by recognizing they have personal values that influence the choice of research problems and methods of studying them and that *could* distort their interpretation of what they see or have found, sociologists may be able to step far enough back from the potentially distorting influence of their personal values to arrive at reasonably accurate or insightful interpretations of reality. We will assume that despite the many possible perceptions of social reality, sociologists as systematic social scientists mindful of their own shortcomings and biases are capable collectively of arriving at relatively consensual interpretations of many aspects of social reality. Thus, if systematically and consensually validated sociological knowledge is assumed to represent a relatively accurate perception of social reality, then it becomes possible to use sociological knowledge to distinguish myths and illusions about sport and the American Dream from reality. We will rely on the sociological perspective and sociological knowledge to examine the relationships between popular beliefs and what is actually known about the pursuit and attainment of social advancement and success in American society through participation in sport.

# Sport and Related Phenomena

The nature of sport is well understood by most of us on an experiential level because sports involvement, either as active participant or as spectator, is extremely popular in the United Stated and in many other nations. However, more than an experiential or intuitive understanding of the meaning of sport is required to be able to analyze its social organization, dynamics, and implications for other parts of society. The special definition of sport used in this analysis emphasizes sociologically interesting qualities, and it distinguishes sport from a number of other types of physical activities that tend to have different meaning and implications for their participants.

Sport is defined here as *institutionalized competitive activity involving two or more opponents and stressing physical exertion by serious competitors who represent or are part of formally organized associations*[4] This definition implies that an activity is sport when: (a) it is characterized by relatively persistent patterns of social organization; (b) it is serious competition (whose outcome is not pre-arranged) between two or more opponents; (c) it stresses the physical skill factor; and (d) it occurs within a formal organizational framework of teams, leagues, divisions, coaches, commissioners, sponsorship, formalized recruitment and replacement of personnel, rule books, and regulatory bodies. The total complex of sports-related values, beliefs, attitudes, roles, and relationships existing in a society is the sports institution of that society. To say that sport is an institutionalized activity emphasizes the standardization of rules, formal sponsorship by clubs and organizations, official enforcement of rules by regulatory bodies, stress on formal organization and technological aspects, formalized socialization into or desocialization out of roles, and the presence of spectators[5]

Institutionalization, bureaucratic organization, rational calculation in the pursuit of goals, emphasis on task performance, and seriousness distinguish sport from other types of physical activities such as play, recreation, and games. *Play* can be defined as voluntary, nonutilitarian activity chracterized by the freedom to innovate, spontaneity, and a lack of external regulation. Examples of physical play include children randomly kicking a ball to each other and engaging in a snowball fight.

*Recreation* can be defined as mostly voluntary activity that tends to be separated from the concerns of daily life and is aimed at refreshing the mind and/or body. Jogging and skiing with friends are examples of physical recreation. *Games* are relatively rule-bound and formalized activities that take on collective representations and are based on a combination of elements, which include competition, skill, chance, strategy, physical exertion, and/or pretense. A soccer or baseball contest after school between teams of neighborhood children illustrates the concept of a physical game. These examples of physical play, recreation, and games can be contrasted with examples of sport such as Little League or Major League baseball, interscholastic or intercollegiate athletics, Olympic competition, or the annual bowling tournament

## Figure 1.
## Distinctions among Types of Physical Activities

LOW AUTONOMY, EXPRESSIVENESS, SPONTANEITY,
SEPARATION FROM DAILY LIFE

Institutionalization,
bureaucratization,
rationalization                                                              **SPORT**

Formalization of
rules, external
regulation                                                                   **GAMES**

Development of
internal rules                                                               **RECREATION**

Relatively
unorganized and
unstructured
activity                                                                     **PLAY**

INCREASING ORGANIZATION, EXTERNAL REGULATION AND CONSTRAINT, SERIOUSNESS, INSTITUTIONALIZATION, RATIONALIZATION, BUREAUCRATIZATION, INSTRUMENTAL-TASK ORIENTATION

HIGH AUTONOMY, EXPRESSIVENESS, SPONTANEITY,
SEPARATION FROM DAILY LIFE

sponsored by the local community bowling league. The distinctions among these forms of physical activity might be seen more clearly in Figure 1[6]

A precise conception of sport enables us to make precise, valid, and meaningful assessments of generalizations about its impact on participants and its relationship to the social organization of the society in which it exists. Confusion with other types of physical activities can only lead to confusion about its meaning and implications for those involved in it. Confusion about the nature of sport in modern American society can be avoided not only by distinguishing it from other types of physical activities, but also by contrasting its modern characteristics with those of sport in earlier societies.

# Characteristics of Modern Sport

In his study of sport from ritual to record, Allen Guttmann has identified seven characteristics that have evolved historically to define the essential character of sport today? These characteristics are: secularism; a *principle* of equality of opportunity to compete and in the conditions of competition for contestants, specialization of roles, rationalization, bureaucratic organization, quantification of achievement, and the quest for records. In Guttmann's conception, the evolution of these characteristics from simpler or contrasting qualities has not been random. Rather, he has assumed that these characteristics have evolved in an interrelated pattern to form a coherent whole. For example, the modern quest for records would have little meaning without the practice of measuring performances. The ability to push performances to new record-setting levels often depends on greater specialization of athletic roles and greater rationalization of training and athletic technique. Specialization and rationalization, in turn, usually are associated with bureaucracy, which organizes championship events, establishes rules for them, and certifies records attained during them.

The replacement of the religious significance of sporting events with secular motivation can be seen in the modern tendency to pursue records rather than to try to achieve salvation or to glorify God through athletic performance. Some observers of modern sport in the United States[8] have seen its passions, rituals, and myths as components of a new "secular religion." However, Guttmann has argued that despite this characterization, the attachment of modern sports to the realm of the transcendent no longer exists. If sports are not pursued because athletes want to set records—or because they are professionals paid to compete or bureaucratic employees obligated to compete—sports may be pursued for their own sake. However, sports for their own sake still do ideological commitment or commitment *in principle* in modern societies to equalize opportunities to participate and to assure that the conditions of actual competition are the same for all participants, the reality of modern sport has failed to live up to this egalitarian principle. In American society, race, color, religion, sex, age, occupation, social class, sports background, and physical stature or other physical characteristics have affected opportunities for involvement and achievement in a variety of sports roles and domains. Not only are these various forms of social discrimination inconsistent with the egalitarian ideology of American democracy, they also fail to conform to the emphases on merit and evenhandedness that are supposed to characterize the dominant organizational form of modern American society and sport, which is rational-legal bureaucracy. Of course, an irony of modern sport is that the emphasis on equality *of opportunity*, which itself is not completely realized, coexists with an inherent tendency toward inequality *of results*. In sports events, there is a precise and unmistakable inequality in the ranking of winners and losers. Guttmann has pointed out that this inequality in the outcome of sports events often is used to justify inequality or social stratification in other areas of society, such as education and the workplace, where opportunity and the conditions of competition are more unequal than in sport.

Since a belief in equality of opportunity is a basic aspect of the American Dream, the "equality" characteristic of modern sport has special relevance to our assessment of the validity of the American Dream as it relates to sport. Concrete sports systems or domains of sport in the United States embody in varying degrees this equality characteristic and other defining qualities of modern sport that have been identified here. A major focus of this examination of sport and the American Dream will be to analyze how and why different sports systems in the United States—from youth leagues to interscholastic and intercollegiate athletics, high-level amateur sports outside the school, and professional competition—enhance or inhibit the *actual practice* of equality of opportunity and the attainment of success and social advancement by the enthusiastic, dedicated, hard-working, and talented.

# The American Dream: An Ideology of Opportunity, Social Advancement, and Success in American Society

At the beginning of this chapter, it was suggested that the themes of equality of opportunity, achievement, success, striving, hard work, and social advancement form a vision of the "good life" in American society, which has come to be known as the American Dream. The attainment of upward social or economic mobility, or the improvement of one's position or status in society, that is at the heart of the American Dream can be seen as more than a perceived privilege or birthright of every American. It can be viewed as an *obligation*. In a society with a fundamental value of, or ideological commitment to, individual achievement and success, it is expected that an effort will be made to improve one's social and economic status. Those who remain content with their status or achievements are perceived by others as deviant[9] Thus, the American Dream is both a source of hope for the striving and ambitious and a form of social control over those who might be tempted to reject such values and the institutional structure built on them.

The American Dream helps reinforce commitment to America's traditional value system, which has been referred to as the work ethic, the Protestant Ethic, the achievement ideology, and the ideology of individualism. This value system, or ideology, has given legitimacy to the fundamental social institutions of American society, and it can be seen as comprising the following core beliefs:[10]

- Each individual should work hard and try to succeed in competition with others.
- Individuals who work hard should be rewarded with symbols of success such as money, property, fame, and power.
- The existence of widespread and equal opportunity will enable those who work hard to be rewarded with success.
- Social or economic failure is an individual's own fault and reflects a lack of effort and other deficiencies in character.

In proposing that the American Dream of equal opportunity for all who have ability is a powerful ideological force in American society, Ephraim Mizruchi[11] chose the term "ideological" with a clear understanding of what it implies. The American Dream as an ideology has the capacity to help less successful groups to adjust to the disparity between their objective social circumstances and the dream of success by being a set of beliefs and sentiments that provide such groups with a continuing source of hope, which may be quite unrealistic but still gives their lives meaning *within* the *existing* value system and structure of their society. In this sense, the ideology of the American Dream is an *argument* for the virtues of the American way of life, and as an ideology, the American Dream performs a social control function.

The ideology of the American Dream helps discourage dissent by blaming those who do not succeed for their own failure. Without wanting to rationalize or excuse failure, it still must be recognized that explaining failure almost entirely in terms of individual deficiencies ignores the influence of external or structural obstacles to advancement and success.[12] However, as long as one accepts the ideology of the American Dream, failure, like success, will be viewed as an individual matter. In direct contrast to success, though, the experience of failure could have a shattering effect on self-esteem while posing little threat to existing social structures that may be the most significant reason why ambition has been frustrated. Biases in the social structure against blacks, women, Jews, the poor, those with the "wrong" social background, those who are older, or those with physical disabilities often prevent members of these groups from gaining access to the avenues to success or from fully attaining the resources needed to attain success. The ideology of the Americajn Dream tends to obscure these biases or obstacles, but the sociological perspective draws attention to them because they are aspects of social organization.

The goal of success that is the ultimate aim of the pursuers of the American Dream has a variety of possible interpretations. For politicians, it may be political power. For businessmen, it may be profits. For teachers, it may be the nurturing of educated minds. For the religiously devout, it may be salvation. Transcending many of these specific interpretations is a general interpretation of success that derives from American capitalism and its emphasis on the individual accumulation of private property or material possessions. It is the equating of success with money. In American society, money is valued not only as an end in itself and as a means of buying goods, but also as a means of symbolically representing one's social rank and personal worth.

Although some form of success is the pot of gold at the end of the road to the American Dream, it is success *by achievement* that is legitimized by this ideology. Robin Williams[13] has offered a useful distinction between "achievement" and "success" by proposing that achievement refers to valued accomplishments or performances and is associated with work, while success is represented by rewards as money, power, and fame. This distinction implies that success can be attained illegitimately without valued accomplishments or performances as well as legitimately by achievement. It also implies that achievement is not necessarily associated with a proportionate level of success, as in the case of the artistic or musical genius whose work is largely unappreciated during his or her lifetime. In sport, it can be seen that the strong emphasis on success as winning and the large sums of money and substantial fame or honor that reward athletic success often undermine the desire for legitimate achievement, encourage the pursuit of success by illegitimate or deviant means such as cheating, and leave many honest achievers with little more than their personal integrity as reward.

It may be that American values generally have evolved to the point where throughout society, success often is pursued without regard for achievement. Christopher Lasch has argued in his recent critique of American life and culture that a new ideal of success has evolved, and this ideal has no content.[14] "Success equals success." That is, success is the projection of an image, or more precisely, a winning image. It is a creation of professional image-makers, whether in sports, business, politics, or elsewhere in society, and it may have little or no relevance to actual or legitimate accomplishments. We all are familiar with the packaging and polishing of the public image of political candidates whose stands on issues remain fuzzy even as their personalities are presented to us as "winners" or as "leaders" whom we can trust.[15] If Lasch is correct, equality of opportunity, achievement, and mobility would seem to have new or diminished meaning in relation to success, and the ideology of the American Dream would seem to be on shaky ground. This possibility makes the assessment of the American Dream in regard to sport, where a winning image is so important, especially interesting.

# The Dominant American Sports Creed: Beliefs about the Functions of Sport in America

If the American Dream is an expression of traditional beliefs about the virtues of American society, then it should be possible to see components of this ideology in traditional beliefs about the virtues of organized sports participation in American society. In fact, free and open competition for advancement and success, which is what the ideology of the American Dream assumes about the nature of opportunity in American society in general, has been identified *in principle* as a defining characteristic of the nature of modern American sport. The belief that sport provides opportunities for individuals to enhance their status and achieve success is part of the set of beliefs about the functions of American sport that Harry Edwards has called the "dominant American sports creed."[16] The degree of integration of this sports creed with the ideology of the American Dream and dominant American value orientations in general can be seen more clearly by looking more closely at the full expression of creedal themes.

Harry Edwards has conducted the most systematic investigation of beliefs about American sport. He surveyed statements about the nature and consequences of sport in America that had appeared in newspapers, magazines, and a leading athletic journal, and he formulated his conception of the dominant American sports creed on the basis of that research. Like the set of beliefs that represents the American Dream, the beliefs about the effects of American sport contained in this sports creed were seen by Edwards as an ideology aimed at convincing people of the benefits or virtues of organized sports participation. Presumably, public adherence to the various core themes of the American sports creed will help resolve conflicts, alleviate anxieties, and overcome doubts engendered by sports involvement. Widespread public adherence to this creed may be expected to reinforce the institutional stability of sport. To the degree the creed is integrated with the value system of American society in general, popular acceptance of the creed may be expected to reflect or reinforce acceptance of traditional American value systems, such as the ideology of the American Dream, and contribute to acceptance of established institutional patterns throughout the society.

The creedal beliefs identified by Edwards are expressed by the following seven central themes, which encompass twelve specific categories of belief:

1. Sports builds *character*, which implies that sport (a) contributes to the development of such character traits as "redbloodedness," clean living, and proper grooming; (b) teaches loyalty; and (c) encourages altruism.
2. Sport teaches *discipline*, including (d) both self-control and obedience to authority.
3. Sport provides *competition* and develops competitiveness, which (e) help create fortitude, courage, perseverance, and aggressiveness; (f) prepare athletes to meet the challenges of life in the larger society outside sport; and (g) enable them to improve themselves and "get ahead" in both sport and the larger society.
4. Sport (h) enhances *physical fitness*.
5. Sport enhances *mental fitness* by (i) contributing to mental alertness and (j) encouraging educational achievement.
6. Sport contributes to *religiosity* by (k) encouraging acceptance of traditional religious precepts of American Christianity.
7. Sport contributes to *nationalism* by (l) encouraging acceptance of patriotic values and expression of patriotic symbols.

It is interesting that winning is not explicitly included in Edwards' conception of major creedal themes. He has explained the absence of this theme by proposing that its significance is *implicitly* understood by all who participate in sport. After all, the challenge and excitement of sports competition generallly are thought to result from opponents trying as hard as they can to win the contest. Of course, those who view sport as an honorable enterprise would add that participants in American sport learn that the attempt to win must not go beyond the rules of the competition and the code of sportsmanship that define the limits of fair play. Such believers in American sport and its dominant creed are likely to assume, or at least publicly claim, that superior development and demonstration of the central creedal qualities of character, discipline, competitiveness, physical and mental fitness, religiosity, and nationalism will lead to victory and success for sports participants. Apparently, it is not necessary to mention winning explicitly as part of the dominant American sports creed as long as one believes that virtue will be rewarded. The sports creed is similar to the ideology of the American Dream in this regard because both ideologies imply that virtuous striving within culturally approved channels will be appropriately rewarded.

Although the value of winning may not explicitly appear as a central theme in the dominant American sports creed, there have been a number of prominent coaches who have candidly expressed some rather emphatic views about the importance of winning. For example, legendary Green Bay Packer football coach Vince Lombardi said that "Winning is not everything; it is the only thing"; and his words almost have become a cliché among followers of sport. His sentiments have been publicly shared by others in his profession, such as George Allen, who said that "Winning is living." He also said that "Every time you win, you're reborn; when you lose, you die a little." To these comments can be added another set in a similar vein by Don Shula, who said that "No one ever learns anything by losing."[17] At times, statements about winning have turned from the emphatic to the outrageous as in the cases of former major league baseball manager Leo Durocher, who said, "Show me a good loser in professional sports, and I'll show you an idiot. Show me a sportman, and I'll show you a player I'm looking to trade," and former University of Minnesota basketball coach Bill Musselman, who posted this message over the entrance to his team's shower: "Defeat Is Worse Than Death Because You Have To Live With Defeat."[18]

Those who have expressed relatively extreme views about the significance of winning often have made their living from the accumulation of entries in the victory column, and might be excused or at least understood for this reason. However, it should not be thought that the value of winning in sport has been emphasized only by those who earn their livelihood from sport. For example, former President Gerald Ford, once a star football player at the University of Michigan, may have spoken for many followers of sport not professionally involved in it when he said: "It is not enough to just compete. Winning is very important . . . In athletics and in most other worthwhile pursuits first place is the manifestation of the desire to excel, and how else can you achieve anything?"[19] He added that winning may even be more important in politics than sports because if you do not win elections you do not get to play the game.

Despite the widely acknowledged importance of winning, or perhaps a winning image, in sport and elsewhere in American society, singleminded devotion to winning at any cost makes many people uneasy. Even professional coaches and others whose jobs depend on their ability to win usually temper their comments about winning with claims about the virtues of sports participation expressed in the dominant American sports creed. Success without virtuous achievement does not conform to the sports creed. Promoters of the creed, such as physical educators, sports administrators, those who market sport or are responsible for its public image, speakers on the sports banquet circuit, and devoted sports fans, are likely to minimize the more unsavory connotations of the pursuit of victory and emphasize instead the virtues or benefits that derive from competition and the excitement generated by a hard-fought but fairly-played contest. As long as the reputation of sport can be protected from offensive, embarrassing, or unsavory excesses by emphasizing its connection to dominant value orientations such as the American Dream, its appeal will be preserved and the dominant values it is perceived to represent will be reinforced.

In expressing his faith in organized sports, Gerald Ford asserted that: "... outside of a national character and an educated society, there are few things more important to a country's growth and well-being than competitive athletics. If it is a cliché to say athletics build character as well as muscle, then I subscribe to the cliché."[20] On the basis of his search for evidence to test the beliefs contained in the dominant American sports creed, Edwards concluded that the creedal themes may indeed be nothing more than clichés. He was unable to find a consistent pattern of systematic evidence to support any of the beliefs in the creed. One of these beliefs even seemed to be refuted by existing evidence. The rejection of this belief concerning physical fitness may be particularly surprising because it is the one we are most likely to take for granted. However, Edwards argued that the injury rate for organized sports participation makes it a rather risky undertaking for our physical well-being.

A limited amount of systematic research may account for the lack of substantiation of most of the beliefs of the dominant American sports creed. Nevertheless, Edwards' assessment of its validity is striking because it suggest that the absence of substantiation has not deterred proponents of sport—including Gerald Ford—from expressing unqualified faith in its claimed virtues. This type of faith, typical of ideologies, makes the validity of the creed difficult to challenge or even test. Yet, the testing of ideological assumptions about opportunity, social advancement, and success embodied in the American Dream by looking at the actual structure, dynamics, and functions of participation in sport is precisely the aim of this book. This testing of the ideology of the American Dream is bound to subject certain explicit and implicit beliefs of the dominant American sports creed to critical scrutiny as well because the basic tenets of both ideologies are so closely intertwined.

# Avenues of Social Mobility and Success in and through Sport

The picture of American sport provided by the dominant American sports creed suggests that the American Dream is alive in organized sport. However, even if we overlook the obstacles to sports success, achievement, and participation in the United States, the manner by which the American Dream might be achieved in or through sports participation may not be evident. In fact, there are a variety of possible avenues of social advancement or mobility and success in and through sport in America.

To understand how sport might provide opportunities for social mobility, it is necessary to understand a few basic facts about the concept of mobility. First, people may move up the social hierarchy to higher-ranking positions. For example, bat boys may grow up to become major league baseball stars or managers. People also may slip down the social hierarchy, as in the case of onetime boxing champions returning penniless to the mean streets from which they came. Social mobility can be measured *intra*generationally in terms of the ups and downs in a person's own lifetime, or *inter*generationally in terms of the relationship between a person's position in the social hierarchy and the position attained by this person's parents. In the latter regard, people may rise above or sink below their social origins.

Social mobility is possible when the social hierarchy of a society or social system is open, allowing people to move up or down by their own accomplishments or failures, by sponsorship, assistance, or interference from others, or by other means. A basic distinction can be drawn between equal opportunity or "circulation" mobility and structural or "forced" mobility[21] Circulation mobility is brought about by hard work, ability, and an assortment of other achievement-related personal attributes under conditions of equal opportunity and equal competition. This concept of mobility readily comes to mind when thinking about the American Dream.

In the case of forced mobility, people move up or down the social hierarchy because the number of available higher-ranking positions has expanded or contracted or because demand for their specialized skills, training, or other performance attributes has increased or decreased. Illustrations of expansion and contraction of opportunities for prestige and success in sport are the creation and elimination of professional sports leagues and clubs and the addition and subtraction of tournaments in sports such as professional golf and tennis. Demand may be influenced by patterns of expansion or contraction in sport and by changes in the rules of particular sports that make their division of labor more or less complex. A rule change in the American League of Major League Baseball that made its division of labor more complex involved the creation of the position of "designated hitter." As a result of this new position, a number of aging batting stars have had their careers extended and some good hitters with less than flawless fielding skills have been given a chance to play major league baseball.

John Loy has suggested that there are at least four avenues to upward social mobility that can be pursued by sports participants.[22]

- Early athletic involvement and development of athletic skills could lead to recruitment or direct entry into professional sport.
- Athletic participation could directly or indirectly enhance educational attainment by motivating better academic achievement to maintain athletic eligibility, by increasing the possibility of graduation as a result of a commitment to remain in school to participate in sports, or by providing an athletic scholarship.
- Participation in sports could lead to various forms of "occupational sponsorship" by which a former athlete is given special treatment in hiring or promotion.
- Sports participation could facilitate upward mobility by teaching attitudes and behavior patterns such as achievement orientation or leadership that are valued in the occupational world outside sport. This function of sports participation is implied by the "competition" theme of the dominant American sports creed.

In addition to providing opportunities for mobility in the occupational world, in professional sport, and in or through education, sport provides chances to achieve upward—or downward—mobility in the informal social systems of peers that are so important during childhood and adolescence. The rewards of esteem and social power that accrue to successful child and adolescent athletes may be as meaningful and valuable to them as the fame, riches, or influence associated with athletic achievement in more publicized and commercialized domains of "big-time" sports. Thus, this assessment of the reality and myth of the American Dream and of the implications of pursuing it will include an examination of children's sports as well as "big-time" sports for older youth and adults.

The implicit or explicit stress on winning at all costs has encouraged some sports participants to strive for success by means other than honest achievement. The blocking of avenues of legitimate achievement or success for sports participants highly motivated to achieve and succeed could lead to cheating. This form of deviance, arising from a discrepancy between socially approved goals such as winning and the availability of socially approved avenues of achieving them, has been called "anomie" by Robert Merton.[23] The prevalence of anomie in society can be a significant measure of the extent of actual acceptance of norms, values, and other beliefs legitimizing the basic institutional structure of society. Extensive anomic cheating in sport could indicate a decline in influence of the dominant ideologies of sport and society, and a breakdown in cultural integration and in the legitimacy of authority in sport and in other major institutions of society. Therefore, the pattern of choice of means by which sports participants strive for mobility and success could indicate the institutional stability of sport and other social institutions by reflecting the amount of commitment to values such as hard work and achievement, which are central components of dominant ideologies in sport and the larger society.

# Summary and a Glance Ahead

This book is an attempt to assess the validity and implications of faith in the American Dream through an analysis of opportunity, mobility, and success in various realms of American sport. Sport is an appropriate vehicle for testing the ideology of the American Dream because the legitimizing beliefs of the sports institution mirror basic tenets of the American Dream. The American Dream conjures up images of "rags to riches" success stories, of self-made men, and of virtuous achievement by sweat and hard work being duly rewarded. The spectacular financial success and fame of athletes from modest social origins would seem to give substance to these images and reinforce the ideology that explains them. Indeed, professional sports careers and athletic scholarships to attend college have been counted among the most important tickets to success for black American males. Despite the strong faith in such visions of the American Dream, there may be some question about the factual basis for this faith.[24] The actual structures of sports opportunity and patterns of sports striving, mobility, and success must be systematically examined and analyzed to determine whether faith in the American Dream in regard to sport is justified. The debunking perspective of the sociologist will be used here to test the validity of this ideology through sport.

The chapters following this one will look at various dimensions of the American Dream in different realms of organized sport in the United States. In the next chapter, opportunity, achievement and success orientations, and social advancement in children's sports outside the school will be examined. Interscholastic and intercollegiate athletics will be the subjects of the third and fourth chapters, respectively. In the fifth chapter, the pursuit of the American Dream in professional and Olympic sports will be examined. Since considerably more research and writing have focused on the professional than Olympic realm, the main focus of the fifth chapter will be on professional sports. However, Olympic sports merit consideration along with professional sports because these two sports worlds can be seen as sharing the top rung of the organized sports hierarchy in the United States. For amateur athletes in sports such as speed skating, cross country skiing, swimming, and rowing, which offer no chance of professional competitive careers, Olympic competition is the highest realm of sport to which they can aspire. In each of the first five chapters, special attention will be paid to structural obstacles and forms of discrimination blocking realization of the American Dream by groups such as minorities, women, and the lower classes. In the sixth chapter, the focus will shift to the boom in leisure "sports" and recreation over the past decade in relation to American life styles and the pursuit of personal happiness and fulfillment. In the final chapter, the implications of the previous chapters for faith in the American Dream will be explored.

# *Footnotes*

[1]Among these studies are Robin M. Williams, Jr., *American Society*, 3rd ed. (New York: Knopf, 1970); Ephraim H. Mizruchi, *Success and Opportunity* (New York: Free Press, 1964); Milton Rokeach, *The Nature of Human Values* (New York: Free Press, 1973); H. Kent Geiger, "American values through the eyes of expert observers" (Unpublished manuscript, Department of Sociology, University of Wisconsin, 1974); and Kay Lehman Schlozman and Sidney Verba, *Injury to Insult* (Cambridge: Harvard University Press, 1979).

[2]Peter Berger, *Invitation to Sociology* (New York: Anchor Books, 1963), pp. 25-53.

[3]The topic "Divergent theoretical perspectives and the problem of values (in sport and sociology)" is discussed in Richard S. Gruneau's article "Sport as an area of sociological study: an introduction to major themes and perspectives," which appeared in Gruneau's coedited volume (with John G. Albinson) *Canadian Sport: Sociological Perspectives* (Don Mills, Ontario: Addison-Wesley Canada Ltd., 1976). Gruneau notes the difference between "objectivity" and "value neutrality," and he discusses the problems associated with both mechanistic applications of a natural scientific model of sociological inquiry and attempts to discard the guise of scientific objectivity in favor of ideological criticism. Gruneau proposes that the link between personal values and interpretations of evidence should be identified and that conclusions should be reached only after reflexively and critically examining what is known from several dimensions of opposing theoretical perspectives.

[4]This definition of sport originally was presented in Howard L. Nixon II, *Sport and Social Organization* (Indianapolis: Bobbs-Merrill, 1976), p. 8.

[5]These dimensions of the institutionalization of sport have been discussed by Jay J. Coakley in *Sport in Society: Issues and controversies* (St. Louis: C.V. Mosby, 1978), pp. 9-10.

[6]The definitions of forms of physical activities and the figure portraying differences among these forms have been influenced by the work of Harry Edwards, *Sociology of Sport* (Homewood, Illinois: Dorsey Press, 1973) and Gruneau (in Gruneau and Albinson) as well as by Nixon's *Sport and Social Organization*.

[7]Allen Guttmann, *From Ritual to Record: The Nature of Modern Sports* (New York: Columbia University Press, 1978), ch. 2.

[8]Edwards, *Sociology of Sport* and Michael Novak, *The Joy of Sports* (New York: Basic Books, 1976).

[9]For an analysis of this theme, see Irvin Wyllie, *The Self Made Man in America* (New Brunswick: Rutgers University Press, 1954); Robert K. Merton, "Social structure and anomie," *Social Theory and Social Structure* (New York: Free Press, 1957); and Mizruchi, *Success and Opportunity*.

[10]These interpretations of the American value system and this statement of its core beliefs have been drawn from Joe R. Feagin, "The ideology of individualism: views of the poor," *Subordinating the Poor: Welfare and American Beliefs* (Englewood Cliffs, New Jersey: Prentice-Hall, 1975). Feagin, in turn, developed his conception of this

value system by drawing from the work of Robin Williams, *American Society,* and Harold L. Wilensky and Charles N. Lebeaux, *Industrial Society and Social Welfare* (New York: Free Press, 1965), pp. 34-35.

[11]Ephraim H. Mizruchi, "Social class and social values," *Stratification and Mobility,* by Mark Abrahamson, Ephraim H. Mizruchi, and Carlton A. Hornung (New York: Macmillan, 1976), p. 245. Reprinted from Mizruchi, *Success and Opportunity.*

[12]Alvin Boskoff (in "Social failure in modern society: a reformulation and a tentative theoretical framework," *Sociological Inquiry,* 52 [Spring 1982]: 89-105) discusses the phenomenon of social failure as a normal accompaniment of social systems in the form of categorical blockage of opportunity as well as that of social incompetence or social misfitting. In his discussion, Boskoff reviews the apparent structural sources of social misfitting (where the abilities and/or performances of people are unequal to the social demands or goals of their social positions), analyzes problematic deviant or dysfunctional consequences of social misfitting, and identifies general patterns of adaptive behavior among social incompetents. Boskoff notes that the ideology of upward mobility—or the American Dream, in our terms—emphasizes the more positive aspects of one's qualifications, which we may see as a source of deception about the genuine capacity of many individuals to perform well enough to be successful and attain their American Dream.

[13]Williams, *American Society,* 2nd ed. (1960), p. 419.

[14]Christopher Lasch, *The Culture of Narcissism: American Life in An Age of Diminishing Expectations* (New York: Warner Books, 1979), p. 96.

[15]In *The Selling of the President 1968* (New York: Trident, 1969), Joe McGinniss has written about how the Nixon presidential candidacy was created and sold to the public through skillful advertising and public relations techniques often devoid of real political substance. Though one might argue with McGinniss' portrait of Richard Nixon's personality or motives, there is little question that Nixon's skillful use of TV advertising techniques helped get him elected or that media-oriented campaigns geared to market an attractive "package" have become common in American politics since Nixon's success in 1968.

[16]Edwards, *Sociology of Sport.* This brief overview of the dominant American sports creed relies heavily on Nixon's summary (in *Sport and Social Organization*) of Edwards' work.

[17]These quotes were taken from the discussion of competition and success values in sport by D. Stanley Eitzen and George H. Sage, *Sociology of American Sport* (Dubuque, Iowa: Wm. C. Brown, 1978), pp. 66-67.

[18]These quotes were included in a discussion of symptoms of the craze for winning by Thomas Tutko and William Bruns, *Winning is Everything and Other American Myths* (New York: Macmillan, 1976), ch. 2.

[19]Gerald R. Ford with John Underwood, "In defense of the competitive urge," *Sports Illustrated* (July 8, 1974).

[20]*Ibid.*

[21]This discussion of facts about social mobility was drawn from the work of Abrahamson, Mizruchi, and Hornung, *Stratification and Mobility,* ch. 7, and Daniel W. Rossides, *The American Class System: An Introduction to Social Stratification* (Boston: Houghton Mifflin, 1976), pp. 89-94.

[22]John W. Loy, "The study of sport and social mobility," *Aspects of Contemporary Sport Sociology,* ed. by Gerald S. Kenyon (Chicago: Athletic Institute, 1969).

[23]Robert K. Merton, "Social structure and anomie," *American Sociological Review,* 3 (1938): 672-682.

[24]Schlozman and Verba (in *Injury to Insult*) found substantial and widespread acceptance of the American Dream, even among those in lower occupational groups and those who were unemployed. Their research was based on a survey of a representative sample of members of the metropolitan labor force—including those out of work—in the United States in the mid-1970s.

# 2

# Children and Sport

# *Introduction*

Jerry Izenberg grew up with a passionate love for sport "as a kind of wall-to-wall Camelot." However, he wrote *How Many Miles to Camelot? The American Sport Myth*[1] after over twenty years in the press box. In this book, he looked beyond his boyhood myths and illusions about sport and beyond sport's public face of glamour, excitement, and virtue that is all many of us ever see. Instead of Camelot, he found a world with the same warts that are elsewhere in society. Surely, there were inspiring acts of courage and remarkable people who embodied the best the American Dream is meant to convey. Along with these noble efforts and great accomplishments, though, he found misguided ambition, selfishness, dishonesty, hypocrisy, exploitation, violence, and prejudice. Perhaps surprisingly, the warts Isenberg saw were not confined to adult sports.

Izenberg did not find Camelot in the world of children's sports. Symbolic of what bothered him about children's sports is the picture of tears streaming down the cheeks of a ten, eleven, or twelve year-old whose team has just lost the Little League World Series, the Pop Warner Championship, or some other cherished title for preadolescent athletes. The tears evoke our sympathy because they reflect obvious disappoint-ment and emotional pain, but they also might raise questions about the nature of ostensibly playful activities that can leave such a deep emotional mark on children.

Of course, Little League baseball, Pop Warner football, Pee Wee hockey, and even the annual swimming race for children at the town beach are not play at all. They are *sports* activities that are organized, sponsored, and run by adults. The presence of adult influence in children's physical activities injects elements of organization, seriousness, and ambition that transform these activities from playlike ones into more institutionalized and rationalized sports. In emphasizing hard work, competition, achievement, improvement, and success, the adults who control these sports programs are unwittingly or intentionally thrusting the young participants into a world of adult emotions, aspirations, and responsibilities. They also are teaching these youngsters about the ideology of the American Dream. Since this ideology accentuates the importance of success and ascribes failure or defeat to individual shortcomings, it is little wonder that young athletes who have been taught it strive so hard to win, or at least to avoid defeat, and react so emotionally to losing.

In this chapter, we will look more closely at the nature of adult-controlled sports programs for children and at the meanings children learn to attribute to core elements of the American Dream such as effort, achievement, ambition, and success as a result of sports participation. We also will look at the opportunities for achievement and success provided to children by sports and at the types of motivation, ambition, and social adjustment that are shaped by exposure to adult models of the American Dream in sports programs such as Little League.

# Decline of the Play Element in Children's Physical Activities

Edward Devereux has argued that Little League baseball and other similar major sports programs for children are threatening to wipe out the spontaneous culture of play, recreation, and games among children.[1] He also has contended that children deprived of opportunities to create and experience their own play culture may miss valuable developmental learning experiences as well as the enjoyment of playing in a world of their own making. By organizing and supervising programs such as Little League for children, adults deprive children of chances for autonomy, initiative, expressiveness, creativity, rule-making and enforcement, and conflict resolution that are needed to establish independent and mature moral judgment and a secure and socially adjusted personality. In addition, the dominance of children's sports by adult rules, values, and emotions that may be highly complex or inconsistent and by adult ambitions that may be unrealistic or unreasonable for most children could cause a "loss of childhood innocence" that the young athletes are not yet mature enough to handle. This premature loss of innocence could lead to cynicism, insecurity, or confusion about values, rules, and self-identity.

If "Little Leaguism"[3]—or adult-controlled children's sports—prematurely thrusts children into a world of adults, it could confront them with responsibilities for effort, achievement, and success they are not yet physically or emotionally equipped to assume. The obligation to fulfill the American Dream of success as a sports champion is a big responsibility for a ten year-old Little Leaguer. Devereux has pointed out that children need to experiment with their skills and emotions in a relatively safe environment to master their anxieties and to develop a sense of security and self-confidence. In the world of children's play, recreation, and games, where kids temporarily suspend reality and make and alter their own rules, there is the kind of safety or freedom children need for experimentation and socio-emotional development. In the world of adult-controlled sports programs, children often perform under the critical eyes of adults and they learn their actions often will have serious consequences for the way they will be seen and treated by others. Thus, in the environment of sports programs controlled by adults, children may miss the chance to learn and develop valuable skills and qualities that could enhance their sense of personal competence, social adjustment. and maturity. Ironically, these are skills and qualities claimed by the dominant American sport creed to be benefits of organized sports participation. As Devereux has suggested,

Little League baseball is superior to the more informal games of "backyard baseball" as a vehicle of anticipatory socialization for high school, college, and professional sports, but these gains in sports "professionalization" are achieved at the expense of a number of valuable and enjoyable developmental and educational experiences that are more closely associated with play, recreation, or games.

Even though Little Leaguism may prepare youngsters for adult roles in and out of sport and teach them about the serious pursuit of the American Dream, it may provide only a relatively narrow concept of strategies for coping and success in a competitive society or activity. John Roberts and Brian Sutton-Smith[4] have observed that different types of games represent microcosms of social systems in which varied styles of competing and of winning and losing are incorporated into the social structure. By participating in a wide variety of game types, in which elements of skill, chance, and strategy are combined in different structures of varying complexity, children have an opportunity to experiment with a range of *different* success styles as well as experience a number of new and different ways of thinking and expressing feelings about the world and their relationships with other people. Thus, the spontaneous, self-initiated, and self-organized culture of play, recreation, and games of children, with its potentially infinite variety, allows children to learn how to cope, achieve, and be successful in a variety of contexts and at varying levels of complexity *appropriate to their stage of development.* The constriction of the culture of children through the increasing imposition of a narrowly and formally defined Little Leaguism model on their culture of physical activity and fun could lead to the constriction of the coping styles, achievement orientations, and success strategies they follow as adults. It could lead to an unimaginative and limited vision of the pursuitof the American Dream.

In general, then, the decline of the play element in children's physical activities represented by the growth of Little Leaguism could deprive many children of valuable developmental and educational benefits they would gain from activities they initiate and control themselves, and it could teach them a very limited conception of achievement and success. In addition, the growth of Little Leaguism, with its emphasis on winning and excellence, could leave many children on the sidelines in the race to capture the American Dream. As Devereux has observed, "Almost inevitably, in a highly organized, competitive sport, the focus is on winning and the eye is on the ball. How often does the well-intentioned volunteer coach ... really think about what kind of total experience his boys are having, including those who have warmed the bench all afternoon, or who were not selected for League competition?"[5] The meaning, implications, and problems of the growth of Little Leaguism in the lives of American children and the conception of the American Dream it conveys to them will be examined more fully after looking at the emergence and structure of adult-controlled sports programs for children.

# The Emergence and Structure of Little Leaguism in the United States

At the beginning of this century, American sports programs generally were organized and supervised by professional educators in the schools.[6] However, as a result of philosophical questioning of the value of highly organized sports competition for preadolescents, American educators in the 1930s decided against providing organized sports programs for this age group in the schools. The sentiments of educators at that time were not fully shared by adults outside the schools. Consequently, many boys' clubs were formed to assume responsibility for organizing sports opportunities for children and adolescents. The voluntary sector, consisting mostly of parents, acted to fill a perceived void in the experiences of children that was created by the decision by the schools not to sponsor sports programs for children. The results of their action has been the establishment of the adult-controlled sports programs for children to which the term "Little Leaguism" refers.

The growth of Little League itself hardly qualifies it as a "voluntary" organization today. In fact, Little League Baseball was established in 1939 and is now an incorporated business organization with a staff of full-time professional employees. This organization has grown from one league in its inaugural year to 3,976 leagues in 1955 and 6,887 leagues in 1976[6] The entire network of officially sponsored Little League competition includes children from eight to eighteen years of age, and Little League constitutes the world's largest sports organization for children and youth. It has leagues in thirty-one nations, and it has more than two and one-half million competitors. Its annual centerpiece event, the Little League World Series in Williamsport, Pennsylvania, receives national television coverage in the United States and in other competing countries.

Although Little League Baseball, Inc. is the largest adult-controlled sports program for children and rightfully merits recognition in the term used here—i.e., "Little Leaguism"—to characterize such programs in general, it is not the only large children's sports program in the United States. Figures presented in 1974[8] revealed that about one million boys played tackle football in organized leagues such as Pop Warner programs, 1.2 million entrants aged eight to thirteen were involved in the Ford Motor Company's "Punt, Pass, and Kick" contest in 1973, organized golf and bowling associations each listed about 1.2 million junior members, including youths of high school age, and Boy's Clubs of America had 1,100 affiliates with more than one million members, of whom a large share were involved in pre-high school team sports. In addition, there has been a recent boom in youth ice hockey programs. The teams registered with the American Hockey Association of the

United States increased from 2,654 in 1965-66 to 10,982 in 1976-77.[9] Staff members of the "U.S. News & World Report" magazine, who in 1974 surveyed the interest in organized sports in the United States for children fourteen years of age and under found, that there was a tremendous surge in participation covering at least twenty-seven sports.

Major structural characteristics of most of the established large-scale children's sports programs include selection of participants through competitive tryouts, restriction of participants to children of a specified age range, and involvement of teams in league or tournament competition.[10] Participation by coaches and players may involve many hours a week and many weeks of the year in practices and official competition. Parents not involved in coaching or administration still may be obliged to spend substantial sums of money on equipment and travel for their athletic offspring as well as a substantial amount of time as chauffeurs transporting their kids to and from practices and games and as spectators watching them perform—or sit on the bench.

Organized and supervised by adults, Little Leaguism tends to mirror the general structural form of sports programs in the older adolescent and adult worlds. Thus, they may be characterized more or less by emphases on secularism, the principle of equality, specialization, rationalization, bureaucracy, quantification, and records. With such emphases, it is not surprising to find Little Leaguism encouraging children to imitate or internalize the values, attitudes, ambitions, and actions of their elders. Indeed, It has been argued that the untested assumption that Little Leaguism promotes "character-building" or the learning of values, characteristics, and behaviors approved by the adult community has been responsible at least indirectly for the continuing expansion of this sports phenomenon.[11] We will examine in the remainder of this chapter whether the the things Little Leaguism teaches children to believe, be, and do embody or distort the idealization of the American Dream and the related principles of the dominant American sports creed. We will examine what Little Leaguism teaches about effort, achievement, and success and how children react to their experiences in a sports world not created or run by themselves.

# Learning the American Dream through Children's Sports

## 1. Adult Values and Expectations in Little Leaguism

According to the official book of rules and regulations of Little League Baseball, the organization exists to provide service to youth. "It is geared to provide an outlet of healthful activity and training under good leadership in the atmosphere of wholesome community participation.[12] Its stated purposes also include character-building, inspiration of goal-directed behavior, life enrichment, preparation for adult responsibilities, and exposure to the fundamentals of teamwork and fair play. Thus, in its conception of itself, the organization of Little League Baseball exists to fulfill many of the basic tenets of the dominant American sports creed. Furthermore, in aiming to provide opportunities to develop and demonstrate virtuous qualities such as good character, motivation, teamwork, and fair play in a competitive setting, Little League at least implicitly is seeking to provide an early proving ground for the pursuit of the American Dream.

Coaches and managers have extensive contact with their players in Little League and other sports programs of this type, and they tend to assume the most direct responsibility for implementing the official purposes of these programs. Therefore, we can understand better the extent to which Little Leaguism actually is represented to children in terms of lofty principles such as Little League's motto of "Character, Courage, Loyalty" by examining the types of values, goals and behavior coaches in children's sports stress to their players. Gary Alan Fine offers a picture of some of the basic themes these coaches emphasize to their young players in a report of his research concerning five Little League "major leagues" in New England and Minnesota, which he studied over a three-year period.[13] What is more interesting than *what* themes they stress is *how* these basic themes are handled.

Fine focused on four major themes, which he viewed as central elements in the "moral order" of Little League Baseball. These are (a) effort, (b) sportsmanship, (c) teamwork, and (d) coping with victory and defeat. Certainly these are major moral or cultural themes in American society as well as children's sports. Fine viewed exposure to these themes in Little League as having general implications for the child's mastering of presentation of self for subsequent participation in adult society. It is easy to imagine how the Little Leaguer's exposure to these ideas and the complexes of values, attitudes, and behaviors they represent could have an influence on his or her broader orientation to society and future conduct and beliefs.

Effort often was stressed to the Little Leaguers in Fine's study through the concept of "hustle." Coaches expected their players to do their best, and some clearly distinguished effort from winning by suggesting that they did not really care about winning or losing as long as their players did their best. However, defeat may have been seen as an indication of lack of "hustle" in many instances. Coaches seldom praised their teams for good effort in defeat. Such praise generally occurred when a hopelessly outclassed team almost defeated its superior foe.

Emphasis on hustle was an important motivational device for Fine's Little League coaches because it could be manipulated more easily than physical ability. Thus, lack of hustle was used to explain players' errors even when insufficient ability was a more suitable explanation: "If you hadn't loafed on the way to first, you would have made it." An interpretation of hustle was used in cases of successful effort as a compliment to reinforce future desire to perform well: "You're pitching like you mean it" (uttered by a coach to his pitcher in the course of a good performance that followed a losing effort in the prior outing).

Criticism for lack of hustle can be an especially powerful tool for the coach because it is so difficult for players to make an adequate response to it. It is almost impossible to prove conclusively to others that one has performed as well and hard as possible, and often there is reason to doubt oneself.

The athletic slogan that "you are only limited by your desire," which grossly oversimplifies the achievement process, reflects the perceived significance of effort, motivation, or hustle. It also implicitly reflects a connection among effort, achievement, and success that is a basic message of the ideology of the American Dream. Fine found that coaches defined situations for their players so that effort by individuals and the team as a whole was made an essential component for the formula for victory. With effort the only available variable for coaches to manipulate in the quest for victory, it is little wonder that it received substantial emphasis, that coaches used lack of hustle to blame players for failure and defeat, or that players made their teammates scapegoats for ostensible or actual lapses in team effort and performance. In a setting where effort was emphasized more than ability, few escaped criticism. The physically unable were blamed, just as the more able were, because they were defined as unmotivated rather than unable.

In an atmosphere where players often were driven to perform at maximum potential and were blamed when their effort did not seem to reach that peak, it is not surprising that sportsmanship—a theme in the official Little League code—was seldom explicitly mentiond by coaches during the season. However, they generally began the season with a few words about the importance of being a "good sport" or a "gentleman." Unlike lack of hustle, which coaches tended to view as a potentially major issue, lack of sportsmanship tended to be treated as a more minor and temporary problem. In fact, coaches generally saw their players as well-mannered, while several criticized their team for insufficient effort. Coaches' handling of the cases of bad sportsmanship depended on the situation in which it was perceived to happen. The coaches' desire to criticize actions such as hostile emotional outbursts, displays of anger in response to personal frustration, of harrassment of the other team to gain an advantage over it might depend on situational factors such as the coaches' own state of agitation, the emotional state of the "bad sport," the importance of the contest, the score, and the sense of rivalry with the other team. Under such circumstances, Little Leaguers are likely to learn that a particular action is not necessarily sportsmanlike or unsportsmanlike, but that its legitimacy depends on the situation. Furthermore, they may learn that sportsmanship as a principle is neither important nor unimportant in itself. Rather, "sportsmanship" is part of a rhetoric that may be raised on certain occasions to express approval or disapproval of behavior.

It is relevant to add here that in a study of third, sixth, eighth, tenth, and twelfth graders in public and parochial schools in Battle Creek, Michigan, Harry Webb found that a sense of fairness or sportsmanship became less important to young people as they got older.[14] In particular, he found that as children grew older, their "playful" activities became more "professionalized." That is, playing as well as possible, which is related to Fine's "effort" theme, was substituted for fairness as the paramount factor, and winning assumed increasing importance. It should be reiterated, though, that at least in the presence of adults, the Little Leaguers Fine observed generally gave the impression of being "well-mannered."

Along with effort and sportsmanship, teamwork was identified by Fine as a central element in the moral order of sport perceived by coaches. Coaches often felt the need to stress teamwork because they believed their players tended to think more in terms of impressing their friends or gaining personal glory than in terms of coordination or fitting their individual efforts into a collective effort. Of course, there was a practical dimension of this emphasis on teamwork because teamwork was thought to be associated with winning, but coaches also believed that learning team play was an important value in itself. Fine noted that the rhetoric of teamwork and team spirit was linked to that of effort on a number of occasions. One can see this linkage in a comment made by a coach after a come-from-behind victory: "Isn't that nice to come back and win it. It was a team effort. Everybody played well." Teamwork and effort also may be linked in valiant performances that fall short of victory, as in the case of a team that tied for third place in the Minnseota Little League tournament: "I'm proud of you guys. You guys showed more togetherness and guts than any team in the tournament . . . You gave it everything you had; I'm proud of every one of you. . ."

The final theme identified by Fine, which concerns winning and losing, often poses a moral dilemma for coaches because even though the structure of Little League competition underscores the significance of winning through attention to league standings, playoffs, champion-ships, and awards for victory, coaches may feel it is their responsibility to represent Little Leaguism as a valuable or enjoyable learning experience whether they win or lose. Of course, coaches often find it difficult to disguise their own desire to win, and frequently, they stress other values such as effort and teamwork, which have merit in themselves, because they are believed to be ingredients of successful performance. The actual reasons for victory in competition at this age may be difficult to identify or may reflect luck or idiosyncratic factors such as the absence of a star player who is away on vacation. Thus, coaches may only be able to speak vaguely about the specific skills that led to victory and may instead simply teach the child that whatever he or she did in a winning effort was good. In this way, Little Leaguers could learn that winning is important in itself, *however* it may be attained. If so, these children could develop a distorted conception of the American Dream in which the end of success—or winning in this case—becomes separated from a process of fair, diligent, and virtuous achievement.

The professionalization of children's sports by adults and their emphasis on winning in these sports programs have caused a great deal of controversy since the beginning of Little Leaguism over forty years ago. Critics of Little Leaguism often complain that coaches and administrators in children's sports programs are using professional athletes and the competitive ethos of professional sports as models for kids' programs that ought to be oriented toward providing fun and education of a broader sort. These and other criticisms will be examined more closely later in this chapter. However, it is important to state at this point in discussing the basic values adults convey to children through Little Leaguism that an emphasis on winning does not necessarily obscure the attention given to other values such as effort, teamwork, and even sportsmanship and fun by adults involved in children's sports. Furthermore, research has suggested that there are variations in the values and expectations adults associate with sports programs for their children.

In his study of family organization and Little League Baseball, Geoffrey Watson[15] discovered that parents with children in Little League or similar sports programs were more concerned than other parents with the successful development of their children within highly institutionalized community settings. Little League parents tended to see organized sports participation as an important vehicle of socialization for children to enrich or extend what they learned in the family. In addition, parents tended to use participation in institutionalized community activities such as Little League as a means of measuring their children's social and emotional development in relation to their peers along with their relative athletic development. However, the ends of socialization these parents hoped their children would achieve through Little Leaguism depended on their social class.

Watson found that middle class parents of Little Leaguers viewed sports involvement as training in cooperative interaction, which is an important value in the middle class status system, and as a source of enjoyment derived from learning game skills. Working class parents of Little Leaguers tended to see involvement in Little League as a means of learning how to compete as well as how to cooperate and conform or obey. Thus, for the middle class parents, Little Leaguism was "adaptive" training for cooperative forms of interaction that make possible successful participation in the middle class system. For the working class parents, Little League participation provided "integrative" training through which their children learned to conform to the expectations of others in a highly competitive setting. An important element in this setting for them was the "risk" involved in gaining access to opportunities for potential social mobility and the chance to learn to accept victory or defeat. Thus, perhaps even more for the working class than middle class Little League parents in Watson's research, Little Leaguism was a means of learning about the attainment of the American Dream. Since working class offspring have a longer climb up the status ladder, this social class difference in orientation might be expected.[16]

A study of the goal perceptions of parents of children in another form of Little Leaguism, youth hockey, suggests that parents of "Little Leaguers" see a discrepancy between the objectives they would like the sports programs to serve and the objectives actually served by these programs.[17] David Larson, Elmer Spreitzer, and Eldon Snyder found that the parents in their study, who were not examined in terms of social class differences, believed that winning and learning to compete were the actual major goals of youth hockey programs: 25% listed "importance of winning" and 21% listed "learning to compete" as current major objectives in these programs. However, none of these parents believed that winning should be the major goal, and only 7% felt that learning to compete should be the major objective.

Since parents often believe strongly in success themselves and in a variety of ways transmit this belief to their children, the unwillingness of parents to subscribe openly to the winning ethos in relation to their children's sports participation may seem curious. However, we are reminded of the implicit rather tham explicit emphasis on winning that Harry Edwards found in his study of the dominant American sports creed.[18] Furthermore, parents—including those who become coaches— may encourage or tolerate things in pratice that they say they do not condone or accept in principle. In addition, they might not see that what they are doing is exactly what they say they do not like. In this regard, Jerry Izenberg noted that every time he spoke to a group of adults about the excesses or problems of Little Leaguism, he would find all the heads in the audience nodding in agreement. However, he also diecovered that there was universal agreement that "They do not do those things in our league. We're different."[19]

# 2. Living Up to the Adult Model: Children's Reactions to Adult Values and Expectations

Gary Alan Fine has argued that Little League teaches its young participants not only how to do what adults think best but also how to manipulate these values in the management of impressions of themselves.[20] For example, Little Leaguers may learn to use rhetoric and create appearances that are meant to show their serious dedication and willingness to work hard and sacrifice for the good of the team. They also might aim the moralistic rhetoric they have learned from adults at the adults themselves when they feel their elders are not living up to these standards or are being hypocritical about them. The idea of sportsmanship was used in this way by a twelve year-old first baseman in Fine's study who sarcastically made the following remarks to his teammates about the opposing coach: "Real sportsmanship. He says to the catcher: 'If that guy in the batter's box doesn't get out of the way (when the catcher is throwing to second base, trying to catch a base runner), I want you to take his head off.'"

Obviously, then, children judge adults as well as themselves and their peers by the moral principles adults idealistically espouse to them. They also may be unwilling to accept the moral disapproval adults use to influence and control them. For example, when a coach in Fine's study emphasized teamwork to his players and attributed his team's disappointing third-place finish the previous year to having "a lot of prima donnas" on the team, he was met by a deliberate belch from one of his returning twelve year-olds. The boy's reaction provoked uproarious laughter from his teammates, suggesting that the coach's charge was not readily accepted by team members. In fact, Fine observed that this team subsequently suffered from poor teamwork and had an even worse record than the year before. Their response to their coach's urging of teamwork could be interpreted as a reason for their lack of success. More fundamentally, it could be seen as a rejection of the moral order of competitive Little League baseball.

Rejection of the competitive ethos of Little Leaguism probably is fairly unusual among its young participants since there is a tendency for them to become professionalized as they become more involved in institutionalized games and sport. Thus, even though they often are able to see through the transparent moral rhetoric of their elders who coach them and urge them on, they also are influenced and molded by the institutionalized and competitive structure of Little Leaguism that adults have created for them. Children recognize the value of the rule structure of their sports. In the words of one twelve year-old centerfielder in Watson and Kando's study of Little Leaguers, "If we didn't have rules things would be so messed up it wouldn't be no fun any more."[21] Of course, these rules represent a key element of external, adult control over the young athletes' activities since they are the creation of adults and reflect models of competition and success found in the adult world. So, as Watson and Kando have suggested, learning the rules of Little League and other adult-controlled children's sports is a means for children, especially those of the middle class, to adapt to the adult environment of achievement and success. It is a more subtle form of socialization than the moral rhetoric explicitly expressed by coaches and parents to teach and control them.

The institutionalized rituals of Little Leaguism also mold and control Little Leaguers. Watson and Kando found a number of adult-originated rituals in their research. The rituals included preparing for games with initial silence by parents followed by their enthusiastic shouting of support after the umpire had called "Play ball" and the first pitch had been thrown, parents sitting adjacent to their child's dugout to give support, punishing inferior performance with laps to run, and rewarding superior performance with an after-game visit to the Dairy Queen for ice cream. Watson and Kando argued that these sorts of rituals were a form of normative control in dramatizing displays of success, encouraging collective commitment to success, and enabling the meaning of success to be collectively shared and enjoyed. Thus, in the absence of spontaneity, autonomy, and rules of their own making, Little Leaguers tend to interpret institutionalized adult-made rules and rituals as a means of adapting to an adult environment and gaining access to goals valued by adults such as winning and success.

Earlier it was mentioned that middle class Little League parents in Watson's research tended to value the adaptive training offered to their children by sports involvement, while working class Little League parents tended to value the integrative and mobility training provided by Little Leaguism. The attraction of Little League to middle and working class Little Leaguers themselves was found by Watson[22] to parallel their parents' values. Middle class players tended to be attracted by the more intrinsic forms of motivation and social reciprocity—such as "fun"and "friendship"—and by the chance to display skill in a highly competitive setting. Working class players were attracted by the more instrumental character of Little Leaguism as a vehicle to learn skilled performance conducive to middle class acceptance—that is, learning to be a winner in a structured competitive setting. Working class players especially appreciated the chance to "belong" to the highly organized structure of Little League. Thus, it appears that parental socialization desires tend to be reinforced by involvement of their children in Little League.

# 3. The Success Ethic and Little Leaguism

Although Little Leaguism may fulfill different values for children—and parents— of different social classes, there is a pervasive emphasis on success built into the structure of competition and at least the implicit value system of adult-controlled children's sports that crosses social class lines. Despite the stated ideology of Little Leaguism, it is evident to all who look closely with objective eyes that the aim of competition is to win and that winners are rewarded handsomely while losers are criticized, ridiculed, rejected, or ignored. But how do the kids respond to this emphasis on winning and success? The tendency for children to become professionalized as they get older indicates they are influenced by adult expectations or models from professional and other highly publicized sports realms where winning often is the central concern. However, even when a collection of misfits is turned into winners by their coach, the young athletes do not necessarily become as impressed by status and victory as their parents, adult fans, and coach. This is the story told by the *Bad News Bears,* a popular film about Little Leaguism that is described in the commentary on the following page. The commentary should reveal that there is often a great deal of fact in ostensible fiction.

*    *    *    *    *

## Hollywood's Bad News for the Little League
## Frank Manchel *

Prior to 1976, American filmmakers rarely concerned themselves with the subject of organized sports for children. On those few occasions when it crept into the storyline—e.g., *Boys Town* (1938) and *Angels with Dirty Faces* (1939)—the message was clear: adult supervision had a positive effect on young people, particularly on ghetto youth with anti-social values. Stock situations featured the clergy and social reformers using organized team sports as a method for reinforcing the ideology of the American dream. Makeshift gymnasiums or vacant lots, transformed by well-meaning adults into facilities for structured athletic programs, became the means for helping cynical youngsters become socially-adjusted, achievement-oriented members of the community. Through adult role models stressing traditional values of hard work, self-confidence, and teamwork, the organized sports program admirably provided the educational experiences deemed necessary for success in our competitive society. That traditional screen ideology is still visible today in the recent CBS TV-sports film *Aunt Mary* (1979).

The major exception to the formula came in 1976 with *The Bad News Bears*. Based upon Bill Lancaster's satirical screenplay, director Michael Ritchie portrayed what happens to rag-tag Little Leaguers when their beer-guzzling manager (Walter Matthau) has a change of heart and turns them into a winning team. In the process, the film takes a critical look at how the Little League structure shapes the lives and values of parents, administrators, managers, and players.

Even as the opening credits flash on the screen, Ritchie prepares us for the highly-structured and deeply-serious nature of this particular Little League. Numerous sprinkling systems methodically arranged are carefully watering an expertly manicured baseball field. Professionalism is evident everywhere, as we see the various teams strenuously preparing themselves for the upcoming season. Except for the age differences, the scene could well be the training camp of a major league baseball team.

It is also clear that the adult influences are a perversion of the American dream ideology. Councilman Bob Whitewood (Ben Piazza), for example, has brought a class action suit against the League in order to get his son's team to play. Furthermore, his intense desire for a winning team motivates him to clandestinely hire an ex-professional baseball player (Matthau) as the Bear's manager. But Morris

---

*Frank Manchel is the author of *Great Sports Movies* (New York: Franklin Watts, 1980).

** For a novelized version, see Richard Woodley's *The Bad News Bears,* based on the screenplay by Bill Lancaster (New York: Dell Publishing Co., Inc., 1976).

Buttermaker's only concern is the money, not the team. This is evident to the over-zealous Yankee manager, Roy Turner (Vic Morrow), who opposes the new team because they aren't good enough ball players for the highly competitive League. Even the League administrator, Pigtails Cleveland (Joyce Van Patten), resents the Bears, as she does any attempt at making the League less professional and more responsive to equal opportunities for all youngster.

In each and every instance, hypocrisy masks the adult actions. Whitewood justifies the insidious hiring of Buttermaker on the grounds that all the boys' fathers were too busy to coach the Bears. "I think we're doing a really fine thing," he intones to the disinterested Buttermaker. Turner's wife (Shari Summers) apologizes for her husband's behavior on the grounds that he cares so much about the kids. And Turner, himself, rationalizing about his unchecked competitiveness, argues, "It's not us; it's the boys, the boys themselves who want it that way, and that's the way they want to keep it." Cleveland's concern, she claims, is only to have good ballplayers. Although she objected to letting girls participate (the result of an earlier class action suit), they could at least play ball.

The Bears, on the other hand, pose a formidable problem even to the best intentioned coach. Described by their shortstop, Tanner (Chris Barnes), as a bunch of "Jews, spics, pansies, and one booger-eating moron," the multi-racial team has an extremely low opinion of itself. They have come to understand their narrow world as a place where winning and ability count far more than effort and growth. Parents don't watch them work out, spectators ridicule their efforts, and the best they can get for a coach is an ex-professional baseball player who passes out drunk during practice. Instead of learning about hustle, teamwork, sportsmanship, and effort, the boys travel about with Buttermaker, helping him with his pool-cleaning jobs and becoming expert at making dry martinis.

Humor aside, the point remains that never once does any parent worry about his son's educational experiences. The assumption remains that as long as the boy belongs to a team in an organized League there is no cause for concern. The parents' obligations consist of attending a kick-off pizza party, contributing financially to the League's fund-raising drive, chauffering, and showing up periodically at the games. Not once in the entire film does a single Bears' parent try to help his child deal with failure or to understand that winning isn't everything. In fact, the boys have no rapport with their fathers. In the season opener, for example, when Buttermaker forfeits the game rather than let the Yankees continue their 26-run first inning, the Bears' right fielder, Ahmad (Erin Blunt), flees from the field, climbs up a tree, and takes off all his uniform, hiding rather than leaving to face his family. It remains for the coach, rather than the boy's father, to help Ahmad cope with defeat.

Ahmad's humiliation acts as a microcosm of how the adult world's misguided values are first transmitted and then accepted by the Little Leaguers. Amid opening day festivities, complete with the dedication of a new scoreboard, an impressive marching band, and sanctimonious ceremonies, the stress is on winning. When the Bears throw their gloves, taunt each other for errors, no one admonishes them for bad sportsmanship. The Yankees mock their opponents, spectators jeer and boo the weaker club, and League administrators urge Buttermaker to get his clumsy team out of the competition.

Underlying the confused values are the misguided adults' stress on appearances. Parents preoccupy themselves with how their children look in their uniforms. Whitewood, viewing the large crowd and impressive-looking facilities, hypocritically observes how important it is to have boys following "the American spirit... playing the great game of baseball." Turner gives his team a pep talk, reminding them to "look like champions, because you're going to be champions." Later on, he argues against a forfeit, telling Buttermaker that it's important that the boys don't feel like "quitters." The final touch to all this superficiality comes when the fans greet the forfeit announcement with cheers.

*The Bad News Bears* then quickly turns its attention to how children are taught to cope with defeat. Whitewood's solution against further humiliation consists of paying off Buttermaker and insisting the team be disbanded. The Bears thenselves take a similar posture. Rather than stand up to peer pressure and ridicule, they vote to quit. Turner, too, agrees that continuing to place the boys in a situation they can't seem to handle is sadistic. Thus after only one game, almost everyone seems eager to "retreat from the American dream." Everyone, that is, but Buttermaker. He convinces the boys not to quit, arguing that it's "a hard habit to break once you start."

Director Ritchie gives us the momentary impression that Buttermaker now represents what a good coach should be. Following the team's second defeat, he shows more concern with the boys' emotional state rather than with winning. He praises their efforts, comments on their athletic development, and reminds the team that success doesn't come overnight. Everyone seems better adjusted, more positively motivated.

Then Buttermaker shows his true values. His desire for victory takes precedence over fair play, sportsmanship and teamwork. Winning becomes paramount. Knowing that pitching is the key to the team's success, Buttermaker bribes his ex-star pitcher, Amanda (Tatum O'Neal), to play for the Bears. In her first outing, the manager boasts to his club how he taught Amanda to use spitballs, concealing vaseline on her baseball cap. Pitching now set, the determined coach uses his attractive star as bait to entice the area's best athlete, the anti-social Kelly (Jackie Earle Haley), to play for the Bears. Initially, Buttermaker's misguided actions appear justified by the team's miraculous transformation. Victory follows victory, while their self-confidence soars. But when a crucial game arrives, he orders Kelly to hog the ball. He is interested in winning, not morale. And when victory puts the Bears into the championship game, he feels his strategy more than compensates for the team's resentment and frustration.

The pre-game activities on championship day serve as a reminder that for most people, Buttermaker's methods need no apology. The stands are packed with proud parents and relatives, the players themselves exude pride in their achievement, and Coach Turner lectures his team on the painful price of losing. Even Buttermaker, sensing the team's hostility over his instructions to Kelly, chides the boys, "You want to win don't ya? That's what you showed up for."

As the game proceeds, we discover how much of the adults' negative values have been adopted by the players. The rivalry between the coaches produces blatant hostility on the ball field. Turner's stress on professionalism rather than on sportsmanship results in a Yankee runner spiking Amanda during a close play, and then a brawl between both teams. Blinded by the passion to win and ignoring the damage already done to the Little Leaguers, the coaches abandon any pretense of being interested in the children. Buttermaker, for example, instructs a batter on how to get himself hit by a pitch in order to make first base. He refuses to change pitchers, even though Amanda risks serious arm injury as a result of a sore pitching elbow. When Ahmad swings on a 3-0 count and makes out, Buttermaker screams unmercifully at him. He also humiliates Rudi (David Pollock) for disobeying orders. Rather than allow himself to be struck again by a pitched ball, the youngster tries to get a hit and fails. For Buttermaker, these defiant acts are intolerable. Gathering his team together in the dugout, the distraught coach berates the players for not listening, making bonehead plays and mistakes. "Don't you want to beat these bastards," he yells at the kids. Up to this point, director Ritchie demonstrates that Buttermaker and Turner share the same inexorable desire for victory. Neither one reveals any real concern for the children's physical or mental well-being. They both fail to understand how their win-at-all-cost attitudes are destructive.

But Buttermaker, as we have seen earlier, is different fron the other adults. Maybe because he once played professional ball, or because he occupies a lower-class status in the adult world, and thus knows better how to be a loser, or because *The Bad News Bears'* commercial success is dependent on its attracting the widest possible audience (made up mostly of people highly supportive of Little Leagues), Buttermaker gets a reprieve.

Ritchie shows us the stunned Bears looking quizzically at their coach. They are confused, bewildered, and disppointed in the one adult whom they had hoped was different. To his credit, Buttermaker finally understands what his team really needs. Sobered by the experience, he quietly tells the youngsters to get out on the field and do the best they can.

Turner, in contrast, becomes more repugnant, not only as a coach, but also as a father. His anguished wife watches helplessly from the sidelines as first Turner chides their son Joey (Brandon Cruz) for striking out and then knocks him down on the field for pitching what appears to be a bean ball. He still doesn't show any change of heart when Joey decides to defy his father and refuses to throw a batter out, thereby allowing the go-ahead run to score. Even after his son quits the game and his wife calls Turner "a son-of-a-bitch," the die-hard manager preoccupies himself with winning the championship game.

Equally effective are Ritchie's images of the teams' contrasting attitudes. While the Bears stage a silent rebellion against Buttermaker's behavior, the Yankees grapple with Joey in order to get the baseball and throw out the runner. They ignore their pitcher's defiant acts against his father, concentrating only on following Turner to victory. Without overstating their message both director and screenwriter subtly define their argument that the League is neither good nor bad; it is just not appropriate for all children. Those highly motivated youngsters who are intent on stiff competition find a man like Turner an effective coach. Less intense children searching more for physical development and reasonable competition have need of a Buttermaker.

What that alternative represents becomes evident during the last inning of the championship game. Buttermaker takes out his star players, replacing them with the boys who have not yet seen action. Not surprisingly, this confuses everyone. The team still wants to win, and it considers the surprising substitutions tantamount to a forfeit. Ignoring all objections, the transformed coach explains to an unwilling replacement that the youngster "didn't come into this life just to sit around on a dugout bench ...," while dismissing Whitewood's heated protests by stating that "everybody on my team gets a chance to play." And when Buttermaker changes pitchers to protect Amanda's health, player and spectator alike foresee only dire consequences for the Bears.

Most fans, parents, competitors, and even many members of the viewing audience overlook the meaning of the subsequent events. The fact that the Bears' worst fielder is responsible for the Yankees' third out and is carried off by his teammates leads most people to hope that the underdog kids might yet overcome their four-run deficit and win the game. No apparent value is placed either on how much Lupus (Quinn Smith) has grown in self-confidence or on how successfully Buttermaker has brought the team closer together. When Tanner fires up his friends, the anticipation of victory increases, not admiration for the boy's newly found team spirit and acceptance of those with lesser abilities. Hopes dim as Rudi gets thrown out trying to stretch a single into a double. But for viewers who might still misunderstand the change going on, Ritchie has Buttermaker praise Rudi for his hustle, adding, "Put it there. I like that." After Amanda makes the second out, the fans start leaving the stands and the loudspeaker blares a note of thanks for those who have attended the game, underscoring again the adults' real values. Then in quick succession, Ogilvie (Alfred W. Lutter) who had gone 0-14 during the season walks, Ahmad singles, and Miguel (George Gonzales) walks to load the bases, with Kelly coming to the plate. With the crowds once more jamming the stands and cheering, Turner orders his pitcher to intentionally walk the Bears' slugger. What Ritchie achieves by this rapid set of events is to merge both the audiences—those in the flim and those watching the film—as a single force rooting for a Bears' victory. No longer is anyone involved with a child's growth, his enjoyment of a game, or his capacity to play. We want a grand slam, and when Kelly delivers a long hit, we cheer along with everyone else as he speeds around the bases. Then, cleverly, Ritchie dashes our hopes as a perfact Yankee relay gets Kelly at home, giving the better athletes the championship. In thie way we are jolted back to the film's concern with children's needs, not misdirected priorties.

The post-game ceremonies provide a fitting summation to Ritchie's list of Little League abuses and distorted emphases. A giant first place trophy dwarfs the runner-up award, reminding us how much winning means to adults. Turner's right-minded rhetoric about the playing field resolving the teams' differences satirizes the fact that throughout the movie dishonest actions are always rationalized with hypocritical clichés. The final gag, however, belongs to the film's heroes, now drunk on beer provided by their ecstatic coach. Rejecting any pretenses of fitting into this highly structured adult-dominated society, the Bears give the traditional challenge to their opponents, "Wait 'till next year."

Although *The Bad News Bears* provided the mid-seventies with a highly popular set of stereotypes—adults with misguided ambitions, smartalec kids who truly know the score—the film's conventions failed when used in subsequent productions. Two sequels—*The Bad News Bears in Breaking Training* (1977) and *The Bad News Bears in Japan* (1978)—not only missed the talented Matthau and O'Neal, but lacked the original's serious criticisms. A flawed CBS-TV series, *The Bad News Bears* (1978) suffered the same fate. What each adapter missed in stressing the formula's obvious humor was that the prototype satirized a society abusing its children through excessive parental pressure. Equally important, the original film demonstrated that popular films often reveal that there is a great deal of fact in ostensible fiction.

\*     \*     \*     \*     \*

The *Bad News Bears* is a comedy with a serious message about excessive parental pressure in children's sports. There are other treatments of the effects of a professional model on Little Leaguers by writers who see little humor in this phenomenon. Thomas Tutko and William Bruns have written about how this professional model has filtered down to children's sports to affect even four and five year-olds. Their perception of the nature of the emotional effects of this model on children is reflected in a newspaper cartoon they described[23] A little boy is in the outfield preparing to catch a fly ball. "If I catch the ball," he says, "the manager will love me, my friends will think I'm great, my parents will adore me, and I'll be a hero." Then his excited optimism fades as he begins to ponder the consequences of missing the ball. The manager will not like him, the other kids will make fun of him, his parents will not let him in the house, and he'll be considered a "dud." The ball finally drops out of the sky into his outstretched glove—and bounces out. In the final frame, this little boy is shown plodding from the field with his shoulders slumped and head bowed. He thinks to himself: "Six years old and already a failure."

Carolyn Sherif[24] has pointed out that aspirations arise in a social context of "significant others"—such as parents, other influential adults, friends, teachers, and the mass media—and that experiences of success and failure depend on how well we do in relation to these socially-induced aspirations. For many children in adult-controlled sports programs, the standards of success are professional ones. When winning becomes the most important thing or the only thing that matters, children learn that the only genuine experience of achievement and the only real basis for success is winning the championship or leading the team or league in some quantifiable and publicized form of achievement such as scoring, batting, pitching, or number of touchdown passes. A world perceived in these terms allows very few "winners." Thus, for many children in Little Leaguism, losing and failure of some sort or degree are common experiences. Since all children need to have some experience with success and achievement to develop self-esteem and confident, secure, healthy personalities, Little Leaguism could cause psychological damage for participants by creating aspirations relatively few can fulfill. After all, championships are rather exclusive affairs, and even those with athletic talent might form the impression they are "failures" because their team has not won the "big game" or championship or because they have not performed flawlessly.

For many Little Leaguers, especially those with less developed skills or limited confidence in them, emphasis on success in Little Leaguism makes them emotionally intense and anxious in their pursuit of success. Rather than enhancing performance, this emotional intensity and anxiety tends to make performances worse than they would be in a relaxed atmosphere. A study by Randall Lowe revealed that performances by Little Leaguers tended to deteriorate under conditions of high competitive stress.[25] More mature, talented, and self-assured individuals with low need for affiliation seem more able to tolerate the tensions of highly competitive sports and find enjoyment in them.[26] However, even those children most suited for highly competitive sports may be unsettled by the adult criticisms of "lack of hustle," "inadequate desire," or "selfishness" that often follow miscues or losing efforts. If adults create too much pressure to win, they may provoke so much anxiety that the motivation to perform well suffers along with the quality of performance.[27] For less skilled players who cannot possibly meet the lofty expectations of their coaches and parents but whose egos are completely tied up in their performances as athletes, the experience of failure in sport can be so salient that they feel defeated as persons as well as athletes. These less skilled players seem to suffer most from the fanatical dedication to the success ethic in Little Leaguism among coaches and parents because they cannot achieve the aspirations adults have set for them.

When winning is strongly urged, highly rewarded, and impossible for all to achieve, it is not surprising that efforts to win sometimes go beyond the boundaries of sportsmanship and morally acceptable behavior. This is true in children's sports as well as in sports for adolescents and adults. Indeed, the stress on competition and beating the opponent that children learn in Little Leaguism may carry over into hostile interpersonal relationships with sports opponents *off the field* that adults find difficult to minimize or control.

In a series of studies of initially well-adjusted eleven and twelve year-old boys at a summer camp, Muzafer Sherif and his colleagues found that gains in solidarity, morale, and cooperativeness *within* competing groups are achieved at the expense of antagonism *between* the competing groups.[28] Boys in their experiments who had initially been friendly with each other developed increasingly hostile relationships after becoming members of opposing teams in tournaments of games such as baseball, touch football, and tug-of-war. The spirit of sportsmanship that prevailed at the beginning of the competition repidly deteriorated into name-calling, raids to mess up the rivals' cabins, painting the stolen blue jeans of the opponents' leader with derogatory slogans. and the development of extremely prejudiced and hostile attitudes toward members of the opposing team. So much antagonism was created between these rival groups that the researchers were hard-pressed to bring the conflicting groups back into harmony. Shared social events such as attending movies and eating together in the dining room only provided further opportunities for name-calling and scuffles. Even appeals to moral values such as "love thy enemy" by the local minister in religious services organized separately by each group were followed shortly afterward by renewed cursing of their opponents. Only the creation by the experimenters of a series of "superordinate goals," which had a strong appeal to both rival groups and could not be achieved without cooperation between them, ultimately reduced friction between the competing groups[29]

The studies of conflict between competing groups by Sherif and his colleagues demonstrate that the benefits of cohesion, solidarity, morale, teamwork. and even achievement and success that a group gains from intensified rivalry with others may be accompanied by significant costs of hostility and hatred toward others who just happen to be members of a competing group. Certainly, these studies offer a compelling lesson to adults who incite children to "destroy" the opposing team of "enemies" with the greatest possible effort. Unlike professional athletes, who often can compartmentalize their athletic and personal lives and relationships, Little Leaguers may be unable to separate the intense rivalry on the playing field from relationships off the field. Of course, adults often fail to recognize the implications of their own emphasis on success or even the amount of emphasis they are giving to this goal. Thus, we find Little Leaguism sometimes publicly encouraging competition by printing badges for boosters urging them to support their favorite team with cheers such as "Slay the Aces," "Scalp the Apaches," "Batter the Bantams," "Destroy the Blue Devils," "Massacre the Braves," "Crush the Chiefs," "Mangle the Matadors," and "Stomp the Moccasins."[30]

Unfortunately, children sometimes try to follow the urgings of fanatical fans quite literally. Fortunately, however, it appears that competition in children's sports does not necessarily or inevitably produce the kind of hostility and sadistic rivalry that was exhibited in the Sherif experiments. John Burchard[31] found in his research involving eleven and twelve year-olds in a state-wide youth hockey tournament that the boys generally did not display poor sportsmanship toward their opponents. The most competitive players, who were highly motivated to win and hated to lose, were more likely to get upset with the referees, themselves, or their teammates than with the members of the opposing team. There were even some players, whom Burchard referred to as "competence motivated" rather than "competition motivated," who did not mind losing. Furthermore, in some cases, teams had more fun losing than winning. This seemed to happen in those games where a team almost defeated an opponent it was not expected to beat. He inferred from these occasions that kids may derive more fun from playing well against a good team and losing, than from beating a much poorer team. This orientation reflacts a greater interest in demonstrating skill than in winning *per se* that seems to occur at least in the preadolescent stage of the professionalization process described by Webb[32] However, it should be added that winning tends to become relatively more important to kids as they become older and more professionalized. Burchard noted the discrepancy between his results and evidence from other studies such as the Sherif research that revealed more negative consequences of organized sports participation by children, and he suggested that the undesirable effects of competition may be minimized by restructuring the environment in which it occurs.

In Burchard's research, a 15-inch sportsmanship trophy was awarded at the end of the tournament along with the more conventional trophies for the champion and runner-up teams and for the most valuable player and the individuals on the all-star team. The addition of the sportsmanship trophy to the awards ceremony, which is in marked contrast to the limited attention to sportsmanship by coaches in Fine's research, might have created an atmosphere in which "good" behavior toward opponents— but not referees, it seems—became more acceptable as well as more rewarded.

Though there are some encouraging signs in Burchard's findings, he introduced a note of caution for those generalizing from them. He reminds us that while negative attitudes toward opponents were less frequent and intense than expected, competitively motivated players did become upset with referees, themselves, and their own teammates when they were not doing well. Those who had the most fun were "competence motivated" players who were motivated more by intrinsic factors such as the quality of play than by the extrinsic factors such as winning or losing and the rewards of success that tended to drive the "competition motivated" players. Significantly, though, competence motivated players were outnumbered by competition motivated ones in this study by four to one. This could be a result of the fact that despite the explicit attention to sportsmanship in the tournament Burchard studied, he found that many coaches and parents were more likely to emphasize winning than having fun. Indeed, when one parent was told that a competence motivated player was able to have fun even in a losing effort, the parent responded, "That's not competence, that's stupidity."

An excessive emphasis by adults on success or the outcome of competition could encourage children in Little Leaguism to cheat, take potentially dangerous drugs, or engage in other deviant or dubious practices as well as to display unwarranted aggression or poor sportmanship toward opponents. Perhaps one of the most disillusioning examples of cheating in children's sports in recent years for believers in American traditions was the scandal that occurred during the thirty-sixth annual running of the All-American Soap Box Derby in Akron, Ohio in the summer of 1973. The winner was discovered to have used a highly sophisticated car that was propelled by an illegal magnet and was ridden to victory on illegal axles and suspicious tires. The car far exceeded the allowable cost of $75 and also contrary to the derby's rules, was engineered by an adult, the boy's uncle, an inventor and engineer whose son had won the Derby the previous year. The prosecutor in this case was so appalled that he said, "It's like discovering that your Ivory Snow girl has made a blue movie." Robert B. Lange, Sr., the uncle, was ordered by a Colorado court in a "nonjudical" arrangement to pay $2000 to a boys' club. The judge also said Lange owed an apology to the youth of the nation, but Lange admitted only a "serious mistake in judgment." He added that cheating had been so prevalent that all he did was even his nephew's chances in a "dirty system."

The use of diet pills to reduce a child's weight to the allowable limit for the level of competition the child, his or her parents, or coaches want is just one of the ways in which children may endanger their health through Little Leaguism[34] Children may be encouraged to compete at a weight that is below what is healthy for them because it is believed they will have a better chance to excel, dominate, or be a star in a lower weight class. Children also might risk serious injury in the quest for athletic success and recognition by participating in sports or activities for which they are not physically suited. Furthermore, there are obvious risks to all competitors in contact sports such as football and ice hockey and dangerous noncontact sports such as gymnastics as well as less obvious risks such as "Little League elbows" for young baseball pitchers and damaged shoulders and knees for competitive swimmers[35] The risk in these sports is created or compounded by pushing young bodies to do more than they can physically or physiologically tolerate. The pressure to perform at such high or intense levels is influenced by the success ethic children learn from adult models or are explicitly taught by adults.

Shortly before he died, Vince Lombardi reflected on the quote that had driven so many to do so much to win in sports. He told Jerry Izenberg, "I wish to hell I'd never said the damned thing. I meant the effort... I meant having a goal... I sure as hell didn't mean for people to crush values and morality."[36] Curiously, this message seldom has been associated with the memory of Vince Lombardi. Instead, the "Lombardian ethic" of winning remains in the minds of many as winning at any cost. In Little Leaguism, the desire to win and succeed often seems to translate into this Lombardian ethic, especially among the adults who run the programs. When children learn this ethic, they may become extremely intense and serious about activities that the ideology of Little Leaguism says are supposed to be fun. It is a revealing commentary about the effects of the success ethic in Little Leaguism that a former sports editor for the *New York Times* and a longtime observer of children's sports could say that in all his years of watching children in organized sports, he noticed few of them smiling.[37] It is a striking contrast to the unbridled and spontaneous laughter and joy found in the play, recreation, and games kids create for themselves.

# Achieving the American Dream through Little Leaguism: The Rewards and Burdens of Being a Preadolescent Athletic Star

Although the attainment of success as a Little Leaguer may require some unchildlike ambition, effort and sacrifices, there are some valuable rewards for children who become successful athletes in the programs of Little Leaguism. They may receive special recognition from parents, coaches, teachers, and the mass media, and they may earn an honored place in the status systems of their peers. They may develop self-assurance, self-esteem, and security from knowing they have achieved something other people value. Furthermore, they may have trophies, medals, pictures, stories, and other awards and forms of recognition and praise to display as tangible evidence of their accomplishments and honored status. Though they have not yet earned great monetary rewards for their sports achievements, the stars of Little Leaguism in many ways embody a pint-sized version of a fulfillment of the American Dream.

If success in Little Leaguism can be seen as a preadolescent fulfillment of the American Dream, then we might ask how successful Little Leaguers react to their success and whether it prepares them to be successful later in life. Though there is little doubt that many youngsters enjoy being the center of attention and receiving special treatment from parents and other adults and praise, envy, and respect from peers, we must be reminded that for many young athletic stars, the road to success has few smiles. In addition, children who are singled out as having the potential to develop into star athletes in high school, college, or the professional ranks shoulder a tremendous responsibility for continued achievement.

If a young athletic star begins to fall short of others' expectations, and most inevitably do as they get older and the world of the successful becomes smaller, he or she may not have the maturity to admit to personal shortcomings, adjust to the disappointment of others, and develop a well-adjusted personality despite the setbacks in his or her athletic career. When children are pampered and treated as heroes because they have demonstrated apparent athletic gifts, they may find it difficult to accept personal responsibility for setbacks and disappointments. Excessive adulation is likely to encourage a distorted view of reality in which it is believed that special privileges are a right and that "that world owes me a living." Thus, when pampered athletes who are spoiled and made psychologically dependent of the constant attention to their needs by others begin to fall short of expectations, lose their competitive advantage, or fail, they often cannot adjust to their change in status and lash out at others—such as referees, coaches, teammates, and parents—in response to their fall from glory.

The longer children are pampered as athletic stars and are shielded from failure, the more difficult it will be for them to face and adjust maturely to disappointments and setbacks in sport and in life in general. Thus, budding athletes on their way to greater success experience—often without realizing it—the peculiar dilemma of being deprived of chances to deal with mistakes and failures that can contribute to their emotional development and maturity. Of course, when spoiled athletes do begin to falter, their failure seldom escapes the eyes of the public and may be more difficult to handle for that reason. In the words of Bill Bradley, the former professional basketball player who is now a United States Senator, "There is little chance...for a public figure."[38] to fail without people knowing it, and no one grows without failing."[38] The twenty-five year-old tennis star who shouts obscenities at the crowd, referees, or his opponent when victory begins slipping away and the thirty year-old major league baseball pitcher who ignores young autograph seekers or refuses to talk to reporters because he has been losing and has been booed by fans and criticized by the press are illustrations of the kind of immaturity in adulthood that childhood and adolescent sports experiences of pampering and uninterrupted success can produce.

Tutko and Bruns have asserted that treatment by parents plays a crucial role in determining how children respond to their success as athletes.[39] Parents must help counterbalance pressures to succeed from teammates, coaches, the public, and himself or herself. Instead, they often add to those pressures. Children need unqualified love and acceptance from parents to develop happy, healthy, and secure personalities. However, they may receive love with conditions. As Tutko and Bruns observed, "If the parents love the child only because he is a first stringer, a winner, a hero, then the day will come when he will run out of first teams, victories, and heroics, and find he is alone. It is tough to find that our when you are 20 or 30 or 35 years of age, It is deadly, psychologically, to discover it at age 12 or 13."

Parents may believe that pushing their child toward the dream of a college athletic scholarship, a professional sports career, or the Olympics is in the child's best interest or what he or she wants. In fact, they may be seeking for themselves vicarious pleasure or glory or financial compensation from their child's success. In the pursuit of such dreams, some parents even go as far as sending their children away to a full-time, year-round sports academy where sports skills and competitive poise and toughness are refined and parental responsibilities are transferred to a coach. When young and promising tennis players attend Nick Bollettieri's Tennis Academy at the Colony Beach and Tennis Resort near Sarasota, Florida, they are placed under the tutelage of a man who is a self-acknowledged disciple of the "Lombardian success ethic."[40] He allows his students only a spartan life style off the tennis courts; and on the tennis courts, he is a driving task master who screams at those who do not listen to him, insults those who do not meet his rigid standards of achievement, and denies water to sweating, thirsty kids who have just been punished with a run on the beach. His most difficult task is said to be breaking the bond between child and parent. Bollettieri simply exchanges roles with parents ambitious or obsessed about the success of their children as tennis stars. Obviously, the parental role he assumes along with his coaching role is *not* to pamper or spoil his athletes. In fact, it seems deficient in the kind of affection and attention children and young adolescents usually need to develop happy and well-adjusted personalities.

Despite being cut off from their families and subjected to rigid discipline, his students—at least the successful ones—do not seem to mind. Even at twelve, thirteen, or fourteen years of age, they have developed a singleminded devotion to becoming a top player and are willing to make whatever sacrifices seem necessary to achieve that goal. A fourteen year-old with a dream of rising from a good player at the state level to a great player expressed his feelings about his training at Bollettieri's Academy in the following way: "The only reason I came down here is for tennis. I don't really care about anything else, such as girls or cars or television... They make you tough here. You have to want to be No. 1. I can't imagine not wanting that and doing what we do here."[41] Another young star, also totally committed to his training with Bollettieri and the success it promised, admitted that he had no desire to go home and see his family.

Not all young athletes accept the sacrifices of trying to become a national champion or professional athlete, and for those who have sacrificed and missed the glory, the consequences could be quite damaging. Don Schollander, an Olympic champion as a swimmer, wrote that he felt the greatest sacrifice of his life was leaving home at fifteen to further his swimming career, and it was a sacrifice encouraged by his parents but resisted by him. He said, "Today I feel that because I went away at fifteen and stayed away, my parents don't really know me... I wished I could have shared some of the frustrations with them and some of the happiness... Today it bothers me, not that I don't know them very well, but that they don't know me very well.[42]

Even though fulfillment of the success ethic of Little Leaguism may bring more burdens and sacrifices than rewards, adult proponents of Little Leaguism who acknowledge these costs are likely to justify them as valuable preparation for adulthood in a competitive, success-oriented society. Martin Ralbovsky's interviews of nine men who had been members of a Schenectady team that won the Little League World Series twenty years earlier in 1954 offer some revealing insights into the kind of preparation for adult society that attainment of the American Dream in children's sports may provide.[43] The story of these former Little Leaguers also indicates the rewards of success that can be earned by young champions of sport. Upon their return from Williamsport to Schenectady, New York, these young baseball players were given a triumphant reception on the steps of the city hall; they were given the keys to the city; they attended fifteen banquets at which they received bicycles, radios, watches, and clothing; they attended a World Series game in New York City at which the first ball was thrown out by one of them; one of the players made a series of tapes for national radio; the team appeared on the *Today* television show; one of the players appeared on the Perry Como show; and the team posed for a color photograph that appeared in *Collier's* and was the subject of a long article in *Sports Illustrated* magazine.[44] They were called "destiny's darlings," and when they returned to public view five years after their Little League glory days as high school sports stars on their way to college with athletic scholarships in hand, it appeared that they were preparing to catch the American Dream once again as young adults.

Of course, not everyone on the team had a college scholarship in hand, and as it turned out, none would achieve a piece of the American Dream as big as he had achieved as a young champion of Little League. Nevertheless, at least one of those whom Ralbovsky interviewed looks back with unreserved praise and pride on his experience twenty years before. Chuck Neidel, the first baseman, spoke of the kind of discipline he learned from Mike Maietta, the manager of the 1954 team, and its payoffs later in life. He told Ralbovsky that his manager had purposely tried to break the kids on his team by screaming and yelling at them and putting a great deal of pressure on them in practice. These tactics were These tactics were meant to discover who would and would not be able to handle the demands and pressures of actual game competition. In reflecting on this experience, Neidel said, "I don't think it hurt me a bit because that's what life is all about anyway, pressure and competition." He also said he would like his son to go through a similar experience. For Chuck Neidel, the values he learned from Mike Maietta and his Little League experience continued to be important to him as an adult in his work as a salesman. He felt that he was "winning in life"—just as he had won in sport—because he had been able to apply the lessons of competition and hard work from sport to his job, where he had learned to outsell competing salesmen. In Niedel's mind, life really had not changed much since his days as a Little Leaguer. In adulthood, he was preoccupied with his work and as a Little Leaguer, he had felt he was going to work when he put on his baseball uniform.

Pete Fennicks, the only black player on the team, also felt his life had not changed in twenty years, but his perspective differed from that of Chuch Neidel. He said that his mother worked all the time and his father worked all the time, but they still had nothing. The key to the city he received after the Little League championship did not open a single door of opportunity for him or his family in the ensuing twenty years. He never got to college and he worked at assorted jobs before becoming a machinist at a G.E. factory, the job he held as a thirty-one year-old. He was divorced and living with his mother at her place. He felt trapped, and saw no hope for a better future. His one wish in life was to be twelve years old again, playing Little League baseball. Apparently, the discrimination and prejudice that have excluded so many black Americans from pursuit of the American Dream were less salient for Pete Fennicks as a twelve year-old Little League champion than as an adult. The twenty years following his glory days seemed to be spent drifting hopelessly away from another chance at an American Dream of a life of good things and contentment. It is difficult to know whether the bitterness he felt at thirty-one was caused or restrained by the success he experienced as a twelve year-old Little Leaguer.

Jimmy Barbieri was the team captain and star center fielder who had the honor of throwing out the first ball in the Major League World Series of 1954. He spoke of the "killer instinct," the urge to destroy opponents by as many runs as possible, that had consumed him during his drive to the Little League championship. He recalled that the competition in Williamsport was not fun, and that he felt incredible pressure to win, especially since they had lost there the previous year. He felt that they were the meanest team in the tournament, and that Mike Maietta had encouraged them to be that way—to knock down or even hurt opposing players if they got in the way on the basepaths or elsewhere on the field. Jimmy Barbieri made it to the Major Leagues in 1966. He received a bonus of $1000 in 1960 to sign a contract with the Los Angeles Dodgers.

He struck out in his only appearance in the World Series that year. He subsequently was farmed out to the minor leagues, played in Japan, and ended his career there in 1970 after a fist fight with his manager in the dugout. In thinking back on his experience, he felt that Mike Maietta wanted to win the the championship for himself, "for his own glory," and not for the experience it provided his players. "We were pawns on the chessboard, and he made all the moves."

Bill Masucci was the winning pitcher in the championship game. He pitched the entire series with a very painful elbow. Twenty years later, he retained the vestiges of that "Little League elbow." Glancing out a window, he said, "I can't throw a baseball from here to the street now."

Johnny Palmer was the left fielder. He remembered that as a kid in his neighborhood in Schenectady, if you weren't in Little League, "you were nothing." Though he recognized the importance associated with Little League stardom where he lived, he had mixed feelings about his championship experience. He felt that the team had been exploited by Mike Maietta. Maietta had diminished the significance of the champion-ship for him as a player because the manager had played such a prominent role in the accomplishment. The championship would have meant more to Johnny Palmer if the players had been able to win it on their own or with less direction from Mike Maietta. The year after Johnny Palmer was a Little League hero, he tried out for the Babe Ruth League and was cut, while the son of the man in charge of the tryouts made the team. Because he felt betrayed by this seemingly ridiculous and unfair turn of events, he quit baseball then, at age thirteen. Throughout high school. he avoided commitments that could lead to similar letdowns. He joined the Marines after high school to impress people in his hometown that he could do something much tougher than going to college or playing professional baseball. As thirty-one years of age, he regretted that decision. He said that if he had not played on the championship team and if he had not had his ego inflated by tht experience, he would have been able to accept being cut by the Babe Ruth League a lot better. He also felt he would have thought about college more seriously than he did because the other members of the team were thinking about college and getting scholarships. However, he turned his back on all organized sports after being cut because he did not want to "risk the humiliation of being cut again..."

Although Chuck Neidel expressed a clearly contrary view, the men interviewed by Ralbovsky generally seemed to have mixed or negative feelings about their experience as Little League champions and the opportunities it opened for them later. While they may have basked in the temporary glory of being Little League heroes, many felt their success was Mike Maietta's prize more than their own. Ernie Lotano, another of destiny's darlings, said about his former manager that he was "probably the best manager in the history of Little League baseball up to that point." While extolling his coaching genuis, Lotano also noted that Mike Maietta seemed to have little concern for the feelings of his players or for the effects of the championship experience on their later lives. To Ernie Lotano, the manager had drawn from the lessons and tricks of his prior pro baseball career to create a hardened and professionalized team of twelve-year-olds who could fulfill *his* desire for a Little League championship.

After becoming a Little League manager in 1951, Mike Maietta quickly learned some valuable lessons about winning in Little League. First, he learned that a lot of guys would do anything to win. Second, he learned that it was necessary to have tough kids who were fighters and were not going to be pushed around. What Mike Maietta learned translated into a tough, demanding, authoritarian style of leadership in which he sought to make his players hate him so they would build up anger that could be directed at the opposing team. In view of his approach, it might seem surprising that Mike Maietta said to Martin Ralbovsky, "It's funny, but you have those kids for a summer or two, you accomplish something with them, and then they grow up and you never hear from them again, but that's life, I guess. . ." In going through his scrapbook, he wondered what had happened to his former players. What happened to Chuck Neidel and some of the others might have pleased him. However, for many of the members of Mike Maietta's championship team, tha American Dream they found as twelve year-olds was a mixed blessing at best, and it was never to be found again later in their lives.

# Exclusion, Dropping Out, and Failure: The American Dream in Retreat?

The experience of Johnny Palmer after his championship days as a Little Leaguer reveals a face of Little League that often is obscured by the emphasis on winning and success. It is the experience of being screened out, not chosen, or excluded. Johnny Palmer's failure to make a Babe Ruth League team was especially bitter and emotionally shattering to him because it came only one year after he had reached the top of the mountain in Little League. His sudden fall from the mountain left him with a fear of future failure coupled with a somewhat paradoxical need to prove himself to others. It also killed his future interest in organized sports. Johnny Palmer's experience could be called a "retreat from the American Dream," and it has been shared by many other children who have never been successful athletes as well as by those who have tasted success.

In view of the stated ideological aim of Little League and many other sports programs for children to prepare participants for life, as well as provide them with fun, their practice of excluding all but the most talented—and the offspring of those who run the programs—would seem to leave out many of the children who might benefit most from such experiences. In fact, many children who recognize the highly competitive emphasis on skill and success in Little Leaguism never try out at all because they feel they cannot meet the criteria of achievement. Evidence from a study by Terry Orlick indicated that 75% of the children he interviewed who had never participated in organized sports said they would go out for a team if they thought they would surely make it, but none felt good enough to be selected.[45] Thus, children lacking skills or confidence never get a chance to develop these qualities in competitive sports either because the adults who run Little Leaguism exclude them from participation or because these children exclude themselves. Of course, the stress on winning in Little Leaguism and the pressures associated with becoming and remaining successful as Little League participants lead many children who are involved in adult-controlled sports programs to decide to drop out. Orlick and Botterill have suggested that the negative experiences that cause children to drop out of sports tend to be associated with perfection, especially at an early age.[46] Successful, winning Little Leaguers may become competition motivated and enjoy the experience of winning and its attendant rewards, though Ralbovsky's interviews indicate that success in Little Leaguism can have its drawbacks and that the fruits of success may be short-lived. However, sitting on the bench, being ignored, or being yelled at for mistakes take the fun out of sport for many children and leave them with little motivation to continue participation.

The successful who drop out may be "burned out." Jim Nelson, a veteran of over two decades of coaching football at a small Missouri college, lamented the professionalization of Little Leaguism for this reason. He said, "Now you see kids who've played little league five or six years. By the time they get to high school they've already been to bowl games and all-star games and had all that attention. What's left?"[47]

Unfortunately, many children who have lost interest and would like to drop out of sports are prevented from doing so by implicit or explicit pressure from parents, coaches, or peers to remain involved. Dropouts often are stigmatized as "quitters" or "losers," and parents frequently fear that children who drop out of sports will not be able to succeed in other areas. However, Bryant Cratty has written in *Children and Youth in Competitive Sports* that there is no evidence indicating that children unwilling to endure the physical demands of sport are likely to fail in tasks involving intellectual of artistic persistence. Indeed, in these other areas, they may display abilities more likely to be beneficial in adulthood than sports skills.[48]

Cratty's remarks are interesting because they suggest that dropping out of Little Leaguism *might* have beneficial consequences *if* children direct their creative and productive energies toward other areas. This possibility is a striking counterpoint to the list of negative cousequences of failure as a Little Leaguer that previously were cited: the frustrations from unfulfilled dreams, the personally shattering realizations of inadequacy, the tarnished self-images, the sacrifices made in vain, and the often difficult process of resocialization that comes after failure. However, the failure to make it in the competitive world of Little Leaguism could lead to a sense of freedom instead of disappointment or despair. In a study of growing up with youth hockey in Canada, it was proposed that, "...there are many who give in to (the) pressure (to compete in youth hockey) who not only lack talent...but who also lack interest... These are the ones likely to react with relief rather than despair to the realization that they are not good enough to go on."[49]

# The Female Challenge to Little Leaguism

For most boys in the United States, there is an obligation felt at least to try-out for some form of Little Leaguism. Sports participation traditionally has been seen as part of their *rite de passage* into manhood in American society. Sport in America, with its emphasis on aggressiveness, toughness, effort, ambition, achievement, and success, generally has been a male preserve. Adult-controlled sports programs for children generally have categorically excluded females in an effort to protect the masculine image of sport or to protect young females from physical, physiological, or psychological harm that would ostensibly result from intense physical competition, especially with males. Whatever the reasons for excluding females from Little Leaguism in the past, these reasons have come under increasing attack and many previously all-male programs have yielded to these pressures and included females in recent years.

The female challenge to Little League Baseball began in the spring of 1972 in Hoboken, New Jersey, when a twelve year-old girl named Maria Pepe demonstrated in her tryout that she was good enough to participate in the local Little League.[50] After learning about her enrollment, the national headquarters of Little League, Inc. in Williamsport, Pennsylvania, revoked the charter of the team for which Maria played because it had violated the boys-only policy that had been confirmed by action of the United States Congress when it granted a national charter to Little League. Instead of accepting the League's decision, Maria Pepe's family challenged it. They took their case to the Civil Rights Division of the State of New Jersey. Five days of arguments were heard, and no definite proof was presented to demonstrate that boys of Little League ages-from eight to twelve—were superior to girls of those ages in characteristics such as muscle strength and reaction time that were relevant to participation in baseball. Indeed, girls in this age group tend to be two inches taller and four or five pounds heavier on the average than their male counterparts. Girls at these ages also tend to have a lower center of gravity and a better sense of balance, which makes it harder to knock them off balance when they are in motion[51]

On the basis of the testimony presented in this case, the hearing officer, Sylvia Pressler, decided that Little League was practicing sex discrimination by excluding Maria Pepe. Though she left it to her superior, the Director of the New Jersey Civil Rights Division, to decide how to respond to this discrimination, she made a strong statement challenging the traditional Little League and Congressional policy that excluded girls from Little League. For example, she said that, "The sooner little boys begin to realize that there are many areas of life in which girls are their equal and that it is no great shame, no great burden to be bested by a girl, then perhaps we come that much closer to the legislative ideal of sexual equality as well as to relieving a source of emotional difficulty for men."[52]

The terms of the administrative order issued by Gilbert H. Frances for the New Jersey Civil Rights Division on January 30, 1974, were even more compelling a challenge to Little League tradition than Sylvia Pressler's findings. Little League in New Jersey was ordered to admit girls into full membership; to allow girls who had proven their ability to compete for a place on a team and to play in any game that the team played; to inform all local leagues in the state of its intention to comply with the order; and to submit an annual report demonstrating its compliance. In February 1974, Little League appealed to the State Superior Court to stay the order, and was denied the stay. The following month, Little League entered another plea, which was denied by a three-judge panel. On April 11, 1974, the State of New Jersey published the order as an extension of state law. This action prompted a number of local leagues in the state to announce that they would suspend play rather than admit girls. However, Little League officials in Williamsport advised its New Jersey subsidiaries to comply with the state ruling. The conflict ultimately was resolved in December 1974 by an act of Congress that amended tha Little League Federal Charter to allow participation by girls as well as boys. This revision of the eligibility rule was accompanied by a replacement of the League's official aim of "instilling manhood" with the goals of "citizenship" and "sportsmanship."

Two appeals by Little League officials and the intention of several local officials in New Jersey to suspend play before admitting girls indicate the resistance Maria Pepe faced in seeking to play organized baseball with boys. However, Maria Pepe and her family were not alone in their battle to include females in Little League, and they were not alone in facing resistance. Carolyn King earned a position as a centerfielder on a team in the Ypsilanti, Michigan, Little League after demonstrating that she was a better baseball player than over one hundred boys with whom she competed in trying out for the league. However, when the Ypsilanti Little League complied with an order by the City Council to allow her to play or face the loss of city facilities, staff, and financial aid,

Little League officials in the National Office revoked the local league's charter. In June 1973, one month after a suit was filed by Carolyn King, the Ypsilanti American Little League, and the city of Ypsilanti against the National Little Leagues organization over its exclusion of girls, Representative Martha W. Griffiths introduced bill H.R. 8854 into the U.S. House of Representatives. This bill led to the amendment of the Little League charter that allowed girls to play[53]

The legal establishment has not always been of the side of the female Little League aspirants. In a suit brought by Pamela Magill's parents against the Avonworth Baseball Conference, Federal Judge Barron P. McCune ruled that the league had a right to exclude a ten year-old girl from playing. Judge McCune supported the argument of the board of directors of the Conference who contended:[54]

> ...the 45-pound girl's admission to Little League play would downgrade the team she joined talentwise, inhibit the play, complicate the task of getting fathers to volunteer for coaching and managing duties, and greatly embarrass the boys who had to sit on the bench while a girl was on the playing field.

Whether or not Pamela Magill was qualified to play in the Avonworth league, the reaction to her effort to play by league officials and a federal judge reveals the fears and concerns that have been associated with opening up Little Leaguism to females. Along with Victorian arguments about protection of the girls' welfare, these fears and concerns effectively kept half the children in the United States from pursuing organized forms of games many of them may have played informally on their own with male and female friends. The fact that most of these fears, concerns, and arguments have proven groundless or unfair does not minimize their roles in justifying and reinforcing the traditional exclusion of girls from Little Leaguism. Exclusion of girls from the organized, and often well-publicized, sports of Little Leaguism denied them the chance for recognition and status gains many boys have earned from their achievements as Little Leaguers. Indeed, girls who excelled informally as athletes in the games of Little Leaguism such as baseball, football, and soccer, were likely to be stigmatized or labeled as "tomboys" for their athletic interests and accomplishments.

By excluding females, Little Leaguism kept invisible the athletic talents or potential of many young females. Though Little Leaguism can place heavy and dubious pressures on children not yet ready to adapt to them, it may provide opportunities to prepare for the competitive pressures to be experienced later in sport or elsewhere in American society[55] The exclusion of girls from Little Leaguism denied them this possible socialization, and perhaps more importantly, it helped perpetuate the myth that females were not able to compete or achieve. The related normative ideas that females *should not* compete or try too hard to achieve are part of what Judith Zoble referred to as "the woman's dilemma (in American society)": living in an achievement-oriented society, females are discouraged from achieving[56] The destructive effects

of the discouragement or stigmatization of female competitive achievement was noted by Zoble in the case of a little girl who had won her
town's soap box derby. The little girl sobbed when she received her
trophy, but her tears did not reflect joy. Instead, they indicated her *regret*
in winning. "I didn't mean to win" was what she sobbed. In this context,
we can begin to appreciate why the American Dream has been more of
a male than female dream and why females often have had to hitch their
dreams to male horses.

In another part of her decision regarding Maria Pepe, Sylvia Pressler
of the New Jersey Civil Rights Division said, "The institution of Little
League is as American as the hot dog and apple pie. There is no reason
why that part of Americana should be withheld from girls."[57] Since
December 1974, when Congress revised the Little League charter to
allow girls to play, Little Leaguism has not been withheld from females.
Now that there are more opportunities for girls to participate in organized
sports formerly reserved for boys. we might wonder whether emphases
on effort, sportsmanship. achievememt, getting ahead, winning, and
success will change in Little Leaguism to reflect increased female
involvement or whether female aspirations and behavior will change to
reflect increased exposure to traditionally masculine values through
involvement in Little Leaguism. At this point, there have been no obvious
changes in the basic structure of Little Leaguism other than the revised
charter permitting female participation and the revised public ideology
emphasizing citizenship and sportsmanship instead of training for
manhood. However, we do know that a higher proportion of females are
remaining in organized sports through adolescence and adulthood
than in the past. We also know that as a result of the women's movement
in American society, sex roles have undergone a transformation during
the past decade of change in female opportunities in sport. The increased
participation of females in Little Leaguism and later in other forms of
organized sport may be an important element in the resocialization or
new socialization process that has caused more women to think seriously
about pursuing traditionally male careers both inside and outside
sport. Thus, even if increased female participation does not encourage a
more serious commitment to the noble stated purposes of Little Leaguism
and minimize concern with the "Lombardian ethic." if may ease the later
adjustment of females to traditionally male roles and increase the
acceptance and approval by society in general of females who pursue
such roles. In this way, the "female challenge" to Little Leaguism may
help open up the American Dream to assure females a place in its vision
of success.

# Conclusion: An Assessment of the Myth and Reality of the American Dream in Children's Sports

In emphasizing effort, achievement, and personal responsibility for failure and in rewarding achievement with trophies, public recognition, and personal deference, Little Leaguism seems to embody much of the central core of the ideology of the American Dream. However, the reality of Little Leaguism drifts away from this ideology and even its own stated purposes when it gives only lip service to sportsmanship, translates competitive contests into battles where only winning counts, and denies opportunities to all but the talented and those with "connections" in the coaching staffs or administration of the league. Indeed, in the latter regard, for most of its history Little Leaguism forbad all females from participating and Little League itself, with the blessing of the U.S. Congress, even included training for manhood in its public statement of purpose.

Perhaps because it is *not* actually an embodiment of its own ideological aims or a romanticized vision of the American Dream, Little Leaguism may teach young athletes more about the reality of competition in adult American society and about pursuit of an adult version of the American Dream than the adults who control it realize or acknowledge. Certainly, many of "destiny's darlings" whom Martin Ralbovsky interviewed learned that achieving the dream of a Little League championship could be a mixed blessing and that their success faded more rapidly than they wished. They also learned that being a Little League champion offered no guarantee of success in the future—even just a year later as a Babe Ruth League candidate in the case of Johnny Palmer. Some of these Little League champions perceived their championship more as a prize for their manager than themselves. He taught his players to be uncompromising, relentless, and even mean in the pursuit of victory. While one of them appreciated this learning experience as preparation for his adult career, at least two or three others felt cheated or exploited by their manager. They felt they had been used to achieve his ends, and they saw no enduring benefits of this treatment.

Johnny Palmer said that it would have meant a lot more to him as an adult if the kids on his team had won the championship on their own—without the direction of their manager. This reflection on his earlier success touches a central element of the structure of Little Leaguism— the control exercised by adults. On the one hand, the injection of adult values, expectation, actions, and dreams into children's sports programs may cause Little Leaguism to mirror adult society and offer possible preparation for the competitive pursuits and pressures of adulthood, at least for males. On the other hand, though, by thrusting children into a world of competition that only a talented and mature few are prepared to handle, Little Leaguism may cause psychological damage and create more cynicism than idealism about the American Dream. Furthermore, by substituting institutionalized and externally controlled activities for the more spontaneous, expressive, and autonomous play and games of childhood, Little Leaguism may deprive children of opportunities to learn and grow that would serve them well as adults.

It is a tribute to the resilience of many children that they are able to derive fun from Little Leaguism despite the pressures to become professionalized or exclusively committed to winning. It is a tribute to many parents and coaches of Little Leaguers that they are able to emphasize fun, sportsmanship, and the development of skills despite pressures to professionalize and win "at any cost" and the temptation to use their team as a path to glory for themselves. It may be that adult-controlled sports for children provide the most benefits and fun for the children when they do *not* try to mirror adult competitive models and when they do *not* try to be a proving ground for the pursuit of the American Dream. When the competition is open to everyone and the competitors are treated sensitively and supportively by adults as *little* leaguers and not *major* leaguers, Little Leaguism may offer its most valuable rewards of fun, lessons in fair play, and opportunities to test and develop skills without the pressure to be a winner. When winning becomes the yardstick for enjoyment, Little Leaguers lose the chance for genuine fun and may develop a distorted interpretation of the meaning of achievement and success and how they should be pursued later in life. In an atmosphere where only a few can win and even fewer can be winners all the time, many may begin to see themselves as failures at an age when their identities and self-confidence are just beginning to take shape. The developmental consequences of such experiences could be long-lasting.

In general, then, it seems that Little Leaguism often falls short of the kind of competitive experience that the pursuit of the American Dream is envisioned to be in the dominant ideology of American society. In addition, if often falls short of the vision of sport embodied in the dominant American sports creed and in the stated purposes of Little Leaguism itself. For these reasons, this chapter will close with the critical appraisal of Little League baseball offered by former major league baseball pitcher Robin Roberts:[58]

> I still don't know what those three gentlemen in Williamsport had in mind when they organized Little League baseball. I'm sure they didn't want parents arguing with their children about kids' games. I'm sure they didn't want to have family meals disrupted for three months every year. I'm sure they didn't want young boys who don't have much athletic ability made to feel that something is wrong with them because they can't play baseball. I'm sure they didn't want a group of coaches drafting the players each year for different teams. I'm sure they didn't want unqualified men working with

the young players. I'm sure they didn't realize how normal it is for an 8 year-old boy to be scared of a thrown or batted ball. For the life of me, I can't figure out what they had in mind.

# Footnotes

[1]Jerry Izenberg, *How Many Miles to Camelot? The All-American Sport Myth* (New York: Holt, Rinehart, and Winston, 1972).

[2]Edward C. Devereux, "Backyard versus Little League Baseball: the impoverishment of children's games," *Social Problems in Athletics*, ed. by Daniel M. Landers (Urbana: University of Illinois Press, 1976). The assumed historical drift away from loosely structured play activities to more institutionalized games and sport for American boys has been substantiated by the research of B. Sutton-Smith and B. Rosenberg ("Sixty years of historical change in the game preferences of American children," *Child's Play*, ed. by R.E. Herron and B. Sutton-Smith, New York: Wiley, 1971) and of Janet Lever ("Sex differences in the complexity of children's play and games," *American Sociological Review*, 43 (1978): 471-483).

[3]This term is taken from Devereux, "Backyard versus Little League Baseball..."

[4]John M. Roberts and Brian Sutton-Smith, "Child training and game involvement," *Ethnology*, 1 (1962): 166-185.

[5]Devereux, "Backyard versus Little League Baseball...," p. 47.

[6]A fuller discussion of the emergence of children's sports in the U.S. If provided by Jack Berryman, "From the cradle to the playing field: America's emphasis on highly organized competitive sports for preadolescent boys," *Journal of Sport History*, 21 (1975): 112-131. John W. Loy, Barry D. McPherson, and Gerald Kenyon (*Sport and Social Systems*, Reading, Mass.: Addison-Wesley, 1978, p. 239) offer a capsule view of this emergence process, and the disussion in this section closely follows their remarks.

[7]The source of these statistics about Little League Baseball is John D. Burchard, "Competitive youth sports and social competence," *The Primary Prevention of Psychopathology. Promoting Social Competence and Coping in Children*, vol. 3, ed. by M.W. Kent and J.E. Rolf (Hanover, N.H.: University Press of New England, 1979).

[8]*U.S. News & World Report* (February 4, 1974).

[9]Cited in Burchard, "Competitive youth sports and social competence."

[10]*Ibid.*

[11]Loy, McPherson, and Kenyon, *Sport and Social Systems*, p. 239.

[12]*1977 Offical Rules: Little League Rules and Regulations*, p. 2.

[13]Gary Alan Fine, "Preadloescent socialization through organized athletics: the construction of moral meanings in Little League Baseball," *The Dimensions of Sport Sociology*, ed. by March L. Krotee (West Point: Leisure Press, 1979).

[14]Harry Webb, "Professionalization of attitudes toward play among adolescents," *Sociology of Sport*, ed. by Gerald S. Kenyon (Chicago: Athletic Institute, 1969).

[15]Geoffrey G. Watson, "Family organization and Little League Baseball," *International Review of Sport Sociology*, 2/9 (1974): 5-32.

[16]These results concerning social class differences were reported by Geoffrey G. Watson in his article "Games, socialization and parental values: social class differences in parental evaluation of Little League Baseball," *International Review of Sport Sociology*, 1/12 (1977): 17-56.

[17]David L. Larson, Elmer Spreitzer, And Eldon E. Snyder, "Youth hockey programs: a sociological perspective," *Sport Sociology Bulletin*, 4 (1975) 55-63.

[18]Harry Edwards, *Sociology of Sport* (Homewood, Ill.: Dorsey, 1973).

[19]Izenberg, *How Many Miles to Camelot?*, p. 201.

[20]Fine, "Preadolescent socialization through organized athletics...," p. 104.

[21]Geoffrey G. Watson and Thomas M. Kando, "The meaning of rules and rituals in Little League Baseball," *Pacific Sociological Review*, 19 (1976): 291-316.

[22]See Geoffrey G. Watson, "Reward systems in children's games: the attraction of game interaction in Little League Baseball," *Review of Sport & Leisure,* 1 (1976): 93-121, along with Watson, "Games, socialization, and parental values...," p. 45.

[23]Thomas Tutko and William Bruns, *Winning is Everything and Other American Myths* (New York: Macmillan, 1976), p. 78.

[24]Carolyn W. Sherif, "The social context of competition," *Social Problems in Athletics,* ed. by Daniel M. Landers (Urbana: University of Illinois Press, 1976).

[25]Randall H. Lowe, "Stress, arousal, and task performance of Little League baseball players." (Unpublished doctoral dissertation, University of Illinois, 1973).

[26]Jay J. Coakley (*Sport in Society: issues and controversies,* St. Louis: C.V. Mosby, 1978) has supported this general point by citing research reported by Bryant J. Cratty (*Social Dimensions of Physical Activity,* Englewood Cliffs, N.J.: Prentice-Hall, 1967) and by Bruce C. Ogilvie and Thomas A. Tutko ("Sport: if you want to build character, try something else," *Psychology Today* (October 1971): 61-63).

[27]Coakley (*Sport in Society...,* p. 50) has pointed out that the Yerkes-Dodson principle in psychology asserts that when the level of tension arousal is too high or too low, motivation will be low, and that motivation is highest when a certain degree of tension is felt but not to excess. A "winning at all costs" philosophy in Little Leaguism could easily raise tension and anxiety beyond their tolerable limits for children not mature enough to adapt to such stress, with the result being diminished performance and motivation.

[28]See, for example, Muzafer Sherif, "Experiments in group conflict" (*Scientific American,* 195/5 (1956): 54-58), for a summary of some relevant aspects of this research.

[29]For example, the experimenters created a series of emergency situations such as a breakdown in the water supply and of a truck on its way to town for their food. Cooperation on these tasks *gradually* brought the hostile groups into a more harmonious relationship.

[30]These cheers, promoted by Junior League football, were cited in James A. Michener's *Sports in America* (New York: Random House, 1976), p. 100.

[31]Burchard, "Competitive youth sports and social competence."

[32]Webb, "Professionalization of attitudes toward play among adolescents."

[33]Cited in Richard Woodley, "How to win the Soap Box Derby: in which craftsmanship abets the passion for success to produce a tale of moral confusion," *Harper's Magazine* (August 1974): 62-69.

[34]Michael Jay Kaufman and Joseph Popper (in Pee wee pill poppers," *Sport* (December 1976); 16-25) have described instances of this behavior along with the pressures that cause then.

[35]Tutko and Bruns (*Winning is Everything and Other American Myths,* ch. 11) have described the potential injuries for children in these sports in more detail.

[36]Cited in Michener, *Sports in America,* p. 432.

[37]Martin Ralbovsky, *Lords of the Locker Room* (New York: Wyden Books, 1974).

[38]Bill Bradley, *Life on the Run* (New York: Quadrangle, 1976), pp. 120-121.

[39]Tutko and Bruns *(Winning is Everything and Other American Myths)* have written about the consequences of stardom for young athletes in a chapter called "The Superstar: A Curse or a Blessing?" In this chapter, they examined society's fascination with talented young athletes and the funnel effect of high-level competitive sports along with the role of parents and family in the young athlete's development.

[40]See Barry McDermott's "He'll make your child a champ" (in *Sports Illustrated,* June 9, 1980) for a story about Bollettieri's academy and his methods of teaching tennis to talented children and adolescents.

[41]*Ibid.*

[42]Don Schollander and D. Savage, *Deep Water* (New York: Ballantine, 1971), see pp. 10-15.

[43]Martin Ralbovsky, *Destiny's Darlings* (New York: Hawthorn, 1974).

[44]Cited in Michener, *Sports in America,* p. 103.

[45]Cited in Terry Orlick and Cal Botterill, *Every Kid Can Win* (Chicago: Nelson-Hall, 1975).

[46]*Ibid.*

[47]Cited in John Underwood, "Taking the fun out," *Sports Illustrated* (November 17, 1975): 86-98.

[48]Cratty's comments were cited by Tutko and Bruns, *Winning is Everything and Other American Myths,* p.90.

[49]Howard L. Nixon II, "Growing up with hockey in Canada," *International Review of Sport Sociology,* 1/11 (1976): 37-48.

[50]This case was discussed in Michener, *Sports in America,* pp. 130-132.

[51]See Carl E. Klafs and M. Joan Lyon (*The Female Athlete,* St. Louis: C.V. Mosby, 1973, Part II) for a discussion of male and female differences in anatomical and physical factors related to sport.

[52]Cited in Michener, *Sports in America,* p. 131.

[53]This case was discussed in Jan Felshin, "The social view," *The American Woman in Sport,* by E.W. Gerber et al. (Reading, Mass.: Addison-Wesley, 1974), p. 217.

[54]This statement appeared in the *Lehighton Times-News* (July 6, 1973), and it was cited in a discussion of Pamels Magill's case by Felshin, "The social view," p. 201.

[55]Janet Lever (in "Sex differences in the games children play," *Social Problems,* 23 (1976); 478-487) argued that the sex differences she observed in children's games tended to have a conservative influence on the performance of adult roles. That is, the nature of male game involvement has prepared young males for traditional masculine adult roles, while the nature of female game involvement has prepared for traditional feminine roles as adults. Lever found that boys were more likely than girls to play in large groups, to play in age-heterogeneous groups, to play games that lasted longer. She suggested that these differences in game involvement might equip boys with social skills needed in occupational careers in a bureaucratic society and equip girls with social skills needed to raise a family and take care of a home.

[56]Judith E. Zoble, "Femininity and achievement in sports," *Women and Sport: A National Research Conference,* ed. by Dorothy V. Harris (Penn State HPER Series No. 2, The Pennsylvania State University, 1972).

[57]Cited in Felshin, "The social view," p. 217.

[58]Robin Roberts, "Strike out Little League," *Newsweek* (July 21, 1975): 11.

# 3

## *Sport in the School*

# Introduction

In 1971, Stockbridge, Michigan, was a town of about 1,000 people who were consumed by basketball fever. Even on nights when the roads were covered with ice and snow and the opponent was weak, 800 screaming fans filled the Stockbridge High School gym to cheer their beloved Panthers on to victory. The coach of the Panthers, Phil Hora, said, "This just isn't the school's team. It's the town's team. The whole town, everybody, watched these kids grow up and practice basketball together since grade school. They are part of us. This is the best team we've ever had here."[1]

The Stockbridge basketball players were well appreciated by their fans off the court as well as on. Young ladies sought their autographs. They were the focus of morning conversation in the downtown coffee shop and of evening talk at the town's bar and bowling alley. Banners proclaimed Stockbridge "the home of the Panthers," and every downtown store displayed pictures of the starting five in their windows. Tournament victories were announced by the town's fire engine and ambulance sirens, and the young athletic heroes were toasted at banquets sponsored by the American Legion, bowling alley, and school faculty.

Stockbridge may not have called its team "destiny's darlings," but there are a number of elements in the story of these young athletes on the verge of becoming state champions that are reminiscent of the story of the 1954 Schenectady Little League champions. However, it may be recalled that the success earned by winning the Little League World Series offered no guarantee of equivalent success later in sport or in other areas of life. Indeed, for a number of members of the 1954 championship team, life afterward, into adulthood, was filled with disappointments, frustrations, and failures that were absent from the vision of a bright future many in their community anticipated for them. At least some in Stockbridge were more realistic about the future of their young heroes. As one fan put it: "These are the glory days for these kids, right now. After they leave high school, they are has-beens around here . . . just like all the other guys in this town (who remained after *their* high school glory days)."

Of course, for the genuine superstars of small town and big city high school teams, there may be future opportunities to recapture the American Dream as athletic heroes in college or perhaps even in professional sports. However, since relatively few high school athletes have the potential to become collegiate or professional stars, we might wonder what the experience of high school athletics *generally* means and provides to participants, and where this experience tends to lead on the road to the American Dream. This chapter will examine the meaning and consequences of participation, achievement, and success in high school athletics, and it will look especially closely at the prospects for achievement, social mobility, and success on and off the athletic field in high school and afterward for participants in interscholastic athletics.

# The Nature of Interscholastic Athletics

## 1. History, Philosophy, and Structure

One of the most extensive studies of athletics at the college and secondary school levels was conducted by the Carnegie Foundation for the Advancement of Teaching? The investigation began in 1926, and 148 college and secondary schools in the United States and Canada were surveyed. As a result of this study, a series of reports were issued in 1929 and 1931. The reports indicated that the period covering the last decade of the nineteenth century and the first decade of the twentieth had a crucial impact on the developing structure of sport in American colleges and high schools. Before this period, intramural and extramural games were played by school clubs that were under the control of students. Nineteenth century students played competitive team games because they were an enjoyable diversion from the monotony or pressure of school work and other serious activities. In the report of an important Physical Training conference that took place in 1889, there were only two references to competitive athletics or games. At that point in American education, competitive games, athletics, and sports tended to be viewed as leisurely pastimes, while gymnastics or calisthenics were seen as the most important forms of exercise in physical training programs for students in the schools and colleges.

In the final decade of the nineteenth century and the first decade of the twentieth century, rapid and dramatic changes occurred in the physical activity programs of American schools. Following the pattern at the collegiate level, the role of gymnastics in physical education programs in the schools declined in importance as competitive games and sports became more important. Extramural sports became organized as interscholastic athletics under the direction of professional coaches and administrators who saw "educational" or socialization benefits to be derived from these activities.

An early model for the organization of city school athletic competition was the New York Public School Athletic League, which was formed in 1903[3] It resulted largely from the efforts of Luther Halsey Gulick, who was early in his work as director of physical training for the New York public schools. Gulick wanted to broaden the base of participation in organized athletic competition to include more boys with average, rather than exceptional, skills. The PSAL he helped to organize was approved by the Board of Education, but it was a distinct organization that was established through the cooperative efforts of the Superintendent of Schools, the Presidents of the Board of Education and the City College of New York, the Secretary of the Amateur Athletic Union, the Chairman of the Intercollegiate Athletic Association, and several important businessmen who had influence in the political and financial worlds. The operation of the league program was supported financially by membership fees and contributions from citizens, which included such prominent financiers as J. Pierpont Morgan, Andrew Carnegie, John D. Rockefeller, and Harry Payne Whitney. Gulick launched the league with the aid of publicity from nine newspapers in the New York metropolitan area.

In 1910, Arthur Reeve called the PSAL "the world's greatest athletic organization."[4] He applauded the work of the league in developing the character of thousands of boys, and he pointed to the value of athletic competition in improving their school work. The types of sports pursued by participants in league competition included running, relay racing, baseball, basketball, football, soccer, cross-country running, swimming, ice and roller skating, and shooting. Baseball was especially popular, with 106 teams competing in 1907 and 15,000 spectators in attendance at the final game that year. However, according to General George W. Wingate, the first president of the PSAL, none of the league's activities was "likely to have as important an influence upon the country at large as the system of instruction in military rifle shooting."[5] In 1908, 7,000 boys received instruction in this activity. Marksmanship badges were awarded; annual contests between different high schools occurred; prizes were awarded by the duPont Nemours Powder Company to the school team having the highest score; and while he was the President, Theodore Roosevelt always wrote a letter of commendation to the boy demonstrating the greatest marksmanship for the year.

Females initially were excluded from PSAL participation. However, in 1905 the Girls' Branch of the league was organized. Unlike the boys' PSAL, it was not independent from the school system. It was an important part of their physical education program. Girls were not given a chance to participate in interschool competition, but thousands became involved in play days during which less competitive physical activities such as folk dancing were very popular.

It seems evident that the PSAL in its early years was seen by its founders, administrators, and benefactors and by interested observers such as Arthur Reeve as performing some valuable socialization functions. The different types of activities made available to males and females reveals very different expectations about the social develop-ment and responsibilities of the two sexes. Males were encouraged not only to compete, but also to develop skills such as shooting that could prepare them to defend their country. Females were directed into more aesthetically-oriented, and less competitive, activities such as folk dancing.

The PSAL in New York City quickly inspired similar types of public school athletic leagues in a number of other American cities, which included New Orleans, Seattle, Baltimore, Newark, Buffalo, Cleveland, Birmingham, Tacoma, Philadelphia, Chicago, Troy, San Francisco, Kansas City (Kansas), Oakland, and Helena. Thus, the idea of interscholastic athletics already was widespread in the United States very early in the twentieth century. A study done in 1904-1905 that covered 555 American cities of various sizes indicated that 345 had high school athletic associations. The popularity of the major sports was reflected in statistics showing that 432 of these cities had football, 360 had baseball, 213 had basketball, and 161 had track teams. The consolidated school movement, which was occurring at this time, enabled rural children to participate in the types of sports programs found in the large towns and cities.

Although sports programs quickly became popular in the high schools at the beginning of this century, there was a cultural lag in the content of physical education programs during this period[6] Until about the start of World War I, physical education instruction continued to concentrate on gymnastics or calisthenics, while competitive games and sports tended to be confined to the afterschool programs. This lag in the introduction of competitive games into physical education classes may have occurred for a number of reasons. Included among these reasons might be the continuing influence of Puritanical values that were hostile to the ostensibly idle or indulgent pleasures of frivolous play, lack of training in sports skills among physical education teachers who tended to be oriented toward gymnastics instruction, and the inability of many schools to adapt their facilities and scheduled class times to instruction of large numbers of (male) students during physical education classes.

During the second decade of the twentieth century, an "athletics for all" movement emerged. This idea reflected the pattern of athletic participation in English private schools; and in the United States, it probably originated in the private high schools and academies, which were better equipped in personnel and facilities than the public high schools to meet the growing interest in sports early in this century. In the public high schools, pressure at this time to create more oppportunities for sports participation probably came mostly from outside. "The wider use of the school plant" became a slogan of taxpayers and municipal officials, and despite some initial resistance from school officials, there was a gradual opening up of school gymnasiums and playgrounds for a variety of forms of physical recreation and sports during evening, weekends, and summers. Increasing use of public high school facilities for competitive games, sports, and physical recreation of various types reinforced efforts to include these types of activities in regular physical education classes in the schools.

Once public school officials accepted the major role of athletics in their extracurriculum programs, they began to be concerned about the regulation and control of interscholastic athletics. Athletic programs had grown haphazardly in the schools, just as they had in the colleges. To rectify this disorderly condition, there first developed school organizations to establish policies within the schools. Then associations between two or more schools developed, and finally, after some additional intermediate steps, statewide associations were organized to establish uniform rules and regulations for interscholastic athletic competition. The growth of a bureaucracy of educators to regulate and control interscholastic athletics reflected the educators' desire not only to introduce order into the expansion and administration of athletic programs, but also to transfer control of these programs from representatives of colleges, clubs, and promotional associations to themselves. By 1918, the National Education Association had legitimized the inclusion of athletics in the total program of the high school. In their report that year, which was called *"Cardinal Principles of Secondary Education"* and is widely assumed to be the classic statement of the modern comprehensive high school, school leaders called for the "participation of pupils in common activities... such as athletic games..."[7] They saw such activities as means to develop social skills and a sense of social responsibility and group loyalty, which generally were thought by educators to be important qualities needed to nurture good citizenship and maintain the national commitment to democracy.

World War I probably contributed significantly to the spread of interest and participation in athletics in this country. Fears that Congress would require universal military training in the schools and Selective Service statistics showing the poor physical condition of American youth resulted in the passage of state legislation setting up compulsory physical education programs in American schools.[8] Though schools often lacked adequate personnel, equipment, and facilities at this time, a number of states almost immediately followed the lead of California in introducing sports instruction and tests into their physical education programs. Thus, a gradual shift from gymnastics to sports in physical education occurred between World War I and the early 1930s. This shift seemed to be accompanied by an overshadowing of physical education by athletics. the Carnegie survey cited earlier revealed that by the late 1920s, forty-seven states had interscholastic athletic associations, while only seventeen states had directors or departments of physical education. As a result of this discrepancy, the Carnegie study proposed that, "If public recognition be a criterion of judgment, physical education is considered to be far less important than inter-school athletics..."[9]

The pattern of increasing control and coordination of athletic programs and policies by educators led to the founding of a national organization of high school athletics in 1922. The National Federation of State High School Athletic Associations now has members from nearly all the states in the nation. It has played an important role in motivating and helping member associations to agree on matters such as rules of athletic eligibility, elimination of national championships, regulation of interstate meets and tournaments, creation of rules for high school competition and athletes, and national policies regarding equipment and adjustments in sport practices.

The boom in participation in interscholastic athletics and in spectator interest during the 1920s was reversed by the economic depression during the first few years of the 1930s. Budget cuts limited athletic equipment and facilities and reduced the availability of teachers to coach athletic teams. Many schools eliminated competition involving out-of-town travel expenses. Although the depression caused these reversals, it also ultimately had some favorable effects on the expansion of interscholastic athletics. A substantial amount of WPA and PWA money—$75 million by 1937—was spend on the construction of school sports facilities such as gymnasiums, swimming pools, tennis courts, and athletic fields.

The adverse economic effects of the depression on high school sports programs did little to dampen the enthusiasm of high school students and their communities for athletics. By the early 1930s, athletics had become a highly valued segment of the subculture of high school students. In his well-known study of American schools at that time, Willard Waller wrote that, "Of all activities (in the culture of the school) athletics is the chief... It is the most flourishing and the most revered culture pattern... At the head of the list (of competitive athletics) stands football... Then come basketball, baseball, track, lightweight football, lightweight basketball, girl's basketball, girl's track, etc. ..."[10]

The salience of interscholastic athletics carried beyond the depression years because August Hollingshead found in his classic study of *Elmtown's Youth,* which was published at the end of the next decade, that athletic prowess for boys was a source of prestige in the community as well as in the school.[11] His study showed that interscholastic football and basketball generated more public support and school interest than a combination of all other extracurricular activities. Furthermore, this substantial popularity was accompanied by equivalent pressures on school and athletic personnel to "deliver the goods." The superintendent of schools was evaluated by the public in terms of the performance of the schools' teams. Coaches were paid the maximum salary with an understanding that their job future depended on the number of games they won—especially in football and basketball.[12]

The development of professionalized interscholastic programs by the 1940s represented a significant departure from the philosophy that spawned interscholastic athletics and also from the expedient rationales that had given athletics value in military training and during the depression. Gulick had organized the PSAL with the idea of providing athletic opportunities for large numbers of boys, and a democratic idea of "athletics for all" had subsequently inspired the growth of interscholastic athletics throughout the United States in the early part of this century. Though they expected positive socialization consequences from athletic participation, early proponents of interscholastic athletics generally saw these activities as a source of fun—in contrast to the rigorous discipline of gymnastics or calisthenics. With the outbreak of World War I, athletic programs were seen as a means of enhancing the physical fitness of American youth. During the depression, high school and college-age youths who could not find work were encouraged to stay in school and pursue extramural or intramural sports in an effort to keep them out of trouble. By the time of World War II, athletic participation was seen as a means of building morale as well as muscles, character, and physical stamina.

The professionalization of interscholastic athletics during this century has made athletics more serious for the participants and often has encouraged spectatorship at the expense of active participation. Interscholastic athletics became more professionalized because those who controlled it saw commercial and public relations value in athletics. Some school officials believed, or hoped, that gate receipts from interscholastic athletic events such as football and basketball would subsidize athletic facilities and equiment for intramural as well as interscholastic sports programs. In fact, revenue from interscholastic athletics rarely was sufficient to pay for the purchase or maintenance of the school's athletic plant and equipment. Nevertheless, school officials still saw financial gains to be derived *indirectly* from school athletics through the community spirit they were thought to engender.

It was believed that by creating pride in the school, successful athletic programs could encourage taxpayers in the community to support public education expenditures for athletics and other areas in the school budget. Furthermore, increased expenditures for the school were seen as aiding the local economy by directing more business to local merchants. The Carnegie Foundation report summarized the assumed benefits of interscholastic athletic programs in saying that, "a series of fast, hard games at basketball or football, forming a season that culminates in a championship match, whether lost or won, leads to much excitement, town pride, and profits in sales of good by local merchants."[13] To this, we could add Joel Spring's comment from his examination of mass culture and school sports: "Athletics became a form of boosterism, a symbolic representation of the dynamics of the community."[14] Though the words are different, this comment is similar to what the Stockbridge basketball coach said about his team. The symbolic value of high school sports programs probably has been greatest in the smaller communities of America such as Stockbridge, Michigan.

From this brief overview of major aspects of the historical development of interscholastic athletics in the first half of this century, it should be evident that school sports programs became increasingly institutionalized and accepted during this period. Since their acceptance by educators early in this century, interscholastic athletic programs generally have enjoyed a relatively prominent place in the overall program of the high school, which has been threatened only by severe dips in the local or national economy. In communities across the United States, athletics has achieved a central place in the value systems of high school students and their community; and school athletic administrators and coaches of major sports often have become esteemed figures in their community.

Although high school sports programs may have grown as a result of the physical or military training they were seen to offer, the commercial or public relations value they were though to possess, or the prestige that winning performances tended to confer on athletes, schools, and communities, these programs generally have been *publicly* promoted by educators as a significant socialization experience or character-builder. In this vein, educators often have minimized the importance of winning in their statements about interscholastic sports programs. For example, leading educators have said, "In the face of many discordant and unworthy aims, the effort to direct (athletics) toward educational ends is tremendously worthwhile."[15] In addition, a President of the American Association of School Administrators has said, "The athletic program should be based upon its educational value to the participating boys and girls and to the schools in general."[16] It is interesting to consider the extent to which the actual structure of contemporary interscholastic athletics embodies the ideals of this philosophy of athletics.

## 2. Philosophy and Reality in Contemporary Interscholastic Athletics

The most comprehensive and systematically-derived statement from educators about their philosophy or ideology of athletics is a report of the Educational Policies Commission called *School Athletics,* which was published in 1954.[17] The Educational Policies Commission is a division of the National Education Association and the American Association of School Administrators. It was founded in 1935 to serve the purposes of preparing, publishing, and distributing statements of proposed policy regarding American education. The recommendations in *School Athletics* continued to impress prominent American educators many years after they were published, and in 1967, the President's Council on Youth Fitness was encouraged to use these recommendations in setting their own policy for educationally sound interscholastic athletic programs.

The recommendations made by the Educational Policies Commission also were used by John Talamini to represent the dominant philosophy of athletics among educators in his study of the relationship between public policy and actual practice in interscholastic athletics.[18] Talamini's research deserves a closer look not only because it draws attention to major educational ideals and structural dimensions of athletics in the American high school, but also because it reveals the extent to which the architects and administrators of interscholastic athletic programs try to realize the educational potential of these programs in the ways they design and run them. In addition, Talamini's research merits attention simply because it helps bring up to date the historical picture of the development of American high school athletic policy and practice in this century. This picture should be kept in mind in trying to understand the role of interscholastic athletics in the pursuit of the American Dream, the main focus of this chapter.

Talamini gathered his data from sixty athletic directors of public high schools in an eastern state. These high schools were four-year and six-year coeducational institutions, and they ranged in size from 456 students to 2850 students. Interview questions were designed to elicit responses from athletic directors regarding eight of the most important policy statements in the Educational Policies Commission report. Although two of these statements concern intramurals and one deals with physical education, all are relevant to a school's athletic program and are worthy of consideration here. The eight policy statements can be described in the following way:

- *Postseason Tournaments.* The elimination of postseason champion-ships was recommended because from an educational standpoint, these championships tended to do more harm than good. They extended the playing season, which could produce physical and psychological harm for the athletes; they distracted from school work and caused absence from school; and they involved excessive personal and school expenditures for travel.

- *Extramurals.* The commission recommended broadening the base of athletic participation through play days or sports days with other schools in which the emphasis is on fun for males and females and the day's events include social events, such as mixers, as well as athletic contests. There was concern about the limited number of students directly involved in formal interscholastic athletic programs. The commission felt the benefits of new acquaintances and friendships with students from other schools would be more widely shared through extramural contacts such as play days or sports days.

- *Corecreation.* The commission recommended the sponsorship of several corecreational sports—such as bowling, swimming, tennis, archery, volleyball, table tennis, and golf—in the intramural program. Mixed-sex sports of these types were seen as promoting greater respect, understanding, and friendship across the sexes.

- *Carry-over Intramurals.* An emphasis on intramural sports that could be continued through adulthood was recommended.

- *Recruitment and Regulation of Coaches (Role Models).* The commis-sion felt that interscholastic coaches should be models for youth in what they say and do.

- *Recruitment of Coaches (Professional Training).* It was recommended that interscholastic coaches should be certified in physical education. Physical education training was assumed to teach prospective coaches how to foster educational values in athletics and how to deal with adolescent growth and development.

- *Organizational Structure of Athletic Programs.* The commission proposed that all athletics should be part of the physical education program. Through this organizational arrangement, the educational value of athletic participation could be emphasized.

- *Financial Resources.* The commission proposed that since athletic programs existed for educational purposes, they should be financed entirely by taxes—rather than by means of financing such as gate receipts, student fees, tournament revenues, tag sales, dances, and solicitations of contributions. It was feared that outside or special financing procedures would contribute to the commercialization of interscholastic athletics, which the commission viewed as the source of a number of undesirable practices.

Talamini's interview data indicated that the reality of high school athletic programs contrasted sharply with the educational ideals set forth for them by the Educational Policies Commission. Contrary to the commission recommendations about postseason play, it was found that 93% of the schools in Talamini's sample would participate in postseason tournaments if they qualified. Talamini noted in this regard that his results indicated "an overemphasis on winning." He went on to say that, "Success is perhaps America's dominant value and success in school sport, the crest of which is winning a postseason tournament, brings much publicity to the participating athletes, coaches, administrators, and their local communities." Thus, even though high school athletes may be learning about dominant American values contained in the ideology of the American Dream through their drive toward victory and success in postseason competition, this type of orientation toward athletics is not what the members of the Educational Policies Commission had in mind to promote "educational values."

The tendencies of the athletic programs in Talamini's sample to be success-oriented or professionalized and to be oriented toward talented males are reflected in other results uncovered by Talamini. For example, he found that only 23% of his high schools had an extramural program in which both sexes were represented. In programs where girls only were represented in extramurals, such activity may have been a compensation for not having an extensive girls' interscholastic athletic program. Thus, schools with extramurals for girls may have served the less talented females while neglecting the more talented ones by failing to provide higher-level competition for them. Since highly competitive interscholastic programs were emphasized more than extramurals for males, athletics tended to be oriented toward the more talented males while neglecting the less talented, which was the reverse of the situation for females.

Talamini also found that 62% of the high schools in his sample sponsored no corecreational intramural sports, and that only 20% sponsored more than three such sports. He found that of the 42 schools offering intramural sports to boys, only 17% equally sponsored carry-over and non-carry-over sports for them in their intramural program and just two schools emphasized carry-over sports for boys. Of the 44 schools offering intramural sports to girls, only 25% equally sponsored carry-over and non-carry-over sports, while 11% emphasized carry-over sports.

In regard to the policy recommendation concerning the recruitment and regulation of coaches, Talamini discovered that "experience" was the quality most frequently mentioned by athletic directors as a characteristic they looked for in hiring a head coach. "Moral character" was mentioned by only 18% of the athletic directors. It seems, then, that the athletic directors placed less emphasis than the Educational Policies Commission on the importance of their coaches setting a moral example for young people. Further evidence of the limited concern among these administrators with the example set by their coaches is the finding that 75% of the athletic directors had no rule against coaches smoking in the school or anywhere else. Of course, one might argue that "misbehavior" of any sort by coaches is most likely to be noticed and made an issue in a campaign to replace a coach with a losing record. Coaches with odd or dubious habits often are able to escape criticism as long as they can win.

In regard to the recommendation that coaches have training in physical education, Talamini learned that none of the athletic directors he interviewed emphasized certification in physical education in hiring a coach, though three preferred to hire a physical education teacher and two emphasized that a prospective candidate should have *some* physical education credits. Related to this finding is the fact that in 60% of the schools in Talamini's sample, the department of athletics was not part of the organizational structure of the physical education department. This organizational independence of athletics from physical education is contrary to the policy recommended by the commission. However, it may be a remnant of the early history of interscholastic athletics when such afterschool activities were not taught in the instructional curriculum of the school.

The eighth recommendation—that interscholastic athletics should be funded entirely by tax money—was actual policy in 50% of the schools in Talmini's study. Nearly all the remaining schools derived most of their financial support for athletics from taxes, with gate receipts being the major additional funding source for them.

The overall pattern of Talamini's evidence reveals little conformity to the recommendations proposed by the Educational Policies Commission and even less to the *spirit* of the recommendations emphasizing the educational value of athletics and its contribution to the physical, mental, emotional, social, and moral growth of young people. Apparently, the philosophy or ideology of athletics articulated by the small group of distinguished educators who served on the Educational Policies Commission in 1954 has had little influence on the actual design and administration of high school athletic programs. Though Talamini's sample may not represent the total universe of high school athletic programs in the United States at the beginning of the 1980s, there is little evidence that interscholastic athletics in the small towns, suburbs, or cities of America have made a significant move in recent years to conform more closely to the policy recommendations of the commission. Even the opening up of interscholastic athletic opportunities to females has not obviously reoriented the aims or practices of interscholastic athletics in general.

Talamini proposed that the reality of interscholastic athletics is likely to reflect the pressure on school officials and those in athletics from the values of their community. We already have considered how the ideology of the American Dream and its emphasis on winning and success shape the beliefs and actions of adults and children in Little Leaguism. Therefore, the pervasive concern for victory and success in high school athletics should not be surprising. Indeed, Talamini observed that "...the same zealousness (found among parents of Little Leaguers) ...is also found in school athletics among parents and local interest groups." In the next section, we will look at how the winning and success themes are emphasized in school sports. In ensuing sections, we will look at what winning and success mean to high school athletes and also at where achievement and success in high school sports lead on the path to the American Dream.

## 3. Winning and Success Themes in Interscholastic Athletics

Coaches use a variety of techniques to emphasize the importance of winning and to encourage the effort they feel is necessary to achieve victory. One technique used by many high school coaches is to put slogans on their locker room walls. In a study of high school basketball coaches and players in Ohio, Eldon Snyder found that over 70% of the coaches and over 60% of the players he surveyed had slogans on the walls of their locker room.[19] The theme most often emphasized in these slogans concerned "aggressiveness and competitive spirit," and the two specific slogans most often mentioned both by coaches and by players concerned this theme. The two slogans were "A quitter never wins, and a winner never quits" and "When the going gets tough, the tough get going." When these slogans are combined with several others emphasizing the themes of "hustle" and motivation, it becomes evident that the moral emphasis on effort that Gary Alan Fine[20] discovered in Little Leaguism carries through to high school sports. However, Snyder's research indicates that the value of winning to which effort often is vaguely or implicitly linked in Little Leaguism tends to be made more explicit by coaches at the level of high school sports.

From coaches, Snyder received slogans about winning and success such as "Winning isn't everything, it's the only thing"; "Winning beats anything that comes in second"; "Give me five men who hate to lose and I'll give you a winner"; "Be a winner"; "Never be willing to be second best"; "You must win to receive recognition"; "Nice guys don't win ball games"; "They ask not how you played the game but whether you won or lost"; "The greatest aim in life is to win"; "The determination to succeeed is more important than any other single thing"; "No one likes a loser"; "Give them nothing"; and "When they are drowning throw them an anchor." To the coaches' list of winning and success slogans, the players added some others they found on their locker room walls, which included "We don't want excuses, we want results"; "A moral victory is like kissing your sister"; "Show me a good loser and I'll show you a loser"; "Win by as many points as possible"; and "If it doesn't matter if you win or lose, why keep score?" Taken together, the over eighty mentions of "aggressiveness and competitive spirit" slogans by the approximately 125 coaches reporting to Snyder and the nearly one hundred and twenty mentions of slogans of this type by the approximately 165 players reporting leave little doubt about the importance of winning and success in Ohio high school basketball. However, we can be sure that stress on these themes is not confined to basketball or Ohio in interscholastic sports. From Talamini's research, we might assume that winning and success will be paramount concerns in high school athletics wherever there are postseason tournaments, awards for team and individual achievement, procedures that narrow the base of participation to the talented few, coaches who are hired for their experience as winners and are fired if they do not win, spectators and commercialization, and substantial recognition and publicity for those who win and become champions.

An excessive emphasis on winning is not a recent development in high school sports in America. The historical overview earlier in this chapter indicated that interscholastic athletics had become professionalized and oriented toward winning and success several decades ago in at least some areas of the country. In fact, Willard Waller wrote in 1932 that, "A more serious indictment of the social system which allows the livelihood of a man and his family to depend upon the athletic achievements of boys is that the coach is so pressed that he uses his human material recklessly."[21] Waller pointed out that from a "blameless desire" to better their position or salary, coaches in the professionalized system of interscholastic athletics were training their players too hard, using their star athletes in too many events, or scheduling too many demanding games. Thus, while pursuing their own American Dreams, these coaches may have been ignoring the long-term developmental effects of their high-pressure programs on their players.

Alhough coaches may have a greater desire to succeed than their players[22] and may push their players physically and emotionally beyond what they can or want to endure for victory, we should not automatically assume that coaches generally feel compelled by the pressures of their job to try to win at any cost or that all coaches abuse, exploit, or coerce their teams in striving to win in interscholastic athletics. We know there are many high school coaches who are sensitive, concerned about their athletes' overall welfare, and less concerned about winning per se than about other values. However, it is interesting to see how players and communities react to these coaches—even when they are winners. The case of George Davis is instructive in this regard.

George Davis has coached football in a number of California high schools and a junior college, and he has been a big winner?[23] While at St.

Helena High School between 1960 to 1964, his teams had a 45-game winning streak, which was a California state record. However, this string of victories is not what sets George Davis apart from his fellow coaches in interscholastic football. George Davis is unusual because he has tried to instill the desire to work hard and win by sharing the responsibility for his team's performance with his players. His players vote on who should be in the starting lineup, decide what positions they will play, set the guidelines for discipline, and discuss their roles in the context of athletic competition. George Davis has been a great believer in democracy. He believed his job as a high school coach was to teach his players about individual and group responsibility, leadership, and decision making as well as about the specific skills, techniques, and strategies needed to play football. He believed he could concentrate on being a teacher of football, the main role he wanted to play as a coach, if his players were encouraged to be mature, independent, and responsible. He felt that the motivation to do well flowed more strongly from the desire to impress peers than from the threats, harassment, or physical abuse that a coach could impose. He gave up the chance for authoritarian control over his players, which has been the style of authority favored by many of his fellow coaches at all levels of sport, because he wanted football to be an educational experience in the fundamentals of democracy and because he believed that democracy worked in high school football.

George Davis has described the philosophy underlying his approach to coaching in the following terms:[24]

> Life is tough, it is competitive... To live, a person needs to be alert, decisive, know how to project goals and how to work to achieve them...
>
> The importance of the vote is not who gets picked. In the years that I've used the vote, I've hardly ever differed with anybody. The important concept is that the players don't have to do what I want them to do...
>
> What does the vote achieve? It takes the problems of discipline and responsibility and puts them them where they belong, with the players. The coach becomes a teacher, what he is paid to do, a resource unit...

George Davis's special approach to high school coaching is unusual because it teaches young athletes how to win or succeed while also encouraging them to develop character traits and values that will enable them to become self-reliant, responsible, and successful later in life. The fact it is unusual is ironic because the qualities, beliefs, and actions he has tried to induce through his democratic approach to football are precisely what the dominant American sports creed claims to be the *usual* consequences of sports participation. The reactions to his coaching style also are ironic because they have been resentment and opposition from community members as well as some uncertainty and reluctance from his players.

When George Davis moved on from St. Helena to Willits High School, he faced the challenge of turning a team with a losing record and attitude into a winner. He faced an even greater challenge of convincing his new players and community to accept his system of coaching. Initially, his players resented or feared having to make decisions for themselves. In addition, he received some ugly letters and phone calls after some early season losses. The letters and calls belittled him and accused him of shirking his coaching duties by giving up some of his authority to his players. The team at Willits High eventually accepted his system and went on to gain a tie for their league title for the first time. However, it is not certain this achievement satisfied the adults who doubted him. For even in St. Helena, his approach was not fully accepted. In reflecting on the season at Willits, Davis thought that although the season had been successful, the game against St. Helena had been a disappointment because the town of St. Helena had made it a symbol of what he stood for and Willits had lost. He wanted to win for more than professional reasons. There was a matter of pride because he knew that townspeople in St. Helena were saying that beating Willits High School was a defeat for the system George Davis believed in, which they opposed. The game was a hard-fought 20-6 victory for St. Helena over the outmanned Willits team.

George Davis' philosophy of coaching is a relatively pure expression of fundamental elements of the ideology of the American Dream that include hard work, discipline, self-reliance, personal responsibility, achievement, and the drive to succeed. Thus, the rejection of his philosophy by adolescent athletes and adults can be seen as an indication of rejection or lack of understanding of the real meaning of the American Dream. Certainly, rejection of George Davis' philosophy reflects a failure to appreciate how participation in his experiment in democracy can provide adolescents with a potentially valuable lesson in how individuals in a group can take responsibility for their own success—or failure. If high school students cannot handle the responsibilities of choosing the starting lineup and making and enforcing rules of discipline for their football team, one wonders how they will handle much weightier burdens of family and career responsibility and success later in life. However, the need to win seems to lead a substantial number of high school coaches to deprive their players of the opportunity to experiment with such responsibility. They seem to be more con-cerned with avoiding the uncertainty that players' decisions could cause than with providing an educational lesson for their young athletes.

To the extent that opposing or competing philosophies dominate high school athletics, questions may be raised about the conception of the American Dream and success typically learned through participation in interscholastic athletics. In fact, even though high school athletes may not learn to strive for the American Dream in precisely the manner the ideology says it should, these athletes often seem to find themselves on paths to achievement and success either directly or indirectly as a result of their athletic participation. The need to win and succeed, whether coerced or internalized among high school athletes, should not be surprising in view of the nearly universal stress on winning and success in high school sports. Even the George Davises believe in the success ethic along with their faith in democracy. As George Davis himself said,

"No one likes to lose."[25] The meaning of winning, success, and the American Dream for the winners and stars of high school sports is the focus of the next section of this chapter. In ensuing sections, the consequences of high school athletic participation for later achievement, mobility, and success in and out of sport will be examined.

# Achieving the American Dream through Interscholastic Athletics

## 1. Athletes and Scholars in the Status Systems of the High School and Community

In his book *The Sports Factory*, Joseph Durso tells the story of two young men, each of whom had been a star in his own high school realm.[26] Both graduated from high schools in the Bronx in 1974. One, Butch Lee, was a basketball star at DeWitt Clinton High School. He was the most heavily recruited guard in the United States in his senior year. He received over 300 letters from 200 colleges asking him to play basketball for them, and ultimately he chose Marquette University. The other young man, Sandy Climan, was a star scholar at the Bronx High School of Science where the team for which he performed engaged in debating rather than athletics. Sandy was an "All-American" math wizard, the valedictorian of his graduating class of 850, a finalist in the Westinghouse talent search, in the top one percent of the more than one million high school students who had taken the Scholastic Aptitude Tests with him, and the editor-in-chief of his school's yearbook and of its *Math Bulletin*. He also scored 100 in an advanced placement test in calculus, and conducted an independent research project that discovered a new bovine brain compound capable of leading to a better understanding of degenerative brain disease. The college of his choice was Harvard, but Harvard, like the other colleges in which he was interested, did not pursue him as Butch Lee had been pursued and offered him no money because his family's income was too high. His prizes and national scholarship awards covered about one-third of the expenses for his freshman year at Harvard, and after that he and his family were entirely on their own.

Butch Lee and Sandy Climan are an interesting study in contrasts. Though both were outstanding in their respective fields of athletics and scholarship, only Butch had been flooded with offers of free rides to college; only Butch's college intentions had been the focus of great anticipation and publicity; and only Butch went on to capture national attention for his accomplishments in college. These contrasts reveal a curious irony about American values. Those who can entertain us with their physical talent in the athletic arena attract more interest than those who can lead us or solve society's problems with their intellectual gifts. Though educators, community leaders, and parents emphasize the importance of scholarship in the school, the winners and stars of high school sports attract more interest from peers and the public than the stars of the high school classroom. Sandy Climan felt it had a lot to do with "anti-intellectualism." Thus, even though both adolescents and adults generally understand that scholarship—or at least good grades—is a more reliable route to success and the American Dream than sports participation for high school students, sport tends to occupy a more prominent place than scholarship in the value system of the American high school.

Male high school athletes have ranked high in status among their peers since the earliest years of interscholastic athletics in this century. In their sociological classic about Muncie, Indiana, which they called "Middletown," Robert and Helen Lynd wrote that "the highest honor a senior boy (in high school) can have is captaincy of the football or basketball team."[27] The Lynds conducted their investigation of Middletown around 1920. August Hollingshead's famous study of another midwestern community in *Elmtown's Youth* revealed that high school football and basketball still were a central focus of student and public life in the 1940s.[28]

In the late 1950s, James Coleman studied the adolescent subculture in ten midwestern public and private high schools. His findings showed the continuing importance of athletics in the status system of high school students.[29] In particular, Coleman found that among males, there was a greater desire to be remembered as an athletic than academic star. Among females, there was a greater desire to be remembered as a leader in activities or as most popular rather than as a brilliant student. For the females, "leader in activities" took the place of "athletic star," which reflects the opportunity structure for females in high school athletics in the late 1950s. Coleman found that regardless of school size, location, or socioeconomic composition, athletics was a dominant focus of high school life, especially for males. Furthermore, he discovered that athletic prowess obscured the significance of social class background as a basis for membership in the school's "leading crowd" for males. Among females, ascribed characteristics such as class background, physical appearance, and possessions strongly influenced their chances of membership in the school's elite group. For males, popularity among peers was based mostly on being an athlete, then on being in the leading crowd, being a leader in activities, earning high grades and a place on the honor roll, and coming from the right family.

Apparently, the value of athletics among high school students was reinforced by parental praise—for boys as athletes and for girls as cheerleaders. Coleman concluded that the rewards high school students received from their parents may have supported the adolescent value system, but it was not because parents had the same priorities as their children—such as athletics or other extracurricular activities over scholarship. Rather, it was because parents understood adolescent values and wanted their children to become successful and respected among their peers. They encouraged what they felt adolescents valued.

More recent studies have replicated, refined, or extended Coleman's findings. There have been a number of journalistic reports during the past decade showing the fanatical devotion of towns such as Stockbridge, Michigan, to their high school sports teams.[30] There also has been research showing the kinds of factors affecting the amount of importance attributed to athletics by adolescents. For example, Stanley Eitzen replicated Coleman's study sixteen years later with an investigation of fourteen schools, which ranged in size from 92 students to nearly 3,000 and which were in communities ranging in size from 400 to over 600,000.[31] Eitzen found that among males, being remembered as an athlete was just as important for high school males in the 1970s as it had been for them in the 1950s. In Coleman's study, 44% of the males wanted to be remembered as an athletic star—as opposed to 31% who wanted to be remembered as a brilliant student, and 25% who wanted to be remembered as most popular. In Eitzen's study, 45% wanted to be remembered as an athletic star, 25% as a brilliant student, and 30% as most popular.

Eitzen also found that although being an athlete still was an important source of status for males, it was not the paramount status criterion it had been in the late 1950s. The males in Eitzen's research ranked being in the leading crowd as the most important criterion making males popular with them. This criterion was followed very closely by being an athlete, then by being a leader in activities, receiving high grades and mention on the honor roll, and coming from the right family. When Eitzen asked females to rank the criteria that made males popular with them, they said that being in the leading crowd was most important, being an athlete was second, having a nice car was third, coming from the right family was fourth, and earning high grades and a place on the honor roll was fifth. Eitzen also asked females whether they would prefer to date a star athlete, the best student, the best looking guy in the class, or the lead guitarist in the local band. He found that the best student was preferred by 11%, the star athlete by 18%, the lead guitarist by 19%, and the best looking by 52%. Evidently, a prospective dating partner's looks are more important than his accomplishments for high school girls.

Although the slight shift in relative emphasis on athletics among high school students is an important finding of Eitzen's research, more important are his findings showing factors associated with variations in high school males' interest in athletic participation.[32] Eitzen found that athletic participation tended to be more highly valued by males who were nonwhite rather than white, younger, sons of less educated fathers, more centrally involved in school activities, more encouraged to participate in sports by their parents, and in the noncollege—versus college—track in school. In addition, athletic participation was more highly valued by males in Eitzen's study who attended smaller schools with a more rigid authoritarian authority structure that were located in smaller, more rural, and less affluent communities. Surprisingly, there was little difference between males at schools with good and poor winning traditions in the importance they attributed to athletics.

Eitzen's results concerning female dating preferences seem to imply that female high school students are not greatly impressed with the athletic conquests of their male classmates. These results also seem to suggest that adolescent females are inclined to be as unimpressed as the male population traditionally has been with *females* involved in high school sports. In fact, neither of these assumptions is necessarily warranted. Although Eitzen found that high school girls preferred to date good looking males over ones simply talented in sports, he also found that being an athlete contributed substantially to a boy's popularity with girls in high school. In regard to the second assumption, there is evidence that at least in some high schools athletic participation has become a source of respect and popularity for females, too.

Admittedly, very few studies have concentrated on females in high school athletics and at least one recent study by Deborah Feltz has shown that female high school students rank being in the leading crowd, being an activity leader, being a cheerleader, and wearing nice clothes above being an athlete (and having the right family background or excelling academically) as criteria for a girl's popularity with them.[33] Feltz's respondents were female students at three western New York State high schools, and they also indicated they would prefer first to be remembered as most popular, then as a leader in activities, as a brilliant student, and as an athletic star. However, the difference between the 28% who wanted to be remembered as most popular and the nearly 21% who wanted to be remembered as an athletic star is not huge. Futhermore, when given a choice of spending an extra hour in school taking a course of their own choosing, participating in sports, participating in a club or some other activity, or attending a study hall for study or for other purposes, more females in Feltz's research preferred sports participation over any of the other choices. Feltz concluded that high school girls enjoy sports but still may have fears about the stigmatizing effects of being seen as a "serious jock."

Although acceptance and recognition for the female high school athlete may not yet equal the acceptance and recognition typically enjoyed by male high school athletes, there are high schools where being an athlete has elevated females as well as males into membership in the school's leading crowd. For example, in a study of rural and small town Iowa high schools, where girls' interscholastic sports have long been popular and well-integrated in the school program, Hans Buhrmann and M.S. Jarvis found that female high school athletes received consistently higher status ratings from male and female peers—and from teachers—than their nonathlete counterparts[34] In another study, done with Robert Bratton in Alberta, Canada, Buhrmann discovered once again that female participants in interscholastic athletics were more popular with their male and female classmates and more often members of the leading crowd as perceived by their peers and teachers than nonathletes[35] Buhrmann and Bratton also discovered that both quality and amount of athletic participation were significantly associated with female status in the high school, but being a good athlete appeared to be more important than being in a number of sports as a source of status.

The parallels between the Iowa and Alberta high school results are interesting because while Iowa has had a tradition of supporting and promoting interscholastic athletics for high school girls, Canada has not. In fact, Canadian high schools have been perceived as placing relatively more emphasis than American schools on the pursuit of knowledge and scholarship;[36] and this apparent difference in values showed up in a study of Canadian high school students by David Friesen, which was conducted in the mid-1960s[37] Both males and females in his study indicated that being remembered as an outstanding student was more important than being remembered as an athletic star. In addition, academic achievement and popularity were chosen substantially more often than athletics as the most satisfying aspect of school life, and academic achievement—rather than popularity or athletics and cheerleading—was the overwhelming choice of over 80% of both male and female students as the factor most important for their future.

Friesen's sample was predominantly urban, but even the segment of his sample that included rural high schools in midwestern Canada valued being remembered as a scholar over being remembered as a star athlete by 61% to 23%. These results seem to be at odds with what Buhrmann and Bratton found five or six years later in their research in Alberta high schools. However, Friesen's results do not necessarily imply that athletes—male or female—were unpopular, unrecognized, or disparaged. Instead, in combination with Eitzen's findings, the apparent discrepancy between the results of Friesen and of Buhrmann and Stratton seems to underscore the notion that the value systems of adolescents and of schools differ across communities and shift over time.

Eitzen's evidence suggests that by the middle of the 1970s in the United States, the place of interscholastic athletics at the top of the hierarchy of adolescent male values was eroding somewhat in urban and suburban schools, but in rural and small town America, athletics retained its paramount importance for high school boys, their schools, and their communities. Of course, in towns such as Stockbridge, Michigan, high school athletics may be, as Eitzen observed, "the only show in town." In general, therefore, it appears that athletics provide the most status recognition, popularity, and success in the small, rural, and less affluent communities of America where the cultural life and social structure tend to be least diverse, and for boys of less affluent and minority backgrounds for whom alternative roads to recognition, success, and the American Dream are most often perceived to be scarce. However, despite variations in the relative importance of high school athletics, athletes seem to remain at least close to the center of male activities in most American high schools, and athletic achievement has become an increasingly important source of acceptance, respect, and popularity for adolescent females in the past decade.

Although the Butch Lees generally are bigger stars than the Sandy Climans in the American high school, it should not be concluded that athletic participation precludes an interest in scholarship. In fact, in a study of males who graduated in 1970 from seven urban and suburban, public and private school systems in southern New York, Richard Rehberg and Michael Cohen[38] found that 17% of all the senior males, 40% of the senior males who participated in interscholastic athletics, and 70% of the senior males who were members of an academic honorary society or club were members of *both* an athletic team *and* an academic society or club. Thus, even though males who combined athletic participation with scholarship as "athlete-scholars" were not prevalent in their class a whole, they were a substantial minority of the athletes and a majority of the scholars.

Rehberg and Cohen found that the combined academic and social characteristics of athlete-scholars placed them above the male student body as a whole as well as above "pure athletes" (who were not members of an academic society or club). On the contrary, despite the positive image enjoyed by athletes among the student body, pure athletes tended to fall substantially short of athlete-scholars, "pure scholars" (who were not athletes), and their class as a whole on a variety of measures concerning commitment to scholarship, academic aspirations, and reputation with teachers. the combination of Rehberg and Cohen's findings with evidence from recent studies of athletics and scholarship in the high school status system suggests that the status model for adolescent males may be *neither* the scholar *nor* the athlete. Instead, the paragon of adolescent male success may be the better-rounded athlete-scholar.

Athlete-scholars may be greatly admired and liked by their adolescent peers—or at least by their teachers and parents. However, in most American high schools, visibility, esteem, and popularity are likely to derive relatively more from being an athlete than from being a scholar for the athlete-scholar. Indeed, even for the pure athletes, who may be deficient on a number of academic and social qualities in relation to their fellow students, there is little doubt that life as a high school athlete can be quite rewarding wherever athletic achievement is highly valued. Nevertheless, the stories of Stockbridge, Michigan, and other towns where high school athletes are heroes generally leave us with only a vague impression, or perhaps some apprehension, about where high school athletic success leads on the path to the American Dream for those athletes who were *not* scholars as well. The paths to later success followed or tried by high school athletes will be the focus of the remainder of this chapter.

# 2. Paths to Success through High School Athletics

For the genuine superstars of high school athletics in the small town, suburbs, and cities of America, there may be future opportunities to prove themselves in "big-time" college sports or, perhaps, even in the professional sports world. However, the likelihood that the heroes of high school athletics will be able to support themselvess or earn a living from their athletic endeavors at higher levels of sport may be much more limited than they can imagine during the heady days of their high school success. As one who "escaped" an eastern Pennsylvania coal-mining town with the aid of a college athletic scholarship, Jack Scott has written with special insight about the chances of riding high school athletic accomplishments to future sports success:[39]

> ... My high school produced some of the finest athletic teams in the State, yet few of my teammates found athletics to be a means for social advancement ... School-boys who spend four years of high school dreaming of collegiate gridiron glory are suddenly confronted by reality on graduation day. For every Broadway Joe Namath there are hundreds of sad, disillusioned men standing on the street corners and sitting in the beer halls of Pennsylvania towns such as Scranton, Beaver Falls, and Altoona.

There are hard statistics to reinforce Scott's argument. For example, statistics from 1972 indicated that in male interscholastic athletics there were 600,000 football players, 600,000 basketball players, and 400,000 baseball players; in male intercollegiate athletics there were 40,000 football players, 17,000 basketball players, and 25,000 baseball players; and in major league professional sports, 157 rookies were added to football rosters, 60 rookies were added to basketball rosters, and 100 rookies were added to baseball rosters[40] From these statistics, a clear picture of a funnel emerges. This funnel awaits the graduates of high school athletics who aspire to go on in sport, and it allows only a small proportion of high school athletes to go on to college sports, a smaller proportion to earn college athletic scholarships, an even smaller proportion to achieve recognition in college athletics, and a tiny proportion to earn a place on a professional sports team. The existence of this funnel should make it evident that for high school athletics to play a role in enhancing opportunities for future advancement and success in the lives of most high school athletes, sports participation must lead these athletes to a route outside athletics. Unfortunately, for the "pure athletes" who devote themselves to high school athletics but lack the talent to go much further in sport, failure to appreciate their athletic limitations is likely to close these alternative routes and create prospects for a future no better than their past. They may not end up on street corners or in beer halls, but they are not likely to find the American Dream either.

Singleminded commitment to the dream of a career in sport seems especially risky for black high school athletes. Many black children have grown up to believe that sport is one of the very few avenues of social advancement and success in a society that is prejudiced and discriminates against them. Thus, failure to make it in sport may be even more crushing for the "pure athletes" of high school who are black than for those who are white.[41] Jack Scott[42] has observed that gifted black athletes usually will achieve some degree of success in sport, but he wondered what happened to the thousands of young unathletic black children whose only heroes were in the world of sport? He wondered how many potentially brilliant black doctors, lawyers, teachers, poets, and artists were lost because intelligent but unathletic black children were led by their society to believe that their only route to upward mobility and success was through sport.

To the black, or white, high school athletes who pin all their hopes for the future on their sports skills, the future is likely to be disappointing and the American Dream is likely to elude them. For participation in interscholastic athletics to serve as a springboard to social advancement and success for those without exceptional athletic talent, athletics must directly or indirectly lead to achievements, skills, or aspirations in other areas. That is, for the vast majority of high school athletes, the combination of athletic participation with other aspects of the high school educational experience, most notably scholarship, is much more likely to be a route to the American Dream than exclusive reliance on athletic accomplishments. However, there is some question about how or how much interscholastic athletic participation contributes to the other achievements, skills, or aspirations assumed to be needed in the climb to success.

## 3. Athletics, Education, and the American Dream

There are a variety of theories indicating possible paths to later educational and career success through interscholastic athletics. Most of these theories suggest a route from athletic participation to academic achievement in high school, college aspirations and attendance, a college degree, and career success.[43] The link between athletic participation and career success through educational attainment and aspirations seems to be contrary to Coleman's assumption that an emphasis on athletics in the adolescent subculture would distract athletes from academic matters.[44] In fact, Rehberg and Cohen's research has shown that athletics and scholarship are not necessarily incompatible in the high school.[45] In addition, there is a considerable amount of research showing that participation in interscholastic athletics by males is associated with better academic performance in high school and higher educational and occupational aspirations. There also has been some research showing that high school athletes ultimately graduate from college at a higher rate and make more money than their nonathlete counterparts from the same social class and IQ range.[46] There have been very few studies in this area concerning females or minority students, but their findings suggest at least a weak approximation to the male results regarding educational attainment and aspirations for females[47] and a closer approximation to the white male results, especially concerning educational plans, for black males.[48]

These results seem to paint a compelling picture of the significance of high school athletic participation for male mobility and success. However, a closer look reveals that the connection between high school athletics and the American Dream may be less significant than first thought because there is no consistent evidence that athletic participation *causes* higher levels of educational achievement, aspiration, and success later in life. For example, two studies—by Lloyd Lueptow and Brian Kayser and by William Hauser and Lueptow[49]—have shown that between the sophomore and senior years of high school, nonathletes improved their grades but athletes did not. The athletes were better students to begin with, but they lost some of their advantage during the years of their high school athletic careers. These results call into question the assumpion that participation in interscholastic athletics *causes* an improvement in scholarship. They suggest instead that athletes are more serious and academically-oriented students with higher educational and career aspirations than nonathletes because they are different in personality or other characteristics *before* they become involved in interscholastic athletics, *not* because they are socialized by athletic participation to become different. Perhaps males with poor academic records or orientations often are discouraged from entering high school athletics or are screened out by coaches or fellow athletes when they try to participate. At any rate, if it is generally true that athletes do not improve their academic records during high school while nonathletes do, there may be some truth in Coleman's argument that athletics distracts from academic performance.

It frequently has been assumed that high school students who are disadvantaged by their social backgrounds or academic preparation will benefit most from athletic participation in scholarship, educational aspirations, and career plans. Certainly, this is part of the imagery of the American Dream in regard to athletics. However, it appears that this assumption may not be completely true. The studies by Lueptow and Kayser and by Hauser and Lueptow compared improvement in academic performance of students at disadvantaged and advantaged high schools. Their analyses indicated that athletic participation was no more beneficial for students at the disadvantaged schools than for those at the advantaged schools. Nevertheless, it still may be possible that when disadvantaged students associate with advantaged ones in athletic programs of advantaged schools, their academic performance and aspirations are inflated. It seems quite plausible that athletes from less affluent homes who receive little academic encouragement at home will be motivated by the recognition they receive as athletes and the encouragement they receive from other athletes and coaches to remain in school and at least to do well enough academically to remain eligible for athletic participation. They also may be encouraged by the influence of their middle class peers and their coaches to aspire to college. However, unless they are better than merely passing students—or are lucky enough to obtain an athletic scholarship because they are outstanding athletes—these disadvantages athletes, like the "pure athletes" in Rehberg and Cohen's research, may find they are not really equipped to handle the academic pressure of higher education—especially if they remain in athletics.

In a recent investigation of male and female high school students, Daniel Landers and his colleagues looked at the effects on educational achievement of participation in athletics alone and of participation in service or leadership activities in the extracurricular program as well as in athletics[50] They found that males who concentrated on athletics seemed to be deficient in the academic skills needed to fulfill aspirations for higher education. This finding is similar to what Rehbeg and Cohen found for their "pure athletes." In the reearch by Landers and his associates, the Scholastic Aptitude Test (SAT) scores of the male athlete-only group were significantly lower than the scores of the athlete-service group, and also significantly lower than the national average for high school boys in their grade cohort. These researchers proposed that their results suggested that athletics only provides a context for forming attitudes and skills from which status goals evolve and upon which future success is based when athletic participation is combined with other extracurricular activities. Their results also imply that athletics alone may provide too limited an educational background for higher education. Thus, even though athletic participation might divert some attention from studies, it still is possible to be a good student, an athlete, *and* a participant in other extracurricular activities.

The greater educational attainment of males in the athlete-service group—evidenced by their higher SAT scores—might be explained by their high peer group status and the example it encourages them to set or by direct or indirect encouragement from significant others. Research has shown that male athletes are encouraged by teachers and counselors more than nonathletes to continue their education; it also has shown that athletes rank their coaches behind only their parents in their influence on their educational and occupational plans[51]

Evidence of the influence of perceived peer status seems less convincing than results showing the influence of significant others. However, it should be added that significant others may not always have a positive long-term effect on educational attainment. Coaches have been known to discourage their top athletes from the "distraction" of other extracurricular activities so that they can commit themselves fully to the achievement of success in their sports specialty. This concentration on athletics could deprive athletes of the opportunity to have experiences, develop attitudes and skills, and form contacts that might enhance the probability of later academic and occupational success, especially if they enter athletics with limited academic interest or skills.

The results concerning females in Landers and his associates' study were inconclusive. However, there was a hint from comparing Maryland data obtained in 1975 with Pennsylvania data collected in 1977 that females involved in athletics were slipping significantly below the national SAT average while female athletes involved in other extracurricular activities were not. The researchers concluded that there seemed to be "an alarming trend emerging suggesting that females . . . involved only in athletics tend to show the same pattern as males." It probably is more than coincidental that many high school athletic programs for females began to grow increasingly in the direction of the male pattern of seriousness and intense competitiveness in the 1970s.

If the prestige of being an athlete actually has a positive influence on one or more aspects of the educational experience or aspirations of high school athletes, then even athletes with no other extracurricular activities should do better and aspire to more in the academic area at high schools where athletics is more important. In a sophisticated study of nearly 1800 male seniors from 87 high schools, Mary McElroy found that the relationship between athletic participation and educational aspirations was *not* affected by differences in the general athletic (or academic) value climate of a high school[52] However, she suggested that the effects of an emphasis on athletics in the school might be more evident at schools with championship traditions or where the number of students is small enough to allow athletes to interact with the rest of the student body.

An area where effects of differences in the athletic value climate of schools does seem to show up is the perceived preferential treatment of athletes. Eldon Snyder and Elmer Spreitzer found that both male and female athletes were more often perceived by other students to be the recipients of preferential treatment at high schools where athletes were seen as having more prestige[53] That is, in schools where athletic participation was more strongly emphasized as a source of peer prestige, athletes were more often seen as the recipients of special counseling, easier grading, more esteem from school officials, release from classes for reasons other than athletic events, and extra tutoring. The tendency to perceive special treatment for athletes was stronger among nonathletes than athletes, and male athletes were more likely than female athletes to be seen as recipients of special treatment regardless of the importance of athletics in the school.

Despite being more inclined to see athletes as recipients of special consideration, students at high schools where athletics was more emphasized did *not* perceive athletes as better *or worse* scholars than nonathletes. Students at schools where athletic participation was less prestigious had this same view of the relative academic status of athletes. In reality, it appears that athletes *are* likely to be better students and to have higher educational aspirations—at least *if* they combine their athletic participation with other extracurricular activities. One would suspect that athletes involved in other activities will be more motivated than their fellow athletes, involved only in athletics, to conform to the educational expectations of teachers, guidance counselors, and other school officials in response to actual preferential treatment from them. Landers and his colleagues suggested that athletes involved in other activities may be highly ambitious and capable people who are more aware of the expectations of school authorities than other students.[54]

Students committed totally to athletics are likely to have a smaller social world in the high school and to know fewer significant others among teachers and other school authorities, and they are likely to be especially influenced by their coaches. Thus, in the absence of strong parental encouragement and close contact with those in the academic realm in the school, athletes who have committed all their energies to sport—unlike those who have not—often may have their educational experiences and plans most strongly influenced by coaches. Unless their coaches encourage them to take their studies seriously, even the stars whom coaches tend to favor with their attention and advice may find that, without a solid academic background, the road to stardom and success ends on the high school athletic field. Thus, a sad irony for the pure athlete who lacks the skills for professional sport—or professionalized college sport—and the academic preparation for college is that there may be few organized opportunities available to display or use his/her athletic ability after high school for status enhancement.

# Conclusion: An Assessment of the Myth and Reality of the American Dream in High School Athletics

The growth of interest and involvement in interscholastic athletics over the course of this century has made athletics a major activity in many American high schools and communities, and it has made many winners and stars of high school sport virtual heroes to friends, teachers, school officials, parents, and members of their community. Especially in the smaller, more rural, and less affluent communities and schools where athletics and athletes are most prized, male and female athletes are at the center of the social world of their adolescent peers and are the focus of much interest and attention from adults at home, in their school, and in their community. Even though schools ostensibly are intended primarily for scholarly pursuits and academic learning, there seem to be relatively few high schools in the United States where excellence in the classroom receives as much recognition and acclaim as excellence in the athletic arena. Lack of prestige for scholarship is unfortunate because it appears that, except for the athletically gifted few, participation in interscholastic athletics will be a path to later mobility and success only if it is combined with a serious commitment to academic work or perhaps with an interst in other extracurricular activities that recognize academic excellence, draw attention to the future benefits of school success, or help nurture skills such as communication that could enhance academic performance. For the high school athlete who forsakes school work and involvement in other activities in the hope of attaining the American Dream through sport, there is a very substantial risk that he or she will find no dream at all but rather a future with limited hope or promise. This risk seems especially great for minority and poor students who need a good or excellent education to combat discrimination or other obstacles their social backgrounds may cause for them in their climb to success outside sport.

It is argued by proponents of the dominant American sports creed that participation in sport builds character and teaches other values and qualities such as competitiveness and the importance of achievement, getting ahead, and success that are essential in becoming successful as an adult in American society. In reality, it seems that relatively few high school coaches of major sports—and perhaps also minor ones—are willing to allow their players to experiment with leadership and personal responsibility in ways that might actually contribute to success as adults or produce the benefits the dominant American sports creed claims for sports participants. There seem to be few George Davises and when they appear, they often seem to cause doubt, criticism, and opposition from players as well as parents—even when they are winners. Of course, many parents have preached the "Lombardian ethic of winning" and many high school athletes have learned it in the realm of Little Leaguism. As a result, when former Little Leaguers become participants in interscholastic athletics, they and their parents often assume that their drive to a championship will *and should* be totally under the control of their coaches who will make all their decisions for them. This attitude may become especially insidious when ambitious coaches encourage their athletes to commit all their energies to *their* team and give little or no attention to the academic and social needs of their players.

There is a tendency for high school athletes to aspire to college. These aspirations may be nurtured by college-oriented peers in athletics, teachers, guidance counselors, other school officials, parents, sports boosters in their community, or coaches. A college education may offer a variety of possible prospects to the aspiring high school athlete. For example, high school athletes may aspire to college because they want to further their athletic careers, because they enjoy the prestige of being an athlete and want more of it in college, because they see a college degree as a ticket to success in life, because they want to continue learning in school, or perhaps simply because they have been told it is the proper or best thing to do. However, unless high school athletes have had the training and experiences needed to handle the academic and social world of college, even the most talented athletes may have difficulty adjusting and surviving as college students. By confining their energies to athletics, high school athletes are likely to find they are unprepared for the climb to success by the college route or by any other means unless they are among a tiny number of high school athletes who are able to compensate for other deficiencies with exceptional athletic talent.

In general, then, high school athletes who dream the American Dream are likely to dream in vain unless they understand that the route to success through sport alone is for a very few. High school athletics appears to contribute most to the pursuit of the American Dream when it directly or indirectly encourages athletes, otherwise unlikely to further their education, to try to better themselves, to broaden their horizons beyond athletics, and to develop the academic and social interests, skills, and aspirations needed to succeed as a college student and in the occupational world after college. Thus, the quest for the American Dream by aspiring high school athletes does not have to end with the discovery that they are not good enough to make their fame and fortune in sport. As long as they can be encouraged—by coaches, mentors, parents, teachers, counselors, or friends—to see beyond the glorious days of their high school success to a world where more than athletic talent is needed, ex-high school athletes should have a chance to rise above their shattered sports dreams to achieve some other kind of success in life.

# *Footnotes*

[1] The story of this top-ranked team during the 1971 Class C Michigan high school basketball competition was told by Tom Ricke in his article, "A town where boys are kings and the court business is basketball," *Detroit Free Press* (March 14, 1971).
[2] The discussion in this section of the history of interscholastic athletics is based on the work of Frederick Cozens and Florence Stumpf (*Sports in American Life*, Chicago: University of Chicago Press, 1953, ch. 6), John Rickards Betts (*America's Sporting Heritage: 1850-1950*, Reading, Mass.: Addison-Wesley, 1974, chs. 7, 8), and Joel H. Spring ("Mass culture and school sports," *History of Education Quarterly*, 14 (1974): 483-498).
[3] Cozens and Stumpf, *Sports in American Life*, ch. 6.
[4] Arthur B. Reeve, "The world's greatest athletic organization," *Outing*, 57 (October 1910): 106-115.
[5] Cited in Cozens and Stumpf, *Sports in American Life*, ch. 6.

[6]Much of the remaining discussion in this section is based on the historical analysis of high school sports development in the United States by Cozens and Stumpf (*Sports in American Life*, ch. 6).

[7]Spring, "Mass culture and school sports."

[8]By 1929, twenty-seven states had enacted public school health and physical education legislation largely in response to World War I and the indignation of the American people regarding the physically unfit draftees.

[9]Spring, "Mass culture and school sports."

[10]Willard Waller, *The Sociology of Teaching* (New York: Wiley, 1932), pp. 112-113.

[11]August B. Hollingshead, *Elmstown's Youth* (New York: Wiley, 1949), pp. 192-193.

[12]These summary comments about Hollingshead's findings regarding athletics in "Elmtown" High School were suggested by Eldon E. Snyder and Elmer Spreitzer (*Social Aspects of Sport*, Englewood Cliffs, N.J.: Prentice-Hall, 1978, p. 45).

[13]Cited in Spring, "Mass culture and school sports."

[14]Spring, "Mass culture and school sports."

[15]Jesse Williams and William Hughes, *Athletics in Education* (Philadelphia: W.B. Saunders, 1930), p. 28.

[16]Jordan L. Larson, "Athletics and good citizenship," *Journal of Educational Sociology*, 28 (1955): 257-259.

[17]Educational Policies Commission, *School Athletics* (Washington, D.C.: National Education Association of the United States, 1954).

[18]John T. Talamini, "School athletics: public policy versus practice," *Sport & Society: An Anthology*, ed. by John T. Talamini and Charles H. Page (Boston: Little, Brown, 1973).

[19]Eldon E. Snyder, "Athletic dressing room slogans as folklore: a means of socialization," *International Review of Sport Sociology*, 7 (1972): 89-102.

[20]Garry Alan Fine, "Preadolescent socialization through organized athletics: the construction of moral meanings in Little League baseball," *The dimensions of Sport Sociology*, ed. by March L. Krotee (West Point: Leisure Press, 1979).

[21]Waller, *The Sociology of Teaching*, pp. 114-115.

[22]There is some research to support this assumption; it has been cited by Donald R. Hellison, *Humanistic Physical Education* (Englewood Cliffs, N.J.: Prentice-Hall, 1973), p. 45. Of course, in view of the possible job implications of winning and losing for high school coaches, their greater concern about winning is hardly surprising.

[23]The story of George Davis and his experiment with democracy in football is told by Neil Amdur in *The Fifth Down: Democracy and the Footbal Revolution* (New York: Delta, 1971). A concise summary of major aspects of his coaching philosophy can be found in D. Stanley Eitzen and George H. Sage's *Sociology of American Sport* (Dubuque, Iowa: Wm. C. Brown, 1978), pp. 103-104.

[24]In Amdur, *The Fifth Down...*, pp. 192, 216, 217, 218.

[25]In Amdur, *The Fifth Down...*, p. 217.

[26]Joseph Durso, *The Sports Factory* (New York: Quadrangle, 1975), pp. 7-9, 32-46, 77, 135.

[27]Robert Lynd and Helen Lynd, *Middletown* (New York: Harcourt, Brace, 1929).

[28]Hollingshead, *Elmtown's Youth*.

[29]James S. Coleman, *The Adolescent Society* (New York: Free Press, 1961).

[30]For example, Eitzen and Sage (in *Sociology of American Sport*, p. 106) have cited stories by Frederick C. Klein ("Hoopster hoopla: high school basketball is a serious matter in a small Illinois town," *Wall Street Journal*, March 1, 1970), William Johnson ("The greatest athlete in Yates Center, Kansas," *Sports Illustrated*, August 9, 1971), and Diana Divoky and Peter Schrag ("Football and cheers," *Saturday Review*, November 11, 1972).

[31]D. Stanley Eitzen, "Sport and social status in American public secondary education," *Review of Sport & Leisure*, 1 (1976): 139-155.

[32]These findings are summarized in Eitzen and Sage, *Sociology of American Sport*, pp. 85-86.

[33]Deborah L. Feltz, "Athletics in the status system of female adolescents," *Review of Sport*

& *Leisure,* 4 (Summer 1979): 110-118.
[34]H.G. Buhrmann and M.S. Jarvis, "Athletics and status," *Journal of the Canadian Association for Health, Physical Education and Recreation,* 37 (1971): 14-17.
[35]Hans G. Buhrmann and Robert D. Bratton, "Athletic participation and status of Alberta high school girls," *International Review of Sport Sociology,* 1/12 (1977): 57-69.
[36]*Ibid.*
[37]David Friesen, "Academic-athletic-popularity syndrome in the Canadian high school society," *Canadian Sport: Sociological Perspectives,* ed. by Richard S. Gruneau and John G. Albinson (Don Mills, Ontario: Addison-Wesley Canada Ltd., 1976).
[38]Richard Rehberg and Michael Cohen, "Athletes and scholars: an analysis of the compositional characteristics and images of these two youth culture categories," *International Review of Sport Sociology,* 1/10 (1975): 91-107.
[39]Jack Scott, *The Athletic Revolution* (New York: Free Press, 1971), pp. 178-179.
[40]These figures were cited by Eitzen and Sage (*Sociology of American Sport,* p. 226); they were taken mainly from a government research report by Harold Blitz ("The drive to win: careers in professional sports," *Occupational Outlook Quarterly,* 17 (Summer 1973): 3-16).
[41]Pete Axthelm (in *The City Game,* New York: Harper's Magazine Press, 170) has written perceptively and poignantly about a number of black basketball stars whose athletic gifts could not elevate them beyond the urban streets and playgrounds from which they came.
[42]Scott, *The Athletic Revolution,* pp. 180-181.
[43]There has been a considerable amount of research concerning high school athletic participation, educational attainment, and aspirations. The discussion in this section will be based mainly on the recent summaries of this research contained in Howard L. Nixon II, *Sport and Social Organization* (Indianapolis: Bobbs-Merrill, 1976), pp. 39-41; Jay J. Coakley, *Sport in Society: issues and controversies* (St. Louis: C.V. Mosby, 1978), pp. 127-146; Eitzen and Sage, *Sociology of American Sport,* pp. 220-221; Daniel M. Landers et al., "Socialization via interscholastic athletics: its effects on educational attainment," *Research Quarterly,* 49 (1978): 475-483; John W. Loy, Barry D. McPherson, and Gerald Kenyon, *Sport and Social Systems* (Reading, Mass.: Addison-Wesley, 1978), pp. 229-234; Snyder and Spreitzer, *Social Aspects of Sport,* pp. 71-76, 79; and Jomills H. Braddock, "Race, sports and social mobility: a critical review," *Sociological Symposium,* 30 (Spring 1980): 18-38.
[44]Coleman, *The Adolescent Society.*
[45]Rehberg and Cohen, "Athletes and scholars..."
[46]Emil Bend, *The Impact of Athletic Participation on Academic and Career Aspiration and Achievement* (Pittsburgh: American Institutes for Research, 1968).
[47]See, e.g, Michael P. Hanks and Bruce K. Eckland, "Athletics and social participation in the educational attainment process," *Sociology of Education,* 49 (1976): 271-294, and Eldon E. Snyder and Elmer Spreitzer, "Participation in sports as related to educational expectations among high school girls," *Sociology of Education,* 50 (1977): 47-55.
[48]See, e.g., J. Stephen Picou, "Race, athletic achievement, and educational aspiration," *Sociological Quarterly,* 19 (1978): 429-438; Braddock, "Race and athletics: attainment enhancer or impediment?" Paper presented at the American Sociological Association Annual Convention, New York City, 1980.
[49]Lloyd B. Lueptow and Brian D. Kayser, "Athletic involvement, academic achievement, and aspiration," *Sociological Focus,* 7 (1973): 24-36, and William J. Hauser and Lloyd B. Lueptow, "Participation in athletics and academic achievement: a replication and extension," *Sociological Quarterly,* 19 (1978): 304-309.
[50]Landers et al., "Socialization via interscholastic athletics..."

[51]Relevant research has been cited by Landers et al., "Socialization via interscholastic athletics..."

[52]Mary A. McElroy, "Sport participation and educational aspiration: an explicit consideration of academic and sport value climates," *Research Quarterly,* 50 (1979): 241-248.

[53]Eldon E. Snyder and Elmer Spreitzer, "High school value climate as related to preferential treatment of athletes," *Research Quarterly,* 50 (1979): 460-467.

[54]Landers et al., "Socialization via interscholastic athletics..."

# 4

# *Sport in College*

# Introduction

Bill McGill sought his American Dream on the basketball court.[1] When he was twelve years old, he was six feet tall and already a basketball star. As a sports hero at his Los Angeles high school, he attended classes but did not study. Neither he, his friends, nor even his teachers worried much about his inattention to academic matters because there was little doubt among them that his fame and fortune would be made with his physical, rather than intellectual, skill. Although he had only a C average in high school, two hundred and fifty colleges offered him a scholarship—in return for his services as a basketball player. He chose the University of Utah and became the second black to attend that institution on a basketball scholarship. He remembers his college years with fondness. "I really enjoyed (college), and I did pretty good in class," he has said. An assistant coach at Utah recalls that McGill attended classes and tried as a student, but that tutors were needed. McGill also tried hard in basketball; the results there were much more impressive. In the 1961-62 season, he was the leading college scorer in the nation with a 38.8 points per game average. His coach, Jack Gardner, said he was "an ideal player, almost a model."

After high school and collegiate careers with a continuous series of high points, Bill McGill achieved his final peak in the 1962 National Basketball Association college draft when he was the first player selected by the professional teams. With a smart agent, a player chosen first in the professional draft a decade later could negotiate a contract assuring many years of wealth and financial security. However, in 1962 with no agent, Bill McGill was very happy with his $5,000 bonus and his two-year contract that would pay him $17,000 each year to play for the Chicago Zephyrs. The $17,000 was the highest salary he would ever earn. The spectacular shooting touch that had earned him stardom in the past was not enough to earn him his niche in professional basketball. He was not strong enough nor quick enough to hold his own in the NBA. He drifted from one team to another, from the NBA to other professional leagues, until 1970 when he played his final professional game with Dallas of the American Basketball Association.

Bill McGill was 28 years old when his professional basketball career ended. He had no money in the bank, and because he dropped out of the University of Utah a semester before graduation, he did not have a college degree. He had been one of those "pure athletes" to whom Richard Rehberg and Michael Cohen[2] had referred. He had known only basketball, and he had been skilled and lucky enough to make it into the professional ranks. However, when his professional basketball career was over, there was nothing else to fall back on to begin a new career or job.

After a couple of years of searching, he finally found a job in 1972—scrubbing floors for a janitorial service for $84 a week. However, he lost that job because he could not master the mopping technique his employer required. "I slept in laundromats, bus stops, you name it, trying to find something. I even contacted the President of Utah to see if I could get an honorary degree, just so I could put it on applications." With the help of a Los Angeles sports editor who had followed his career for many years, McGill found a job at Hughes Aircraft tracking down equipment that had been lost in transit. He held that same job for more than seven years, but he lost it after missing too much work as a result of a back problem that was a remnant of his years in professional basketball. Initial efforts to find another job at Hughes were unsuccessful, and a discrimination suit was filed with the Equal Employment Opportunity Commission because McGill felt he had been treated unfairly by his former employer.

In retrospect, Bill McGill said, "I hung all my dreams on being a basketball player. Basketball was my whole life." Obviously, though, even for the truly gifted heroes of high school and college sports, dreams about success as an athlete may be much too narrow. A college athletic scholarship might give a high school star a chance to move closer to the dream of a professional sports career, but as Bill McGill's story sadly demonstrates, even becoming a star in the college sports world and earning national publicity and recognition offer no guarantee that success will continue into a professional sports career. Indeed, McGill's experience dramatically emphasizes the tremendous risk of hanging dreams exclusively on sports.

There are relatively few opportunities for high school athletes to earn a college athletic scholarship; the proportion of high school and college athletes who become professional athletes is very small; the major league career of a professional athlete in the United States seldom lasts more than six or seven years; and only a handful of the athletes in professional sports earn the kind of financial compensation that will bring them lifelong security[3] Consequently, for both high school and college athletes, athletic participation appears to serve best as a vehicle to achieve later success when athletes are encouraged to take advantage of the broader educational and academic opportunities outside sport. That is, athletes in high school and college generally must be more than athletes if they want to see their American Dream fulfilled. The story of the "education" of Bill McGill as an athlete and afterward raises some of the key issues about intercollegiate athletics, education, and the American Dream that will be addressed in this chapter. In particular, this chapter will examine the environment of modern intercollegiate athletics in the United States and its historical roots, the recruitment and subsidization of athletes in this environment, the experience of college athletes as athletes and as students, and the opportunities for future success opened—or closed—by participation in college sports.

# The Nature of Intercollegiate Athletics

## 1. History and Philosophy

Bureaucratization and commercialization happened sooner and on a larger scale in intercollegiate athletics than in interscholastic athletics[4]. Around the middle of the nineteenth century, forces such as urbanization, industrialization, immigration, and increased prosperity had combined to create an American population that was socially and culturally more diverse, had less commitment to the traditional discipline or puritanical values, and had more leisure time. These changes in the composition, values, interests, and life styles of American people encouraged the development of interest and involvement in sport in America and on American college campuses. College "gentlemen" who had previously held play, recreation, and sport in contempt as frivolous, wasteful, or sinful, became increasingly caught up in the growing interest in physical exercise and athletic competition around the middle of the nineteenth century.

Harvard University played a significant innovative role in spurring the growth of organized athletic competition. By approximately 1850, it had organized intramural and interclass athletic activities and a sports day for its students. The sports day, called "Bloody Monday," soon became a model for similar events at other universities, and it provided a basis for the development of intercollegiate sports competition. Harvard was a competitor against Yale in the first intercollegiate athletic ontest, an eight-oared barge race that took place in 1852. From then until 1880, intramural and intercollegiate sports programs grew slowly but steadily, though most of the growth during this period was in the northeast.

The 1859 game between Williams and Amherst inaugurated intercollegiate baseball in the east, and within a year, over a dozen colleges were involved in this sport. It is generally acknowledged that the first intercollegiate football game pitted Princeton against Rutgers in 1869. Football at that time was more similar to rugby or soccer than the modern version of American football. It was played during its first several years of existence with local rules, which meant that the size of the field, number of players, and time limits varied between games and locations. In 1876, a convention settled a dispute between proponents of the carrying game (rugby) and proponents of the kicking game (soccer) in favor of the former. A succession of rule changes by the intercollegiate football association, formed after the convention, eventually created the unique American game of football from the variant of English rugby originally adopted[5].

In its early years, intercollegiate athletics tended to be student-oriented, student-run, and fairly loosely organized. Coaches were students or volunteers from the faculty. Since there were no eligibility rules, students often competed with faculty in intercollegiate contests. These patterns of participant control and casual organization that characterized college sport's early years shifted toward external regulation and institutionaliza- tion in the 1870s. During that decade, leagues and conferences were established to regulate and promote regular competition between a number of colleges in sports such as track, rowing, baseball, and football. In addition, the formation in 1879 of the National Association of Amateur Athletes of America, which later was reorganized as the National Collegiate Athletic Association or NCAA, helped bring greater stability to the structure of American intercollegiate athletics in general.

Intercollegiate athletics had grown so much by 1880 that in March of that year, *Popular Science Monthly* warned, "a positive and serious evil of athleticism is ... that it tends to become a power in the schools rivaling the constituted authorities."[6] The increasing influence of intercollegiate athletics in the 1880s concerned many educators and observers of higher education because of the direction in which athletics seemed to be moving. During the 1880s, critics already were attacking tendencies in college sports toward brutality, betting, paid coaches, gate receipts, hiring "pseudo-students" to perform on college teams, and alumni solicitation and control. In 1888, three years after banning football for its brutality, Harvard prepared a *Report on Athletics* in which it asserted that, "during recent years a strong, and in every respect objectionable, tendency had developed to break down the line between athletics practiced for sport, social recreation and health, and athletics practiced in a competitive spirit in emulation of professional athletes and players."[7] College officials at that time also were worried about the effects of long trips and lost study time.

One very important reason why intercollegiate athletics became much more popular, influential, serious, bureaucratized, and commer- cialized during the 1880s is the appearance of sports pages in the newspapers of that period.[8] Newspaper accounts of the accomplish- ments of a college's athletic teams held the promise of free publicity to aid in public relations, solicitation of alumni support, and recruitment of students. Thus, while some colleges or college officials were attacking the evils of the expansion of intercollegiate athletics in the late nineteenth century, many others expanded their athletic programs, hired coaches to guide them to victory, and sought talented athletes to perform on their athletic teams.

The potential publicity value of strong and visible athletic programs helped push church-controlled colleges into the professionalized and commercialized world of intercollegiate athletics at the end of the nineteenth century.[9] Until that time, they had condemned physical activi- ties as frivolous. Many of the colleges with a history of student control over athletics usurped that control and gave it to professional athletic administrators, coaches, or other college officials in response to the wave of popularization and commercialization of intercollegiate athletics.

A few colleges resisted this wave and either de-emphasized athletics or dropped their athletic program entirely. However, *very few* colleges were able to resist the expansionary pressures in intercollegiate athletics for long.

In his book *The American College and University,* Frederick Rudolph pointed out that, "By 1900 the relationship between football and public relations had been firmly established and almost everywhere acknowledged as one of the sport's major justifications."[10] Despite this perceived value of football in the colleges, it became a source of great contoversy. Critics of college sports who had earlier objected to the long trips, lost study time, and perversion of academic ideals, shifted their attention around the beginning of the twentieth century to the violence and professionalization in intercollegiate football. "Flying wedges" and "mass play" were dominant aspects of the sport at that time, and they frequently led to serious injuries. "Tramp players" moved from college to college. They ostensibly were students, but in reality they were full-time professional athletes. Some of these "pseudo-students" played for money under assumed names.

Though both the violence and the professionalism aroused critics of college football at the beginning of the twentieth century, it was violence that almost caused the sport to be abolished. Despite reforms in the playing rules, there still were many serious injuries and some deaths. In 1902, deaths of twelve college football players were reported. Although college officials continued to believe that football was more beneficial than detrimental to college life, they faced some strong opposition. by 1905, President Theodore Roosevelt was considering whether college football should be outlawed—in spite of his own interest in the sport. The supporters of the sport were not helped by the stinging criticism by Shailer Mathews, dean of the Divinity School of the University of Chicago, who wrote in *The Nation:* "Football to-day is a social obsession—a boy-killing, education-prostituting, gladiatorial sport. It teaches virility and courage, but so does war. I do not know what should take its place, but the new game should not require the services of a physician, the maintenance of a hospital, and the celebration of funerals."[11]

A number of colleges suspended or considered dropping football, but the sport was given a new lease on life when a conference of thirteen colleges passed a resolution favoring reform instead of abolition, a new Intercollegiate Athletic Association was organized, and the forward pass opened up the game. Love for the reformed game became rooted in the hearts of college students and the American public. After the crisis of college football in 1905 waned, the place of this sport and intercollegiate athletics in general on American college campuses and in American life became increasingly entrenched. The growing popularity of college football stimulated the construction of huge stadiums, a rise in admission prices for football contests, and alumni pressure to recruit strong teams and famous coaches. The financial commitment of colleges to athletics early in this century is indicated by a *New York Times* estimate in 1914 that one hundred and fifty colleges spent a total of $2,000,000 annually for their athletic programs, with Harvard leading the way with an annual expenditure of $160,000.[12]

Though the survival and growth of football at the beginning of this century drained much of the intensity from the attacks on this and other college sports during those years, overemphasis and improper leadership or guidance still were targets of critics. Sports historian John Betts observed that, "Scholastic life, in the eyes of the critic, was undermined by athletics which fostered an excess of distraction to the student, a nonacademic self-advertisement for schools, false conception of the athlete's prominence in university life, an unwanted pressure in collegiate circles, a demand for expert coaches rather than inspiring leaders, a neglect of nonathletes, an inordinate expense for the institution (particularly smaller colleges), a gambling menace, and an undue influence on the lower schools."[13]

Despite such criticism, college athletics continued to expand over the first two decades of the twentieth century into a golden age of the 1920s. During this golden age, football was king and college football heroes began to rival professional baseball stars in national popularity for the first time. The drive by many colleges to become a national football power in this era resulted in widespread violations of the amateur code, especially in regard to the recruitment and subsidization of football players. The rampant professionalism and commercialism in college football prompted more calls for reform, including a strong recommendation for a return to pure amateurism in college athletics in the Carnegie Foundation report of 1929 that was supervised by Howard Savage.[14]

Intercollegiate athletics entered a period of crisis at the time when the Carnegie report was published. However, this crisis was due more to the economic collapse of the Great Depression than to the challenge of social criticism. Spectators and gate receipts declined, causing many colleges to reduce admission prices to bring back lost fans to their huge stadiums as well as to cut back on recruiting efforts to try to save money. However, the decline of "big-time" college sports was temporary. By the mid-1930s, college football again was prospering and interest in a number of other college sports was booming. For example, college basketball became a popular national sport during the 1930s. The inauguration of the National Invitation Championship in 1938 and the NCAA tournament in 1939 contributed substantially to the growing national popularity and prestige of this sport and its stars. Although baseball did not regain its pre-Depression popularity on college campuses, sports such as handball, fencing, badminton, lacrosse, soccer, swimming, rowing, tennis, and golf survived the crisis years and in many cases, increased their appeal among students.

The resurgence of intercollegiate athletics in the mid-1930s did not silence its critics. One figure, Robert Maynard Hutchins, was an uncompromising opponent of intercollegiate atheltics. His crusade against an overemphasis on athletics in the colleges during his tenure as President of the University of Chicago persuaded many other great intellectual centers of higher education—such as the Ivy League schools—to re-evaluate the degree of their commitment to national athletic recognition. Hutchins decried the interference with the proper intellectual mission of the university brought about by an emphasis on intercollegiate athletics. Despite student opposition, his university dropped college football after the 1939 season and intercollegiate athletics in general in 1946. Very few of the other great universities followed Chicago's lead, though a number did de-emphasize athletics. Since the 1930s, football has been dropped at a number of other private and public colleges and universities, but the reason usually has been financial rather than philosophical.

During the 1940s and early 1950s, criticism of the evils of professionalism and commercialism in intercollegiate athletics lost some of its potency as public attention turned more to the problems of fascism, economic restoration, world war, communism, social reform, cold war, and the atomic age. However, the appeal of big-time college sports did not decline as social critics and attention focused more on the dangers of international and domestic issues outside the sports arena. In the 1950s, some of the practices that earlier had been prominently attacked as violations of the amateur code were legalized by the NCAA. Financial aid to athletes in the form of athletic scholarships and grants-in-aid was officially approved in 1952. Any institution could recruit and subsidize athletes from any area of the country, if they had the money for these purposes. National recruiting efforts aimed at landing the best possible athletic prospects are now a major aspect of the highly organized, commercialized, and success-oriented world of big-time college sports.

## 2.  Current Patterns and Problems

George Hanford is a prominent leader in educational circles as President of the College Board, and he has been an influential observer of intercollegiate athletics as a member of the prestigious American Council on Education's Commission on Collegiate Athletics. The recent inquiry into intercollegiate athletics by this commission parallels Howard Savage's work with the Carnegie Commission in the late 1920s. Hanford noted that, "Recently, a backlog of moral, educational, and financial considerations primarily related to big-time college football and basketball led the Council to inquire into the problems of intercollegiate athletics and subsequently to convene a Commission on Collegiate Athletics (in the spring 1977)."[15] The commission was charged with three basic responsibilities: "to clarify the relationships between collegiate athletics and the educational missions of higher education institutions; to assess ways and means of meeting the financial predicament facing collegiate athletic programs; and to develop recommendations for coping with the ethical problems attributed to the athletic programs."[16]

Hanford's own assessment of the key issues of intercollegiate athletics influenced the formation and direction of the Commission on Collegiate Athletics. It also gives us an idea of the central issues affecting the current environment of intercollegiate athletics. Hanford identified four major themes in the evolution of college sports in the United States: the economics of college sports, unethical practices in the recruiting and on-campus care-and-feeding of athletes, the relationship of college athletics to higher education, and the achievement of equal opportunity for women.[17] He suggested that analysis of the role of these themes in the history of intercollegiate athletics was complicated by their connection to a number of other important issues related to college sports such as the risk of injuries, the impact of television, the growth of professional sports, student rebellion in the late 1960s and early 1970s, the exploitation of minority athletes, and the lengthy conflict between the NCAA and the Amateur Athletic Union over control of Olympic sports. In addition, he pointed out that the societal context of the recent history of intercollegiate athletics included such prominent factors as the civil rights movement, public disillusionment with education, the resulting pressure for fiscal accountability, the increasing tendency in our society to engage in litigation, and the related pattern of intervention of courts and legislatures in the affairs of education and sport.

## A. *Economics of College Athletics*

The economics of college athletics today can best be understood if it is recognized that college sports are a business. Perhaps the budgets of intercollegiate athletic programs do not rival the financial operation of the top corporations on the "Fortune 500" list, but in the mid-1970s, these programs consumed about one percent of the $30 billion budget of higher education in the United States or about $300 million. Basic differences in the nature and goals of college athletic programs can be seen in terms of differences in the type of financial support they receive. Hanford identified three categories of support: institutions where athletic activities are integrated in the overall college program and are supported by general funds of the college; institutions where athletic activities are in the extracurricular program and are supported by general college funds; and institutions where major elements of their sports program, always including intercollegiate athletics, are auxiliary enterprises requiring economic self-sufficiency. The third category mainly includes universities with big-time football or basketball programs, or both. These big-time programs are expected to generate enough revenue from gate receipts and other sources to pay for other intercollegiate sports, and perhaps also to pay for intramural sports and help provide and maintain facilities for use in physical education. Hanford estimated that the budgets of the biggest of the big-time programs at institutions such as the University of Michigan, Southern California, Notre Dame, Ohio State, Alabama, and UCLA might have become inflated to over $4 million by the end of the 1970s. In fact, some were $7 million or more by then.[18]

James Koch has suggested that big-time athletic programs operate as an economic cartel to try to generate the huge financial returns needed to run them and support whatever other athletic activities they are supposed to underwrite in their university.[19] The NCAA provides the structure for this cartel. It regulates economic competition among member institutions by:

- setting spending limits for recruiting;
- setting maximum payment levels for student-athletes receiving grants-in-aid;
- regulating the conditions and years of athletic eligibility and the length of time student-athletes can be "redshirted" and held out of competition for future use;
- establishing the rules of athletic competition;
- limiting the number of games in a season;
- pooling and dividing profits from television rights, royalties, and tournament receipts;
- informing member colleges of transactions, market conditions, and business procedures; and
- monitoring rules and punishing rule violators with penalties such as probation and withdrawal of the rights of television exposure and the accompanying revenue.

In addition to the national cartel of the NCAA, cartel-like arrangements in regional conferences such as the Big Ten and PAC-10 impose rules and regulations on intercollegiate competitors. Since it is not possible for every member of these cartels to be a winner, the cartels attempt to encourage equalization of competition and sharing of revenue as much as possible. However, by operating in a monopolistic manner, intercollegiate athletic programs tend to control competition at the expense of the freedom of athletes to participate in college sports when, where, and how they wish.

Despite economic controls, many colleges have had trouble meeting the expenses of their athletic programs, especially in the recent period of spiraling inflation. In fact, Donna Lopiano, Director of Intercollegiate Athletics for Women at the University of Texas at Austin, has cited some statistics revealing the severity of the current financial crisis in college sports:[20]

- 69 percent of all men's athletic programs operate at a deficit, which means they require general fund support;
- 81 percent of all football programs do not pay for themselves;
- among institutions with policies requiring athletics to be economically self-sufficient, 37 percent are not; and
- women's athletics is currently receiving an average of 16 percent of the athletic dollar when approximately 10 percent more is required for Title IX compliance.

These statistics were compiled by the NCAA and the Association for Intercollegiate Athletics for Women or AIAW. These organizations looked at the economic trends for their member institutions and predicted that the coming several years would be even more difficult than the recent past as increasing deficits were projected for the future. Furthermore, additional financial pressure could be expected to come from Title IX mandates requiring equalization of athletic opportunities for men and women and the expansion of many women's athletic programs.

Apparently, if athletic programs are to survive the financial crisis of the coming years, they must either scale down their operations to modest proportions or strive for success at the highest level of intercollegiate competition in one or more of the "big-money" sports of football and basketball. Striving for success at the top level of intercollegiate athletics is a very risky venture because the big-money sports, especially football, are the most expensive. However, at all levels of intercollegiate athletics and for all types of revenue-producing sports, expenditures are likely to exceed income unless major budget items such as travel for recruiting, scouting, competition, grants-in-aid or athletic scholarships, salaries, and expansion or maintenance of the athletic plant can be controlled or reduced. In inflationary times, keeping these items in check becomes increasingly difficult. Colleges that intend to support their athletic programs primarily or exclusively from general institutional funds will have to be satisfied with quite modest programs with few of the trappings of more professionalized programs such as recruiting, extensive scouting, grants-in-aid, training tables, air travel, large and well-paid athletic staffs, and sophisticated athletic facilities and equipment. Support for athletics from general funds is problematic because the current financial crisis in intercollegiate athletics is a part of the more general economic crisis facing the institution as a whole in most of higher education today.

## B. The Recruiting Game and the Subsidization of College Athletes

It already has been made apparent that the professionalism represented by recruitment and subsidization of athletes in intercollegiate athletics has long been a favorite target of critics of college sports. In view of the long history of these professionalized practices in intercollegiate athletics, it is surprising that the NCAA did not officially legitimize financial aid for college athletes until 1952. The NCAA and other regulatory agencies of college athletics such as the National Association of Intercollegiate Athletics (NAIA), the National Junior College Athletic Association, and most recently, the AIAW, have tried to control recruiting and subsidization with rule books that become thicker every year. However, their regulatory efforts have not seemed to deter potential rule breakers.

Factors such as competition from professional sports, selective treatment from the media, and pressure from alumni and the public have combined to push big-time athletic programs into fierce competition with each other to attract the kind of "blue-chip" athletic prospects who will bring victories on the playing field. In the big-time world, and to some extent at lower levels, of college athletics, an intense need to win, nurtured by these sorts of factors and underlying considerations of prestige and money, has driven many institutions to violate the rules of their own cartel and to engage in some very dubious or unethical practices in the pursuit and treatment of student-athletes. These practices were another of the major reasons for the formation of the American Council on Education's Commission on Collegiate Athletes.

Among the major unethical or illegal practices in the recruiting, financial subsidization, and on-campus care-and-feeding of college athletes to prompt concern within the American Council on Education— and elsewhere—are the following: tampering with high school transcripts and admissions test scores; getting grades for athletes in courses they never attended; letting substitutes, including assistant coaches, take admissions tests for recruits; misrepresenting financial aid packages to recruits; using federal work study funds to pay athletes for questionable or nonexistent jobs; "tipping" or paying athletes for athletic performances; providing star athletes with apartments, cars, and other special privileges and rewards; offering jobs to parents or relatives of prospects; and forcing injured athletes to play[21] These sorts of practices have rekindled the kind of criticism of big-time intercollegiate athletics that was com- mon over a half-century ago. In his book about recruiting in intercollegiate athletics, sports geographer John Rooney referred to "the recruiting game"—with its national scope, high costs, reliance on people outside the university community, and pervasive cheating—as "collegiate sport's most miserable affliction."[22] Former Clemson University basketball coach Tates Locke has revealed the personal misery one experiences in the insidious process of becoming "caught in the net" of this underside of big-time college sports[23]

Driven by an intense desire to win and succeed at Clemson and gripped by the feeling he could not win at the highest level of college basketball without breaking the rules, Locke gradually became ensnared in a web of cheating to obtain the athletes and resources he thought he needed to succeed. In his fifth year at Clemson, an NCAA investigation uncovered violations of NCAA rules by the Clemson basketball program that resulted in public reprimand, censure, and probation for Clemson by the NCAA. Among the violations cited by the NCAA report were extra benefits and improper financial aid to student-athletes; improper inducements and pre-college enrollment expenses; improper transportation; and illegal tryouts and out-of-season practice. The public disclosure of these violations and the NCAA penalties for them led to Locke's departure from Clemson. However, he not only lost his job. The considerable stress of his experience at Clemson plunged him into a period of great personal trauma. In Locke's words, "It tore me apart, wrecked my life, both socially and professionally." Thus, Tates Locke's experience clearly illustrates that the pressures to recruit and retain the star athletes needed for successful big-time college sports programs can lead these programs into a world of dubious and risky illicit activities that can have high costs for those coaches, athletes, and schools who are "caught in the net."

Former Notre Dame football player Allen Sack has asserted that, "The most reprehensible feature of college football today is that many universities engage in what amounts to professional football, but hold fast to the illusion that their athletes are amateurs. By persisting in this hypocrisy, whether out of greed or ignorance, they do a tremendous injustice to college athletes. Those who ultimately control college football, i.e., college presidents, boards of governors, faculty and influential alumni— these are the people responsible for the present system and its corruption."[24] Sack went on to argue that grants-in-aid, which ostensibly provide "free rides" through college for their athlete-recipients, actually give the university a free ride by providing subsistence wages to athletes who generate millions of dollars of revenue in the big-time sport of college athletics.

The case of Tates Locke shows that coaches—as well as athletes— may become victims of a college sports sytem in which they are merely actors (with human frailties) rather than playwrights or directors. Former University of Texas football coach Darrell Royal resigned after twenty consecutive winning seasons because "the minuses of coaching outweigh(ed) the pluses." He told an interviewer that, "There's a lot of hypocrisy and outright cheating. The athletic scene must be getting too big. The tail is a whole lot bigger than the dog. Coaches who have won get to feeling all powerful and that the university is in operation just so they can have a football team. Inevitably these people self-destruct."[25] In view of the tremendous pressure on coaches to produce winning and profitable teams, it is not difficult to appreciate why many are tempted to cheat in luring top prospects to campus, easing their academic load during their college careers, and providing them with privileges not available to other college students—or legally available to athletes either. It also is not difficult to understand why many crack under the pressure and voluntarily resign—if they escape being fired.

Though frequently reluctant participants, both coaches and athletes in big-time college sports are part of an entertainment business in which the recruiting game is an essential element. Coaches must recruit top athletes to be able to fulfill the major requirements of their job: to win, to fill the stadium or gymnasium, to make money for their institution, and to satisfy alumni, boosters, and others who might contribute to their school. In this type of system, many coaches no longer are hypocritical about efforts to recruit genuine student-athletes. The University of Alabama's widely respected and highly successful football coach the late Paul "Bear" Bryant, said, "I used to go along with the idea that football players on scholarship were student-athletes which is what the NCAA calls them. Meaning a student first, an athlete second. We are kidding ourselves, trying to make it more palatable to the academicians. We don't have to say that and we shouldn't. At the level we play, the boy is an athlete first and a student second."[26]

## C.  College Athletics and Higher Education

Not all coaches subscribe to Bear Bryant's philosophy—or are as honest about their view of college athletics. However, the prevalence of unethical practices in the highly professionalized and commercialized college sports system raises serious questions about the place of big-time sports in higher *education*. The integration of athletics with education was a third major concern of the Commission on Collegiate Athletics.

College officials, athletic directors, coaches, and the athletic boosters often have tried to justify their school's investment of money and other resources in intercollegiate athletics at least partially in educational terms. In this vein, they have cited the values and virtues ostensibly taught by athletic participation. For example, the late Lou Little, football coach at Columbia University from 1930 to 1956, defended his sport with these words:[27]

> I think football is valuable because it develops in the young men qualified to play characteristics wholly useful to any man ... (The young man) will learn to work with a group, to discipline himself and pick himself off the seat of his pants after he has been knocked down. He will develop a priceless asset—competitive desire. Are there any more valuable things than these that a young man can learn to complement his formal classroom, library and laboratory education?

In Coach Little's eyes, he was as much a teacher as the professors in the classroom, and the course he taught was a demanding one that led to a broadly enriched experience in life.

Many other college coaches over the years and at all levels of college athletics have invoked sections of the dominant American sports creed to give broad educational legitimacy to athletics. Though a number of coaches in recent years have shown Bear Bryant's candor in expressing their priorities concerning the athletic and academic commitments of their athletes, most probably would agree with Lou Little that there was a valuable education to be gained on the athletic field. There also have been coaches at the big-time, as well as lower, levels of college athletics who have expressed a continuing commitment to the academic education of their athletes. For example, Penn State football coach Joe Paterno recently said, "We have an obligation to try to make these athletes better people. If a kid goes through here and can't read and write but can knock people down, is that good? We've got more of an obligation than that."[28]

Arguments in defense of the educational benefits of investment in intercollegiate athletics have been made on grounds other than the dominant American sports creed or the academic gains achieved by student-athletes. On a more practical level, it has been argued that highly publicized and successful athletic programs attract good students to a college or university and attract public and private financial contributions that enable a school to build and maintain a reputation for *academic* excellence. This type of argument may be recalled as one the major justifications for the initial commercialization of intercollegiate athletics at the end of the nineteenth century. However, it appears that it may be as dubious as some of the philosophical or ideological arguments for the educational value of intercollegiate sports.

David Roper and Keith Snow examined the relationship between academic excellence and prominence in the big-time college sports of basketball and football for a larger number of institutions of higher education.[29] They found *negative* correlations between the academic excellence of incoming freshmen and national prominence in basketball and football, between the ranking of an institution's graduate programs and its national prominence in basketball and football, and even between its rankings as a basketball power and as a football power.[30] Thus, contrary to what many boosters of intercollegiate athletics have claimed, prominence in big-time college sports does *not* seem to lead to excellence in an institution's academic programs or reputation. Indeed, not only is it unusual to be nationally prominent in both intercollegiate athletics and scholarship; it also is unusual to rank among the top teams in the country in both of the big-time sports of basketball and football.

The difficulty of maintaining national prominence in more than one sport is not surprising in view of the financial expenditures required to win in big-time intercollegiate athletics. This cost factor brings to light once again the question of the proper relationship between athletics and the educational mission of institutions of higher education. Commercialization and the attendant pressures to win in college sports often undermine educational purposes by causing cheating in the recruitment and subsidization of college athletes and a distortion of the role of the athlete as student. In addition, instead of contributing to general funds for other programs in the college or university, unsuccessful or unprofitable big-time athletic programs could *dilute* the academic quality of an institution by diverting funds from academic programs or facilities. Therefore, the integration of commercialized athletics and higher education may be questioned on philosophical, moral, practical, and financial grounds.

The fact that big-time intercollegiate athletics has been under fire in recent years for all of these types of reasons reflects the state of crisis that many intercollegiate athletic programs are currently experiencing. George Hanford has suggested that the problems of financing, principle, and practice causing this crisis cannot be resolved until college and university officials decide exactly where their athletic programs fit in the educational mission and organizational structure of their institution. Many big-time athletic programs seem to be weathering or deflecting their current problems because their past success, their coating with the dominant American sports creed, or their ostensible practical value has made school officials reluctant or unwilling to control them. If the current problems of big-time college sports persist, a bombardment of the public with publicity about them could cause a loss of ideological support and a willingness by college officials to clamp down or even reduce the emphasis on athletics.

One observer of the college athletic scene has concluded that the current problems reflect a deteriorating environment for college sports that could lead to their decline or demise. James Frey[31] noted that 48 schools had dropped football since the end of the 1960s, and he predicted that this was part of a trend in intercollegiate athletics in which schools would continue to drop their most costly programs. He predicted that competition would be limited from a national to a regional scope and that national championships might even be eliminated. Frey predicted that colleges and universities would seek financial assistance from professional teams for their athletic programs. He predicted the elimination of "frills" such as training tables, recruiting visits, and scouting trips to observe high school prospects. He predicted more faculty control over athletic programs, which would result in pressure either to give more academic credibility to these programs or to separate them entirely from the institution. Finally, he predicted that coaches would be replaced by athletic managers skilled in promotion and administration.

If Frey's predictions become reality, the business of intercollegiate athletics will become something very different from what it is now. Indeed, colleges and universities may no longer be in the business of intercollegiate athletics. Revenue-producing sports may become separated from the functions and authority of higher educational institutions. They may be left to float mainly or entirely on their own as minor league professional franchises located in university communities and using university athletic facilities. Athletes would be expected only to be athletes while competing, but could be given an option during the off-season of attending the school whose name they carry on their uniforms[32] With revenue-producing "college" sports given such autonomy, the remaining sports in college athletic programs could be more closely integrated with the physical education program and overall educational mission of the school. In these less professionalized and commercialized sports, athletes would be expected to be genuine students as well.

# 3. The Opportunity Structure in College Athletics

Even changes considerably less dramatic than the ones envisioned or implied by Frey could substantially alter the perceived role of intercollegiate athletics in the pursuit of the American Dream. A highly commercialized and professionalized world of college sports offers a very different vision of future possibilities than a world of intercollegiate athletics in which the competitors are genuine student-athletes and the competition is for their enjoyment rather than to fulfill the needs of their institution, its athletic program, or spectators. While the overall pattern of change in intercollegiate athletics is important to all participants, it may be especially important to women and minority athletes. During the past decade, Title IX began to open up opportunities to women in intercollegiate athletics that had previously been available only to men.[33] For many decades, black athletes have participated in college sports, first in black colleges and then in predominantly white colleges, as a means of achieving athletic prominence and of reaching for the American Dream.[34] Ironically, then, changes that scale down or de-emphasize athletics in higher education to resolve some of the current problems might cause disappointment or bitterness among college women because they may be deprived of big-time college sports opportunities they never had, and these changes could cause similar reactions among blacks and other minorities because they may be deprived of big-time college sports opportunities many of them have seen as a major route to recognition and success in American society. On the other hand, changes that reinforce professionalism and commercialism and exacerbate existing problems in intercollegiate athletics might be especially welcomed by women, blacks, and other groups seeking to make their fame or fortune through the route of big-time college sports.

## A. The Black Opportunity Structure

Until the end of World War II, black college athletic participation had been confined almost entirely to black colleges. However, the war caused some reassessment of traditional racial policies in the United States, and afterward some of the barriers to racial integration in intercollegiate athletics began to fall. In addition, racial integration—or more precisely, the movement of black athletes from black to white college campuses—was stimulated by the prospect of greater athletic and commercial success made possible by talented black athletes on athletic teams at white colleges. The 1954 Supreme Court decision outlawing separate educational facilities in the nation's schools also helped open up opportunities for black athletes in the big-time world of white intercollegiate athletics, although many institutions were slow to respond to this decision.

An indication of the changing opportunity structure for blacks in intercollegiate athletics since the end of World War II can be seen by looking at college basketball. Wilbert Leonard and Susan Schmidt examined the period from 1948 to 1973, and they found a number of significant changes.[35] The absolute number of black players increased during this period by over 57 times, from 25 to 1,436, and black players as a percentage of the total number of college players went from 1.4 to 29.8. The average number of black players on intercollegiate squads increased from 1.4 to 4.6. Between 1970 and 1973, the percentage of teams with black players went up from 79.8 to 86.3. This period and the period between 1966 and 1970 tended to show the greatest strides for black athlees in intercollegiate athletics. The transition from segregation to integration betwen the late 1960s and the mid-1970s may best illustrated by the University of Alabama. In 1968, Alabama had no blacks on athletic scholarship. By 1975, its basketball team had an all-black starting lineup.[36] Intense political pressure from a potent civil rights movement, pressure from the expansion of professional sports, and competition from other schools probably accelerated the growth of black opportunities in college sports.

Statistics showing similar growth patterns for black participation in other intercollegiate sports over the past three decades may mask the persistence of certain underlying obstacles and problems for blacks in college sports. Surely, they reveal a disproportionate level of current involvement, since black people constitute only about 12% of the American population. In addition, we have seen black athletes lead college teams in a variety of sports to national prominence and championships. However, evidence has been uncovered to suggest that black athletes may have to be better than their white counterparts to be recruited by and play for white colleges. For example, Norman Yetman and Stanley Eitzen found that regardless of the region, the type of college, the level of intercollegiate competition, or the year in school, black college basketball players were overrepresented in starting and starring roles and underrepresented in marginal or substitute roles during the 1969-70 season.[37] It should be added, though, that when Yetman and Forrest Berghorn extended this data analysis, they found a declining pattern of overrepresentation of black players in starting roles.[38] In 1962, 76% of all black college basketball players were starters. By 1975, this percentage had decreased to 61%, which reflects a diminished tendency to recruit only black superstars.

A study conducted at Kansas State University in 1974 by Arthur Evans produced data to reinforce the assumption that black recruits for college sports tend to be better athletes than their white counterparts.[39] Evans found that black members of the Kansas State football team had more high school varsity experience and earned more awards and recognition in high school football than their white teammates. Evans also found that black players evaluated their recruitment experience in less favorable terms than white players did. A substantially lower percentage of blacks than whites on the Kansas State football team rated from good to excellent the knowledge they gained during recruiting about social life, about academic programs, about the football program, and about what life on campus would actually be like. It might safely be assumed that since voices of discontent about social, academic, and athletic life on campus have been raised by black college athletes on other campuses across the nation and in other sports, Evans' results probably apply widely outside football and the big Eight Conference.

Although they continue to experience at least subtle forms of discrimination and prejudice in intercollegiate athletics, black athletes have built a record of substantial achievement and success in big-time college sports over the past three decades. Top black high school athletes have been courted by scores of college athletic recruiters; they have earned college athletic scholarships; and in many cases, they have gone on to star in college sports. Admittedly, there have been too many Bill McGills left by the wayside when their college eligibility has run out or their athletic skills have diminished because no one encouraged them to view college as anything more than a continuation of their athletic journey to professional sports stardom. Nevertheless, *male* black athletes have a history of opportunities to perform and star in the well-publicized and glamorous world of big-time college athletics. The same thing could not be said about *female* college athletes until very recently. Even now, several years after Title IX was passed by Congress, the opportunity structure for women in intercollegiate athletics, though improving, continues to lag far behind the men.

## B. Title IX, Women, and College Athletics

Title IX of the Educational Amendments Act of 1972 has been a major cause of the boom in women's intercollegiate athletics over the past decade. The key regulation of Title IX for female college athletes reads:[40]

> No person shall, on the basis of sex, be excluded from participation in, be denied the benefits of, or be treated differently from another person or otherwise be discriminated against in any interscholastic, intercollegiate, club or intramural athletics offered by a recipient, and no recipient shall provide any such athletics separately on such basis.

The term "recipient" refers to educational institutions and activities receiving federal financial assistance, and recipients who defy Title IX risk the loss of their federal funds. Title IX has been a major weapon against sex discrimination in intercollegiate—and interscholastic—athletic programs because 2,700 colleges and universities—and 16,000 public school districts—receive federal financial aid.[41] It went into effect in July 1975, and high schools and colleges were given three years from that date to bring their programs and activities into compliance with the law.

Although the precise manner in which Title IX would be applied to intercollegiate athletics was uncertain, many colleges and universities began improving their women's athletic programs soon after the passage of Title IX in 1972 in anticipation of possible penalties for noncompliance. For example, in 1972, the University of California at Berkeley budgeted $5,000 for women's athletics. The following year the budget jumped to $50,000. Five years later, it had soared to $448,000, almost 90 times the 1972 figure. In 1974, two years after Title IX became law, an average of 2% of the money allocated by colleges and universities to athletics was for women. By 1977, the average women's share of athletic budgets at these institutions was estimated to be from 4 to 8%. In 1974, about 60 colleges gave athletic scholarships to women; in 1977, 460 colleges had female recipients of athletic scholarships.[42]

By the end of the 1970s, women's intercollegiate athletics was many steps removed from the antipathy toward varsity sports that had been common during most of the history of women's college "sports." the female physical educators who have controlled physical activity programs in America's colleges throughout most of their existence have resisted competitive varsity athletics until relatively recently. In 1951, less than 30% of the colleges had women's varsity teams[43] However, in 1971, 278 colleges and universities became charter members of the Association for Intercollegiate Athletics for Women. By 1976, there were 843 members of the AIAW. By 1979, AIAW membership had expanded further to 930. The number of national championships it sponsored rose from seven in 1972-73 to seventeen at the end of the 1970s. According to AIAW estimates, ther   were about 100,000 women in intercollegiate sports in comparison with approximately 170,000 men by the end of the 1970s[44]

It should not be assumed that the growth in women's intercollegiate athletic opportunities has happened without resistance. In addition to the lingering reluctance of many administrators and coaches in women's college athletics to follow the male lead toward highly competitive, professionalized, and commercialized programs, there has been opposition to the apparent equality mandate of Title IX from the male college athletic establishment. Objections to Title IX have ranged from the demand for total exclusion of athletics from its provisions to arguments for the exclusion of at least revenue-producing sports[45] Male directors of athletics have been especially worried that a directive to provide equal athletic opportunity for both sexes would divert financial support from big-time men's sports that require large and increasing sums of money to continue to operate on their current scale. Those who run these programs seem unlikely to allow their resources and power to be challenged or undercut without a major struggle. Since the process of incremental change accepted by women athletic directors is slow, the strong resistance by the male college athletic establishment is likely to keep women from substantially narrowing the still large gap in resources between them and men in intercollegiate athletics for quite a while. Nevertheless, women in college sports do have many more opportunities to participate in intercollegiate competition, many more athletic scholarships, much better facilities and equipment, better coaching, and much wider acceptance from the male and female population than they had a decade ago.

An understanding of the stratification of opportunities in intercollegiate athletics might focus more appropriately on the division between the spectator-oriented, revenue-producing sports and the participant-oriented ones not intended to make money rather than on the division between men's and women's sports. In fact, men in participant sports may share many of the complaints of inadequate support commonly expressed by women in intercollegiate athletics. At institutions where huge sums of money are spent on college athletics, disproportionately large amounts of that money are spent on football, basketball, hockey, or some other "major" men's sport. If these major sports are removed from the men's budget, men and women would be much closer to equality or at least fairness in their respective shares of the athletic budget. To the extent that only certain women's sports, such as basketball, field hockey, gymnastics, or track and field, receive the athletic scholarships, full-time professional coaching, travel money, and other privileges of "big-time" athletics, the growth of women's intercollegiate sports may involve a growing disparity in support for different women's sports.

If women follow the lead of men, they may find themselves confronted with the men's problems of financing, ethics, and educational priorities before they have had much chance to enjoy the rewards of enhanced athletic opportunity. Ewald Nyquist[46] noted that the AIAW wanted to avoid the mistakes that the men had made in developing costly programs that emphasized high-pressure recruiting, winning seasons, and the enforcement of complex rules; but he believed that women and the AIAW were destined to fail. As evidence for his prophecy, Nyquist cited the expansion of national and regional championships in women's college sports, the increasing use of letters of intent to bind female high school athletic recruits to a particular college, increasing talk about "token awards" versus "full rides," new problems of minority participation and representation in administration and coaching, the appearance of illegal recruiting and inducements to prospective athletes, and pursuit of television dollars. As further evidence, we might add the controversial efforts by the NCAA to sponsor women's championships, which began in the early 1980s and threatened to deprive women of control over their own college sports.

# Intercollegiate Athletics and the American Dream

Nyquist has suggested that three philosophies are responsible for the most serious issues in the professionalized and commercialized world of intercollegiate athletics today: "to win at any cost, moral or otherwise; to make legal accommodations to women in the interests of equity even if it means robbing Peter to pay Paula; and to finance athletics in spite of declining resources and rising costs." These philosophies of "win, women, and money" have led to conflicts and compromises of principles; power struggles to control the future direction of intercollegiate athletics and individual athletic programs; legal battles; and problems of financing, ethics, and morality that have prompted a new round of criticism of big-time college sports. These philosophies also shape the experiences of the many male athletes and the growing number of female athletes who now compete in professionalized and commercialized college sports.

In his recent article about phony transcripts and other forms of academic cheating in college sports, John Underwood[47] called the student-athlete a "victim" of the system of big-time intercollegiate athletics. In recalling the story of Bill McGill once again, it is not difficult to agree with this characterization. However, we also know that despite the problems, pressures, and conflicts in intercollegiate athletics today, there are athletes who seem to capture their dreams on campus or later. They become stars; they receive local or national recognition; and they go on to success in professional sport or some other area of life. Perhaps ironically, the professionalization and commercialization of college athletics that are the source of so much controversy today also create an environment in which many athletes—including some females and numerous blacks—seem to excel and which many seem to use as a springboard for subsequent success. Since there are college athletes who appear to attain at least a part of the American Dream during their college career or afterward, the general relationship between intercollegiate athletics and the American Dream seems to require a close examination. In the ensuing sections, we will look more closely at the experience of the student-athlete and its attendant rewards and pressures and at the consequences of college sports involvement for future success.

## 1. The Rewards and Pressures of Being a College Athlete

The recruitment experience, financial subsidization, special care-and-feeding on campus, intense pressure to perform well and win on the athletic field in front of packed gyms or stadiums, publicity from the mass media, and esteem or scorn from college alumni, boosters, the sports public, and the campus community combine to make the lives of big-time college athletes very different from those of "minor sport" athletes and students not in athletics at all. Big-time college athletes are set apart from other college students by their special or unusual responsibilities, privileges, and pressures as athletes. On some campuses, they also are literally set apart physically and socially by being housed in athletic dormitories.

Allen Sack, formerly a Notre Dame footballer and now a college professor, has provided an insider's view of the distinctive role of the big-time college athlete and the implications of this role for life as a student.[48] In his view, college coaches clearly indicate to their players that their main priority in college as "big-time" athletes is their sport. Thus, in Sack's case, he found that football preoccupied him during most of his waking hours and even in his dreams. Long, tiring practices, films, and team meetings consume many hours and make serious study very difficult. At the level of Notre Dame football, intercollegiate athletic participation often is very stressful as well as time-consuming. Sack observed that the demands on the athlete at this level of college sport can cause a psychic drain, which could deflate the value of the ostensible "free ride" through college for the athlete.

According to Sack, the physical and psychic demands of big-time college sport can force athletes to take academic short-cuts. That is, they may cheat, cut classes, and seek out the least demanding professors. Their course selection, daily schedule of classes, and choice of major often are decided in a way that will minimize the amount of academic interference with athletic commitments. Sack did not want to suggest that athletes were more likely than nonathletes to cheat, take easy courses, or otherwise avoid the academic demands of a college education. However, he did emphasize the point that big-time college athletes seemed more likely than their classmates to be *denied the opportunity* for genuine intellectual development in college, even when they harbored real intellectual interests.

Sack's comments clearly reveal why John Underwood called the student-athlete a "hoax" as well as a victim in big-time college sports. Unlike high school, where athletes can be and often are scholars as well, big-time college athletics often denies its participants the chance for serious academic pursuits. Gary Shaw, a former football player at the University of Texas, wrote about the approach to a "winning education" he learned there, which included "winning grades" from sympathetic professors in relatively undemanding courses that did not interfere with his commitment to football.[49] His description of football and education is strikingly similar to the observations made by Sack about the world of the big-time college "student-athlete."

The priorities openly expressed by college coaches such as Bear Bryant—and privately held by many others—leave little mystery about why college athletes might lack serious scholarly motivation. They might come to campus with little interest in the classroom because they have been recruited as athletes rather than as students. Or, they might lose interest in their studies as a result of the responsibilities, values, and pressures thrust on them as college athletes. Thus, even when coaches urge their athletes to be "winning students," at least for eligibility purposes, the athletes themselves might find it difficult or unimportant to do well academically. The limited evidence available does not provide a clear picture of how college athletes perform academically in comparison with nonathletes.[50] However, it seems unlikely that college athletes in big-time programs do as well academically as their high school counterparts, who tend to be at least slightly better students than nonathletes. Even when college athletes in high-pressure programs receive good grades, there is reason to wonder in what courses or how they were earned and whether they reflect a genuine accumulation of knowledge. The tremendous athletic demands and evidence of academic cheating lead to suspicions about the existence of real student-athletes in the more professionalized and commercialized college sports. Of course, there *are* genuine student-athletes who are able to excel as scholars in demanding academic programs and as big-time athletes, but their ability to meet the demands of being a serious student and an athlete is as much a cause for our amazement as our admiration.

Coaches in big-time college sports frequently try to shield or protect their athletes from "distractions," frustrations, or problems of academic and social life on their campus. The "protection" might involve special dormitories, special food, carefully screened courses, and even influencing professors and fixing grades. However, the protected life of the college athlete ends when he—and perhaps, she, in some instances today—suits up for team practice.

As sport psychologist Thomas Tutko has observed, the life of the college athlete may be quite hard: "Injured part of the time, chronically tired. Travel, disruption of classes, lack of consistency..."[51] College coaches often are highly authoritarian, demanding almost total control over their players' lives, and sometimes they become demeaning or brutal in an effort to motivate better performance or punish unsatisfactory performance. Marginal scholarship athletes, whose performance never met or no longer meets the level expected of them, seem to bear the worst of the humiliation and pain that disgruntled coaches may inflict on their players, especially if the coaching staff has decided to mount a campaign to induce such players to quit and give up their scholarship. Gary Shaw has written about the special drills at Texas that he believed were designed to get marginal players to quit. They included ostensible conditioning drills in a room heated to 120°, running the stadium steps every morning from 4:30 to 5:00 wearing a thirty-pound vest, and physical contact drills involving extremely violent collisions.[52]

The pressures on all athletes in big-time men's intercollegiate athletics seem to be considerable. However, black athletes may experience extra or special pressures and frustrations because they are black. We already have considered evidence indicating that blacks often must outperform whites in interscholastic competition to be pursued by college recruiters and that black college athletes are less likely than their white teammates to feel adequately prepared by recruiters for the academic, social, *and athletic* aspects of life in college. There is additional evidence indicating that college coaches may use racial stereotypes in relegating black athletes more often than white athletes to less central positions demanding less leadership and mental ability. For example, Roger Williams and Zakhour Youssef found that in college football, coaches stereotyped the demands of particular positions and the relative ability of black and white players to meet those demands.[53] The "black positions"—running back, defensive halfback, and wide receiver—were evaluated by coaches in their study as demanding physical speed, physical quickness, and high achievement motivation. These were the same characteristics considered by the coaches to be dominant in blacks. The "white positions"—center, guard, and quarterback—were evaluated as requiring reliability, quick mental comprehension, and thinking ability. These were the same qualities seen by the coaches as dominant in whites.

Black athletes may suffer from the downgrading or underestimation of their intellectual and leadership potential by their college coaches because they may be discouraged from developing these abilities or from pursuing positions, activities, or occupations requiring them in or out of sport. Black college athletes especially may suffer from this demeaning stereotypical treatment because it could easily reinforce the lack of commitment to scholarship that seems to prevail in much of big-time college athletics. In a study of black athletes in the big Ten Conference,[54] it was found that all of the black athletes in the study felt that their coaches expected them to remain eligible, but only seven percent felt that their coaches expected them to earn degrees. Seventy percent of these black athletes reported that their white coaches, white professors, and white classmates expected them to be weak students. Unfortunately, such perceptions often become translated into reality as self-fulfilling prophecies, leaving black athletes who lack the talent for professional sport with little to show for their college attendance and commitment to intercollegiate athletics.

The only fond memories of college for many black athletes may be of their accomplishments in athletic competition because in addition to difficulties in adjusting to academic requirements, black college athletes often experience social isolation on predominantly white campuses. Especially on campuses with few black students, black athletes may have few friends other than fellow black athletes. It may also be difficult for them to find dating partners because white coaches frequently discourage interracial dating.

The experience of women in big-time women's intercollegiate athletics may not yet be as hard as the big-time male athlete's experience. However, their lives as college athletes are bound to become more demanding and their commitment to scholarship is bound to diminish as their athletic environment becomes more professionalized and commercialized. Already in women's college basketball, there are full-time coaches who are hired and fired for their ability to win, intensive recruiting, full-ride scholarships, a weekly Top 20, television exposure, and illegal inducements to entice high school stars or to get stars already in college to transfer elsewhere[55] It may not be long before the more casual participants in women's athletics who saw athletics as a source of fun in a well-rounded college education are replaced by more serious and professionalized scholarship athletes in sports such as tennis, swimming, track and field, gymnastics, skiing, soccer, and field hockey as well as basketball. To the extent women follow men in big-time college sports, they can expect the same problems and pressure. However, without the same lucrative professional sports opportunities, big-time female college athletes may have even less to dream about beyond college than their male counterparts in intercollegiate athletics.

Not all athletes victimized by the demands, pressures, and chicanery of big-time college sports accept their fate with docility or without questions. Some protest; some become serious students despite the obstacles; some quit; and some bring lawsuits to rectify the exploitation they feel they have experienced. In fact, a court case may help define the legal boundaries and legitimate rights and obligations of the student-athlete in college sports. In one case, seven athletes who dropped out of California State at Los Angeles brought a $14 million civil suit against their former school, its president, and their former coaches. They charged breach of contract and misrepresentation. They claimed they were promised basketball scholarships but instead received student loans, for which they were billed after their athletic eligibility ended. They also claimed that the academic courses such as Water Polo, Badminton, and Theory of Movement that were arranged for them by their coaches did not constitute a genuine college education, and that they were denied adequate academic counseling and remedial work. One member of the group of athletes, Randy Echols, contended that the Cal State coaches discouraged players wanting to take serious courses and became "upset" if athletes tried to switch from courses that were guaranteed to keep them eligible but that provided no academic substance.[56]

## 2. College Athletics and Dreams of Future Success

The zeal to win, which may be accompanied by a sincere interest in the future of their best players, may lead college coaches in the men's and women's realms to deprive their athletes of educational experiences that might be useful or necessary for success once their college careers have ended. Coaches in big-time sports actually might do a good job in preparing a few gifted athletes for successful professional sports careers. However, they may do a great disservice to the vast majority of their athletes by discouraging them from academic and social commitments that might interfere with their athletic involvement. These academic and social experiences, rather than athletics, are going to be the springboard to success for all but a relative handful of former college athletes. Coaches and others on campus who cut corners in admissions, who alter high school transcripts, admissions test scores, or college grades, who arrange course schedules that minimally meet athletic eligibility requirements but offer no genuine learning experiences, and who teach that winning in sport is "the only thing," do an especially great disservice to disadvantaged or minority athletes for whom a genuine college education and a college degree are their best chance for social mobility. When the role of athlete as student is a hoax or sham, athletes are provided with very little to start a career after their college eligibility has run out and their athletic skills have faded.

From the days in high school when they were wooed by college recruiters, many college athletes dream of a future in professional sports. However, statistics compiled in 1972[57] show that there were 25,000 collegians playing baseball, 40,000 in college football, and 17,000 in college basketball. Only 100 baseball players, 157 football players, and 60 basketball players were added to major league professional teams that year. The odds against making it from college to professional sport are even more graphically illustrated by the case of baseball alone. There are approximately 120,000 baseball players in the free agent pool each year. These players include high school and college seniors, junior college graduates, college players over 21, and foreign players. Only about 1,200, or one percent, actually are drafted. Most of the players drafted never become major leaguers even for a single day, though many keep their dreams of stardom alive for years as minor leaguers.

The cases of baseball, football, and basketball illustrate how difficult it is for college athletes to move on to any professional sport. The idea that college sports are avenues to professional sports is a cruel illusion for athletes who depend exclusively on their athletic ability to provide a ticket from humble social origins to success. For them and all other college athletes, the path to professional sport is the same kind of upside down funnel confronting high school athletes. Many try, but very few succeed. However, the college "jocks" who do not or cannot take their role as a college *student* seriously suffer more in their fall from athletic glory than those who have good grades or some other educational experience in college to fall back on.

It appears that sports participation is substantially more likely to serve as an indirect than direct route to upward mobility and socioeconomic success for college athletes. That is, the path to the American Dream will be *outside* sport for the vast majority of former college athletes. For athletes at smaller colleges or in participant-oriented sports outside the boundaries of the big-time realm, athletic participation may be just one of several college activities or achievements listed on their résumé or job application. Athletics may have taught them how to compete, persevere, work hard, and strive for goals, but there is no definitive evidence showing that athletic participation is better preparation for success in adult life outside sport than serious involvement in other college endeavors.

The major value of participation in a low-keyed athletic program in college may be that it allows athletes the freedom to be genuine student-athletes. As student-athletes, they can pursue their studies, athletics, and other activities as components of a college education that makes them well-rounded, interesting, and knowledgeable people. Well-rounded, interesting, and knowledgeable people are likely to be attractive job candidates. People with these qualities who want to succeed probably often will succeed, and it may be the experience of achievement in athletics that gives them the confidence to succeed.

The confidence and desire to succeed without the necessary training, knowledge, or skills are not enough to achieve and become successful in the occupational world. Unfortunately, for athletes who have neglected all other aspects of their education in college, athletic training, knowledge, and skills usually do not generalize to jobs outside sport. To be able to aspire realistically to a share of the American Dream after college, college athletes who do not become professional athletes must find a way to learn something other than athletics. Participation in a less professionalized and commercialized athletic program or participation without an athletic scholarship does not guarantee that college athletes will be seriously involved in their course work or other ultimately worthwhile nonathletic activities on or off campus. However, less professionalized roles make less intense and less encompassing athletic demands of college athletes and allow them greater freedom to pursue nonathletic educational experiences during college that may be essential for their success afterward.

The extent to which college athletes actually take advantage of the nonathletic educational experiences in college that can help in pursuing the American Dream outside sport can be measured by their college academic performance, graduation rates, and occupational career patterns in relation to nonathletes. The limited systematic research that has been done offers no clear indication of how much athletic participation interferes with or contributes to academic performance at various levels of college athletics. However, the extensive recent evidence of academic cheating and revelations about the assorted obstacles to serious scholarship confronted by athletes in big-time college sports programs indicate that good grades in a demanding curriculum and normal progress toward a college degree are difficult to achieve for athletes in many big-time programs. Nevertheless, athletic directors, coaches, and college officials often boast of the impressive graduation rates for "student-athletes" at their institution.

Sometimes, as in the case of Penn State football, the boasts are justified. For example, of the 26 players recruited in 1975, 19 earned degrees, two now in professional football could earn their degrees with a few more credits, two transferred, and three quit. Furthermore, the 1979 *Player Register* for the NFL shows that 29 of the 31 former Penn Staters in the league were college graduates, while only 611 of the 1690 players in the league as a whole had earned their undergraduate degrees.[58] Penn State and the stress on scholarship by football coach Joe Paterno appear to be exceptions in big-time college athletics. At many institutions with big-time athletic programs, boasts of impressive graduation rates appear to be exaggerated. For example, when Iowa State University claimed a "76% graduation rate" among its football players in 1979, the former Athletic Academic Adviser at the University of Iowa said it was "a lot of poppycock."[59] He added that any Big Eight program claiming a 70% or 80% graduation rate for its athletes was guilty of hypocrisy. He pointed out that such figures often are very misleading because they may only reflect the percentage of seniors who graduate and may not indicate the attrition rate among freshmen and sophomores, which might be as high as 25 to 30 players for these two years. He noted that Iowa of the Big Eight Conference and Michigan of the Big Ten graduated about 60% of their football players—but that figure included all those who started out in the program as freshmen.

The 60% graduation rate for football players at Iowa and Michigan may be fairly high for big-time football programs. A study of graduation rates for football players who were seniors at seven major universities in 1975-76 revealed that only one of the universities, with 69% of its seniors graduating, had a rate higher than 60%, and it should be emphasized that the study was restricted to seniors. The graduation rates for the other six schools were 25%, 28%, 29%, 32%, 39%, and 56%. Though football players often graduate at a lower rate than other college athletes, graduation rates for scholarship or major sport athletes not in football are not much better in many cases. For example, a study of athletes at the University of Colorado in 1975-76 showed that 39% of the football players graduated, but only 40% of the scholarship athletes in golf and tennis and 55% of the basketball players earned degrees.[60] The graduation rates for scholarship golfers and tennis players seem particularly noteworthy because they involve white middle class sports, and one would expect academic motivation to be inflated by exposure to middle class values. Of course, talented college golfers and tennis players also may be lured off campus by the hope of earning the substantial financial rewards available to top players on the professional golf and tennis tours.

The most important dimension of statistics about college graduation rates is how college athletes compare with nonathletes. In general, the available evidence seems to show that college athletes are less likely to earn degrees than nonathletes.[61] This pattern suggests either that athletes were inferior students at the beginning of their college careers or that college athletics interfered with their academic performance. One would expect to find proportionately more athletes with poorer academic preparation for college and less commitment to scholarship and graduation in more professionalized and commercialized programs where the student-athlete is most likely to be a sham.

In view of the often substantial obstacles to serious scholarship and graduation faced by big-time college athletes, it would not be surprising to find that those *who graduate* ultimately are more upwardly mobile and successful in their careers than their classmates who were not athletes. In fact, a study by John Loy[62] of former UCLA athletes who had earned at least three varsity letters and their college degree showed a significant amount of intergenerational social mobility and career success among these former athletes. The majority were in relatively high prestige occupations, and nearly half went on to earn advanced degrees. Unfortunately, Loy did not employ a control group of nonathletes to show how these ex-athletes did in comparison with their fellow graduates who were not athletes. A few additional studies conducted at other institutions such as the University of Pittsburgh[63] have shown relatively high levels of occupational success for former varsity athletes who had graduated, but these other studies have had similar methodological shortcomings such as neglecting to look at nonathletes or failing to examine the social class origins of the successful former athletes.

Some recent studies of the occupational mobility and attainment of former college athletes have tried to correct the methodological deficiencies of past research in this area. In one of these studies, Allen Sack and Robert Thiel looked at the social origins and career mobility of former Notre Dame football players who graduated between 1946 and 1965.[64] They found that the former athletes, who had lower socioeconomic origins than the average Notre Dame student, tended to achieve the same amount of social mobility as Notre Dame students in general. Both groups experienced a considerable amount of mobility. The former football players differed from the average student at Notre Dame in educational attainment after college. The ex-football players were less likely to have earned graduate or professional degrees. Among those who played football, it was found that first team players experienced more income mobility than members of the second team and reserves. Former starters also were overrepresented as top-ranking executives. Sack and Thiel suggested that the income and business success of these former first team members might have resulted either from the extra career boost provided by their celebrity status on one of the nation's most prestigious college athletic teams or from the entrepreneurial and competitive skills learned in gaining a starting position on a top college football team.

Another recent study, which was conducted by Paul Dubois, indicated that being a star athlete, a participant in a major sport, and even a star in a major sport in college athletics does not necessarily lead to an immediate career boost after college.[65] He surveyed the occupations of males who were college athletes in their senior year at three state universities in the San Francisco Bay area three years earlier. He also surveyed the occupations of a control group of nonathlete senior male classmates of the former athletes in the study. He found that occupational attainment three years after being college seniors was not significantly better or worse for former star athletes than for nonstars or nonathletes, for former participants in the major sports of football and basketball than for participants in minor sports or nonathletes, or for major sport stars than for nonathletes or former athletes who were not major sport stars. In an earlier study,[66] Dubois had shown that former athletes *in general* were not significantly different from classmates who had not been athletes, in early occupational attainment. Dubois concluded from the findings of both studies that at least for early occupational attainment, college sports participation in starting or supporting roles in more or less prestigious sports was not a special steppingstone. Perhaps Notre Dame is among an elite minority of institutions that can provide its major sport stars *who graduate* with the exposure and prestige that initially open doors to attractive career opportunities that may be closed to academically comparable or better graduates without such athletic credentials. In fact, neither initial nor long-term occupational effects of starring in the most prestigious intercollegiate athletic programs have been clearly demonstrated.

A fact about college athletics and social mobility that seems to have been clearly established is that college athletic scholarships and college sports participation seldom justify the faith that many less affluent and minority athletes and their families place in them as mobility escalators. Melvin Oliver has collected data indicating that belief in scholarships as mobility vehicles is more likely to be accepted by blue collar families than white collar families and by black families than white families.[67] For black families, in particular, acceptance of this belief seems a cruel hoax. Admittedly, a disproportionately large number of black athletes have starred in big-time college spors in recent years, and some of these athletes have achieved additional fame and a lot of money in professional sports. However, for all but a tiny fraction of black *and white* college athletes, the end of college athletic eligibility is the top rung of the sports ladder to success. The tendency for black athletes to dream longer and harder about sport as their route to success puts relatively more of them on a path that one observer has called a "treadmill to nowhere."[68] The fact that black people have been denied so many other routes to success in American society explains why successful black professional and college athletes have encouraged the belief in sport as a significant mobility lever. However, this history of discrimination often prevents the treadmill from stopping and depositing black athletes in the land of their dreams.

A college education and a college degree are much more reliable vehicles than sport for achieving long-term mobility and career success for black as well as white athletes. Indeed, even the long-term occupational success of former professional athletes seems to depend more on their educational attainment than their fame in professional sport.[69] Unfortunately, due to a combination of reasons including poor academic preparation, misplaced dreams, poor and misleading guidance from college recruiters and coaches, problems of social adjustment, and the "pampering" of athletes as students, black college athletes tend to graduate at a lower rate than white college athletes. There is evidence indicating that twice as many white athletes graduate than blacks. The results given to *Sports Illustrated* reporters by one university, which understandably wanted to remain anonymous for "recruiting reasons," indicated that of 91 blacks on its varsity teams from 1968 to 1979, only 10 had graduated. Thirteen more were on the verge of graduation, but even if all of them made it, the university's graduation rate for black athletes would be barely over 25%.[70]

Jomills Braddock has cautioned that the relatively lower graduation rate for black athletes may be a reflection of a more general problem of academic survival for blacks at predominantly white colleges, since black students in general tend to graduate at a much lower rate than their white classmates at these institutions.[71] However, his note of caution does not blunt the argument that athletic scholarships and college sports participation fall far short of the hope that black athletes and their families often place in them. Without professional sports prospects and without a solid college education, even blacks who had been stars at one time in college sports are likely to find the climb to a better life a long, hard, and frustrating one.

Not much is known about female college athletes and social mobility because sport traditionally has not been viewed seriously as a career or even as a college activity for women and because the independent career patterns of women—apart from those of their husbands—have not interested students of social mobility until recently. At least female college athletes in the past were saved from illusions about mobility through sport by the lack of serious attention paid to them as athletes and members of the work force. However, in recent years, a number of professional sports opportunities have arisen for women, women have been given athletic scholarships to participate in increasingly professionalized and commercialized college athletic programs, and women have increasingly committed themselves to their own career development. In this context, it will be interesting to see the extent to which college athletic participation hinders or helps the career dreams of women in future years.

# Conclusion: An Assessment of the Myth and Reality of the American Dream in College Athletics

The glamour and glory that can be associated with being a big-time college athlete often lure star high school athletes into a world of dreams destined to dissolve. Big-time college athletics is not a fantasyland. It is a highly professionalized and commercialized business world in which scholarship athletes usually are paid—or underpaid—performers expected to produce victories on the playing field and "win" grades high enough to remain eligible for athletic competition. In too many cases, the student-athlete in big-time college sports is a hoax. The values and pressures in big-time collegiate athletics often make it impossible or unimportant to be a serious student as well as a serious athlete.

The distraction—or "protection"—of athletes from their studies in big or small-time realms of college sport is unfortunate because the sports careers of the vast majority of college athletes will end with the final game of their college careers. To pin one's hopes for the future on professional sport inevitably will end in disappointment and failure for all but a tiny elite of college sports stars. A solid college education and a college degree represent a much more realistic basis for a better future. Even the initial occupational benefits of fame as a professional athlete are likely to fade with the passing of the retirement years unless former athletes possess strong educational credentials and the knowledge and skills they imply. Some former college athletes may find success in coaching, but there are few of these opportunities in professional sport and coaching opportunities in high schools and colleges are limited almost exclusively to the holders of college degrees. In general, then, the path to the American Dream for college athletes is actually the same one pursued by their classmates not involved in intercollegiate athletics. It is through the role of student. College athletes may receive a special boost from an athletic scholarship to get through college. College scholarships could finance college educations too expensive for many athletes' families to afford. However, these scholarships often involve so many nonacademic obligations and diversions that they may be an anchor rather than aid for athletes who want to use them to obtain a genuine college education and a college degree.

The financial, ethical, philosophical, and legal problems currently troubling big-time intercollegiate athletics may be especially salient for blacks and women. Black athletes and their families have looked at college athletic scholarships and prominence in big-time college sports as one of the most important roads to the American Dream for black males. This faith in sport has been fueled by the many individual cases of black athletes who have taken advantage of their *athletic* opportunities in big-time college sports and have gone on to success in professional sport over the past two decades. Thus, many athletically gifted black adolescents and their families probably would be disappointed to see a reduced emphasis on sport in higher education. Many female athletes also probably would be unhappy to see a scaling down of intercollegiate athletics because Title IX has just begun to open up big-time college sports opportunities for them. However, it is not obvious nor even clear that blacks or whites, women or men, derive nearly as much from big-time college athletic participation as they put into it.

The professionalization and commercialization of college athletics place a severe strain on the educational integrity of colleges, and these processes often interfere with the ability or desire of athletes to be students. For the select few who go on to professional sports careers or who are able to use family connections to land a good job after college, the student-athlete sham may not matter. For the less privileged and minority athletes who especially need college as a steppingstone to mobility, sacrificing a serious college education for a college athletic career that will lead nowhere is a tragic mistake. For female athletes who are interested in a career of their own, forsaking a good college education for a college sports career that might even lead to professional sport is also likely to be a regrettable choice. Women's professional sports, it should be noted, provide far fewer chances for stable and financially rewarding careers than professional sports for men.

Intercollegiate athletics may be a route to success in professional sport for its All-Americans, and it may develop qualities in athletes that will help them succeed in other areas of American society. However, it also can permanently damage the lives of participants who are seduced or coerced into giving up their studies for sport or who are encouraged to wait, hope, and plan for professional sports opportunities that will never materialize. One college football coach lamented the tendency for college athletes to dream unrealistically about professional sport and he criticized the system of intercollegiate athletics for promoting such dreams. Utah State coach Bruce Snyder said, "It's a sad commentary that so many are planning to go on to pro ball rather than to get their degree. We've allowed them to think about the pros. It's not just the athlete's problem. There's a system that's been created that encourages them to think it's possible."[72]

The responsibility for assuring that intercollegiate athletics is integrated with the educational mission of colleges and universities and encourages athletes to be genuine student-athletes is in the hands of the college presidents and trustees who ultimately control college sports. Many inside and outside college sports have criticized the excesses, misdeeds, and misplaced values of athletic directors, coaches, athletes, and the college athletic system, but not enough of the people who run the system have implemented changes that might eliminate or bring under control the major sources of these problems: commercialization, subsidization and special on-campus care-and-feeding of athletes, and a "win at all costs" philosophy that drives coaches, athletes, athletic directors, and athletic programs to cheat and make a mockery of the student-athlete. Intercollegiate athletics may be a source of fun and perhaps even personal growth when athletic participation is integrated with the academic and social roles of college students and when the welfare of participants is the primary concern. To the extent that commercial entertainment, public relations, student recruitment, or other external purposes are allowed to dominate in the operation of college sports programs, the welfare of the participants and the educational integrity of the institution are likely to be subverted. The persistence of big-time college athletic programs might mean the persistence of dreams about using college sports fame as a steppingstone to later success, but as we have seen, these dreams usually are only illusions that probably should not be encouraged at all by institutions ostensibly in the business of educating.

The current crisis of morality in intercollegiate athletics has been appreciated by college presidents and others in a position to change athletic programs. For example, in the wake of the extensive bogus credit scandal in the PAC-10 Conference that was uncovered in 1980, one of the PAC-10 presidents, Robert MacVicar of Oregon State, conceded, "Some students, extremely talented in athletic ability, simply do not belong in a four-year, research-oriented type of university. It simply isn't reasonable that they can survive in that environment unless you do things that are improper or irregular. If we can't have athletes who are successful students, intercollegiate athletics is a fraud and we ought not be a party to it."[73] It will be interesting to see whether those with the power to eliminate this fraud will take the necessary steps to do so.

# *Footnotes*

[1]The story of Bill McGill told here was reported by John Underwood in his "Special report: the writing is on the wall," *Sports Illustrated* (May 19, 1980).

[2]Richard A. Rehberg and Michael Cohen, "Athletes and scholars: an analysis of the compositional characteristics and image of these two youth culture categories," *International Review of Sport Sociology,* 1/10 (1975): 91-107.

[3]This argument about the funnel-like opportunity structure for high school athletes aspiring to collegiate and professional sports careers was made in the previous chapter. It has been statistically supported by evidence cited in D. Stanley Eitzen and George H. Sage, *Sociology of American Sport* (Dubuque, Iowa: Wm. C. Brown, 1978), pp. 226-228.

[4]The historical overview of intercollegiate athletics in this section is based mainly on John R. Betts, *America's Sporting Heritage: 1850-1950* (Reading, Mass.: Addison-Wesley, 1974), especially pp. 101-105, 211-218, 346-352, and on John F. Rooney, Jr., *The Recruiting Game: Toward a New System of Intercollegiate Sports* (Lincoln: University of Nebraska Press, 1980), ch. 2.

[5]The influence of American social and cultural patterns on the evolution of a relatively unstandardized game of rugby football into the highly institutionalized and rationalized modern sport of American football has been examined by David Riesman and Reuel Denney, "Football in America: a study in cultural diffusion," *American Quarterly,* 3 (1951): 309-319.

[6]Cited in Betts, *America's Sporting Heritage,* p. 211.

[7]*Ibid.*

[8]Howard Savage, in his comprehensive history of intercollegiate athletics (*American College Athletics,* New York: The Carnegie Foundation, 1929), directly linked the initial appearance of sports pages in newspapers in 1880 with the beginning of the professionalization of American college sports.

[9]Jack Scott, *The Athletic Revolution* (New York: Free Press, 1971), p. 162.

[10]Frederick Rudolph, *The American College and University* (New York: Random House Vintage Books, 1962), p. 385.

[11]Cited in Betts, *America's Sporting Heritage,* p. 127.

[12]Cited in Betts, *America's Sporting Heritage,* p. 130.

[13]Betts, *America's Sporting Heritage,* pp. 215-216.

[14]Savage, *American College Athletics.*

[15]George H. Hanford, "Controversies in college sports," *Educational Record,* 60 (1979): 351-366. Hanford's article appears in a special issue of the *Educational Record* devoted to college athletics. This journal is a publication of the American Council on Education.

[16]*American Council on Education Annual Report, 1977* (Washington, D.C.: The Council, 1978), p. 52.

[17]Hanford, "Controversies in college sports."

[18]An article in *Sports Illustrated* about the University of Missouri athletic program (Bil Gilbert, "Hold that Tiger!" Sports Illustrated, September 1, 1980) indicated how much money is required to operate a big-time program. Operating costs and income for the Missouri program were in approximate balance at $6.9 million. Football was by far the biggest item in the Missouri athletic program. It generated about $5.7 million, or 83%, of the athletic department's annual revenue, but the cost of football was approximately $3.2 million. At Missouri in 1979-80, $800,000 of the athletic budget was spent on women's sports, and the women's program produced $6,000 in revenue.

[19]James V. Koch, "the economics of 'big-time' intercollegiate athletics," *Social Science Quarterly,* 52 (1971): 248-260. Major points in Koch's article are summarized by John W. Loy, Barry D. McPherson, and Gerald Kenyon in *Sport and Social Systems* (Reading, Mass.: Addison-Wesley, 1978), p. 259. This discussion is based mainly on their summary.

[20]Donna A. Lopiano, "Solving the financial crisis in intercollegiate athletics," *Educational Record,* 60 (1979): 394-408.

[21]George H. Hanford, *An Inquiry into the Need for and Feasibility of a National Study of Intercollegiate Athletics* (Washington, D.C.: American Council on Education, 1974), pp. 74-76.

[22]Rooney, *The Recruiting Game . . . ,* p. 144.

[23]Tates Locke and Bob Ibach, *Caught In The Net* (West Point, N.Y.: Leisure Press, 1982).

[24]Allen L. Sack, "Big-time college football: whose free ride?" *Quest,* 27 (1977): 87-96.

[25]Murray Olderman, "Minuses outweigh pluses," *Newspaper Enterprises Association* (December 26, 1976). Cited in Rooney, *The Recruiting Game,* p. 143.

[26]Paul W. Bryant and John Underwood, *Bear: The Hard Life and Good Times of Alabama's Coach Bryant* (Boston: Little, Brown, 1974). Cited in George H. Sage, "The collegiate dilemma of sport and leisure: a sociological perspective—a reaction," *Sport and American Society: Selected Readings,* ed. by George H. Sage, 3rd ed. (Reading, Mass.: Addison-Wesley, 1980).

[27]These comments first appeared in a *Look* magazine article, "Who's to blame for football's troubles?" (December 10, 1957), and they were cited recently by William E. Davis, "The president's role in athletics: leader or figurehead?" *Educational Record,* 60 (1979): 420-430.

[28]Douglas S. Looney, "'There are a lot of people who think I'm a phony and now they think they have the proof,'" *Sports Illustrated* (March 17, 1980).

[29]David Roper and Keith Snow, "Correlation studies of academic excellence and big-time athletics," *International Review of Sport Sociology,* 3/11 (1976): 57-69.

[30]Undergraduate excellence was measured by the average SAT scores of the incoming freshmen at an institution. National prominence in football and basketball was measured by rankings in Associated Press polls and victories in post-season tournaments. Graduate school excellence was measured by an "effectiveness of graduate programs" ranking given by K.D. Roose and C.J. Andersen in *A Rating of Graduate Programs* (Washington, D.C.: American Council on Education, 1970).

[31]James H. Frey, "The coming demise of intercollegiate athletics," *Arena Review,* 3/3 (1979): 34-43.

[32]This radical change in big-time sports was proposed by Rooney (in *The Recruiting Game . . . ,* ch. 11) as a practical solution to the ethical and economic problems and the hypocrisy currently plaguing this realm of intercollegiate athletics.

[33]The experience of women in intercollegiate athletics has been examined by Ellen W. Gerber, "Collegiate sport," *The American Women in Sport.* by Ellen Gerber et al. (Reading, Mass.: Addison-Wesley, 1974), and by assorted writers in Carole A. Oglesby's edited volume *Women and Sport: from myth to reality* (Philadelphia: Lea & Febiger, 1978).

[34]The experience of blacks in intercollegiate athletics has been examined by Harry Edwards in *The Revolt of the Black Athlete* (New York: Free Press, 1969), and in *Sociology of Sport* (Homewood, Ill.: Dorsey, 1973).

[35]Wilbert M. Leonard II and Susan Schmidt, "Observations on the changing social organization of collegiate and professional basketball," *Sport Sociology Bulletin,* 4 (Fall 1975): 13-35.

[36]Cited in Eitzen and Sage, *Sociology of American Sport,* p. 238.

[37]Norman R. Yetman and D. Stanley Eitzen, "Black athletes on intercollegiate basketball teams: an empirical test of discrimination," *Majority and Minority,* ed. by Norman R. Yetman and C. Hoy Steele (Boston: Allyn and Bacon, 1971).

[38]Forest J. Berghorn and Norman R. Yetman, "Black Americans in sports: the changing pattern of collegiate basketball," unpublished paper, University of Kansas, 1976. Cited in Eitzen and Sage, *Sociology of American Sport,* p. 255.

[39]Arthur S. Evans, "Differences in the recruitment of black and white football players at a Big Eight university," *Journal of Sport and Social Issues,* 3 (Fall/Winter 1979): 1-9.

[40]*Federal Register 40* (June 4, 1975), Part II, Washington, D.C.: Department of Health, Education, and Welfare, p. 24142. The general statement of this law covers areas such

as employment, admissions, and financial aid as well as athletic opportunities in schools and colleges.

[41]Figures cited in Eitzen and Sage, *Sociology of American Sport,* p. 283.

[42]Figures cited in Candace Lyle Hogan, "Title IX: from here to equality." *WomenSports,* 4 (September 1977): 16-60.

[43]Figure cited in Gerber, "Collegiate sport," p. 66.

[44]These AIAW statistics are from Eitzen and Sage, *Sociology of American Sport,* p. 280; Wilbert M. Leonard II, *A Sociological Perspective of Sport* (Minneapolis: Burgess, 1980), p. 202; and Ewald B. Nyquist, "Win, women, and money: collegiate athletics today and tomorrow," *Educational Record,* 60 (1979): 374-393.

[45]See George LaNoue, "Athletics and equality: how to comply with Title IX without tearing down the stadium," *Change,* 8 (November 1976): 27-30, 63-65; Patricia Huckle, "Back to the starting line: Title IX and women's intercollegiate athletics," *American Behavioral Scientist,* 21 (1978): 379-392; and Ellen W. Gerber, "The legal basis for the regulation of intercollegiate sport," *Educational Record,* 60 (1979): 467-481, for discussions of the legal and political maneuvering aimed at revising or defining the applicability of Title IX to college sports.

[46]Nyquist, "Win, women, and money..."

[47]Underwood, "Special report..."

[48]Sack, "Big time college football..."

[49]Gary Shaw, *Meat on The Hoof: The hidden world of Texas football* (New York: St. Martin's Press, 1972).

[50]For reviews of relevant research, see e.g., Jay J. Coakley, *Sport in Society: issues and controversies* (St. Louis, C.V. Mosby, 1978), pp. 167-170; and Eldon E. Snyder and Elmer Spreitzer, *Social Aspects of Sport* (Englewood Cliffs, N.J.: Prentice-Hall, 1978), pp. 76-78.

[51]Quoted in Underwood, "Special report..."

[52]Shaw, *Meat on The Hoof...,* pp. 78-91, 122-134. Eitzen and Sage (in *Sociology of American Sport,* pp. 96-98) have summarized some of the authoritarian and "dehumanizing" aspects of college athletics cited by Shaw and others.

[53]Roger L. Williams and Zakhour I. Youssef, "Division of labor in college football along racial lines," *International Journal of Sport Psychology,* 6 (1975): 3-13..

[54]Reported in James A. Michener, *Sports in America* (New York: Random House, 1976), pp. 159-161.

[55]See, e.g., Kent Hannon's "Too far, too fast," *Sports Illustrated* (March 20, 1978), for an indication of current and future problems in big-time women's college basketball.

[56]This case was cited in Underwood, "Special report..." and in Nyquist, "Win, women, and money..."

[57]Cited in Eitzen and Sage, *Sociology of American Sport,* p. 226.

[58]Cited in Looney, "'There are a lot of people who think I'm a phony and now they think they have the proof.'"

[59]Quoted in Underwood, "Special report..."

[60]These graduation statistics are from Mike Madigan, "Graduation academic to college gridders," *Rockey Mountain News* (December 26, 1976), p. 96. They were cited in Eitzen and Sage, *Sociology of American Sport,* p. 225.

[61]This conclusion has been shared by Coakley (in *Sport in Society...,* p. 171), among others.

[62]John W. Loy, "Social origins and occupational mobility patterns of a selected sample of American athletes," *International Review of Sport Sociology,* 7 (1972): 5-23.

[63]Edward H. Litchfield with Myron Cope, "Saturday's hero is doing fine," *Sports Illustrated* (July 8, 1962).

[64]Allen L. Sack and Robert Thiel, "College football and social mobility: a case study of Notre Dame football players," *Sociology of Education,* 52 (1979): 60-66.

[65]Paul E. Dubois, "Participation in sport and occupational attainment: an investigation of selected athlete categories," *Journal of Sport Behavior,* 2 (1979): 103-114.

[66]Paul E. Dubois, "Participation in sports and occupational attainment: a comparative

study," *Research Quarterly,* 49 (1978): 28-37.

[67]Melvin L. Oliver, "Race, class and the family's orientation to mobility through sport," *Sociological Symposium,* 30 (Spring 1980): 62-86.

[68]Quoted in Bob Oates, "The great American tease: sports as a way out of the ghetto," *Los Angeles Times* (May 15, 1979).

[69]Rudolf K. Haerle, Jr., "Education, athletic scholarships, and the occupational career of the professional athlete," *Sociology of Work and Occupations,* 2 (1975): 373-403.

[70]These statistics on black athletes' graduation rates were cited in Underwood, "Special report..."

[71]Jomills Henry Braddock II, "Race, sports and social mobility: a critical review," *Sociological Symposium,* 30 (Spring 1980): 18-38.

[72]Larry Keith, "Sitting, waiting, and hoping," *Sports Illustrated* (March 31, 1980).

[73]Quoted in "Scorecard: crackdown in the PAC-10," *Sports Illustrated* (August 25, 1980).

# 5

# Professional and Olympic Sports in the United States

# *Introduction*

A professional sports career and an Olympic gold medal are the twin peaks in the ascent toward an American Sports Dream pursued by many of the serious and talented athletes in the United States. Indeed, it is not even necessary to be among the most athletically gifted to yearn for and pursue one or both of these pinnacles of sports success. The American Sports Dream, like the broader ideology of the American Dream, encourages aspiring young boys and girls with more limited athletic gifts to compensate for their limitations in natural ability by unceasing dedication, commitment, and hard work. Thus, along with the athletically gifted, athletes with more modest talents dream of the fame, glory, riches, or sense of accomplishment they associate with being a star professional or Olympic athlete in the United States, and they often singlemindedly devote their childhood, adolescence, and even part of their adulthood to the realization of their American Sports Dream.

Many of the athletes who achieve a professional career or earn an Olympic medal find, at least for a while, that the fruits of their sports accomplishments are as sweet as they had anticipated. Perhaps few athletes have enjoyed the status of a star professional athlete as much as major league baseball player Pete Rose, known to fans as "Charlie Hustle" for the tremendous amount of energy and enthusiasm he has put into playing his sport throughout his career. It has been written about him that, "Baseball was what he loved, what he knew, and everything else, except perhaps for money, was superfluous." Approaching his fortieth birthday, Rose, himself, said:

> How do I live through the off-season?... I rest up. Sleep. Watch sports on TV. Don't think about age. And count down the days to spring training!

In Olympic sports, the joy of victory etched on the faces of victors as they receive their medals is adequate testimony to the significance these athletes attribute to their accomplishment.

While there can be little doubt about the great joy and satisfaction that can result when athletes find their American Dream in the professional or Olympic sports arena, it also is true that athletes at the highest levels of professional and amateur sports in America may find their success short-lived, their fame fleeting, and their material rewards less than they expected. Life in the arenas of professional and Olympic sports can produce joy and sadness, fulfillment and frustration, glory and humiliation, wealth and exploitation, ecstasy and pain, intense public scrutiny and loneliness, success and failure.

Though some have been able to sustain excellence past their fortieth birthday, most high-level athletes are long into their quest for an alternative career or job by that age. Professional and Olympic sports typically are for the young, and in some sports such as skating, swimming, and gymnastics, athletes not even out of their teens might be considered "old." In other words, athletes still young by the standards of the larger society may find their greatest hopes and accomplishments in life behind them. The substantial physical and emotional demands and the intense competition from a seemingly endless supply of younger aspiring stars make the worlds of professional and Olympic sports mostly for the young, and the demands and competition help shape the contrasting moods, emotions, and experiences that characterize the pursuit of the American Dream at the highest levels of American sport.

This chapter is about the development, organization, and operation of modern professional and Olympic sports in the United States, and it is about the pursuit of the American Dream by athletes who aspire to be professional stars or Olympic champions. This chapter is also about the contrasting moods, emotions, and experiences that are produced at these highest levels of American sport as new stars rise and former and would-be stars fade with each new season or competition. Since there is no higher rung on the ladder to success for American athletes than a professional sports career or an Olympic medal, the examination of sport and the American Dream in this chapter should reveal most fully and clearly the meaning of the American Dream and the sacrifices it can demand when it is pursued through sport. In doing so, this chapter also might reveal some important insights about the nature and requirements of the pursuit of the American Dream of fame, fortune, and influence in other realms of American society.

# The Development of Modern Sports in the United States

## 1. Historical Background

According to sports historian John Rickard Betts, the roots of the American sporting heritage are in the horse racing and fox hunting of the colonial period, but the major aspects of modern sport were not apparent until the middle of the nineteenth century? In his analysis of the changes in American sport between 1850 and 1900, Betts noted that continuing rural influences, the decline of orthodox Puritan thinking, the English athletic movement, the immigrant, frontier traditions of masculinity and strength, and the contributions of energetic sportsmen all left an impression on the development of sport during this period. He argued, however, that the Industrial Revolution and urbanization were more significant influences on the development of American sport during the second half of the nineteenth century.

Manufacturers in search of cheap labor encouraged immigration and migration to larger towns and cities where their factories could be run most efficiently. The newly urbanized masses, who missed the rural pleasures of hunting and fishing, were drawn to commercialized entertainment and spectator sports. Thus, urbanization created a need for commercialized spectator sports. Industrialization gradually made possible the standard of living and leisure time that allowed the masses to support spectator sports. Revolutionary technological advances in transportation, communication, manufacturing, finance, and various facets of economic life made it easier to attend and follow sports events, enabled sports competition to expand geographically and commercially, and contributed to a more sophisticated quality of play. Betts observed that, "By 1900 sport had attained an unprecedented prominence in the daily lives of millions of Americans."

Some may argue that the rise of sport in the nineteenth *and twentieth* centuries reflected a reaction against the mechanization, division of labor, and standardization of an industrializing society. While acknowledging that this might partially be true, Betts pointed out that "sport in nineteenth-century America was as much a product of industrialization as it was an antidote to it." He went on to say that, "While athletics and outdoor recreation were sought as a release from the confinements of city life, industrialization and the  urban movement were the basic causes for the rise of organized sport."

Baseball was the first sport to have a significant national impact during the initial development of commercialized sports in the United States. The Cincinnati Red Stockings of 1869 are reputed by many baseball observers to have been the first professional baseball team, but baseball historian David Voigt has presented evidence showing the existence of professional baseball teams earlier in the nineteenth century[3] Nevertheless, the transcontinental tour from Maine to California in 1869 by Harry Wright's Cincinnati Red Stockings was a major event in the popularization of this sport as the "national game."

The emergence of professional baseball teams was followed by the emergence of commercialism and professionalism in a number of other sports in the late nineteenth and early twentieth centuries in the United States. By 1903, golf, football, bowling, basketball, and hockey were organized on a professional basis, and in 1926, professional tennis appeared[4]

The rise of commercialism in the "amateur" realm of intercollegiate athletics was reported in the last chapter. At the same time sports were becoming more commercialized in the U.S. (the end of the nineteenth century), there was a movement to advance the ideal of pure amateurism in sport. According to Charles Bucher, "The term ('amateur') was first used to indicate those athletes who won events in the Olympic games but refused to capitalize commercially on their fame."[5] The association of amateurism with the Olympic Games is somewhat ironic because the birth of professionalism in sport can be traced to the ancient Olympics. In 594 B.C., Solon decreed that any Athenian who was a victor in the Olympics should receive 500 drachmae, which was equivalent to 100 oxen.[6] Nevertheless, the modern Olympic Games, which began in Greece in 1896, have come to symbolize at least the *principle* of amateurism in the context of modern sport. Pierre de Coubertin, the French baron who founded the modern Olympics, was quite explicit about what he intended the Games to represent: "I shall do all in my power that the following Olympian Games may revert to the true theory of amateurism, which declares the uselessness of the professional and desires his disappearance."[7]

In the United States, efforts to identify what one must *not* do in order to preserve amateurism accompanied the formation of various amateur sports organizations. The first definition of amateurism adopted by the National Association of Amateur Athletes of America in 1879 stated that:

> An amateur is any person who has never competed in an open contest, or for a stake, or for public money, or for gate money, or under a false name; or with a professional for a prize, or where gate money is charged; nor has ever at any period of his life taught or pursued athletic exercises as a means of livelihood.[8]

An even more restrictive definition of amateur status appeared in the constitutional statement of the U.S. Amateur Athletic Union, or AAU, which was formed in 1888. Despite variations and some vagueness in the definitions of amateurism put forth by amateur sports organizations in their early histories, it is clear that amateur sports officials were trying to separate their sports and athletes from any association with financial compensation—or "professionalism"—and profit-making—or "commercialism."

In the early years of the Olympic movement, the International Olympic Committee (IOC) seemed to recognize its dependence on the various national and international governing bodies controlling the sports included in the Olympic Games. It stated the Olympic ideal of amateurism and then left to these governing bodies the task of ensuring the amateur status of the competitors. However, as Peter McIntosh has pointed out, the Nazi Olympic Games of 1936, which were staged as a spectacle of propaganda to glorify Hitler's regime, "revealed to the IOC that governments and other interested bodies could make the ideal and even the regulations (of amateurism) a mockery. The IOC later tried to be more amateur than the governing bodies."[9]

In 1958, the IOC defined Olympic eligibility in the following way: "An amateur is one who participates and always has participated in sport solely for pleasure and for the physical and mental benefits he derives therefrom, and to whom participation in sport is nothing more than recreation without material gain of any kind, direct or indirect. *In addition,* he must comply with the rules of the International Federation concerned."[10] The phrase "In addition" clearly implies the discrepancy perceived by the IOC between its rules of amateurism and those of the International Federations.

Difficulties in arriving at a consensus about the definition and application of a principle of amateurism at different levels and in different domains of "Olympic sports"[11] were almost inevitable in the United States in the face of growing trends of commercialism and profession- alism in sports. The realities of sport in the twentieth century, especially at the national and international levels, made the ideal of amateurism increasingly anachronistic or unrealistic. Indeed, when sport becomes highly organized, its basic structure tends to be antithetical to any notion implying a playful activity, pursued for its own sake, without concern for external rewards. Furthermore, the strict enforcement of the principle of the Olympic ideal of amateurism throughout amateur sports would restrict these sports to the most privileged. For all its virtues, this ideal is an aristocratic or elitist notion because only the affluent can afford the leisure time or money to pursue excellence in sport as a financially uncompensated avocation.[12] If the Olympic ideal of amateurism were strictly enforced by amateur sports officials, there would be very few athletes able to meet current Olympic standards of performance. A strict enforcement of this amateur ideal would exclude athletes who had engaged in extensive training and competition subsidized by governments, universities, or businesses, or who received direct or indirect, manifest or concealed, payments for their sports participation.[13]

In view of the commercialism, professionalism, bureaucracy, nationalism, politics, and ambiguities in interpretation and enforcement of amateur principles in modern sports, it is not difficult to accept sports philosopher Harold Vander Zwaag's contention that amateurism in sport has almost become an obsolete concept.[14] Even if amateurism is not obsolete, the veneer of amateurism in the major Olympic sports has become nearly transparent. In the United States today, commercialism, professionalism, and bureaucracy have become dominant features of the major Olympic sports as well as professional sports.

## 2. Dominant Aspects of Contemporary Professional and Olympic Sports

Big-time amateur and professional sports and their stars have become increasingly complex and diverse over the past several decades. Simple, pure, romanticized images of the games and the players have been challenged by a seemingly endless stream of changes in the organization and operation of the sports and by apparent changes in the personalities and motives of the athletes and those who run their sports.[15] There now seem to be a multitude of leagues, associations, sports, teams, and athletes to follow. New professional franchises appear to be born, to relocate, and to dissolve in the space of months. In the amateur realm, established associations such as the AAU are replaced by new organizations(or at least new names) such as The Athletics Congress of the U.S. (TAC), while amateur athletes in sports like track and field argue with the officials of their sport about governance and the right to compete openly for prize money. At the international level, huge costs, political demonstrations and boycotts, and controversies over commercial endorsements and amateur eligibility have become routine features of the Olympic Games. In professional sports, new leagues have formed, old ones have dissolved, and mergers have taken place. There have been battles over the control of various sports domains between commissioners of different sports, between different ruling bodies, between commissioners and owners, between management and coaches, and between management or coaches and players and their unions and agents. Professional athletes have sought higher salaries, better fringe benefits, and improved pension plans. They have engaged in strikes when their contract negotiations have gone awry, and they have been locked out by retaliating owners. Few large-scale sports, professional or amateur, have been unaffected by the lure of television money, and they have made a number of accommodations to the demands of the medium. In fact, media coverage in many sports spans almost the entire calendar as athletes are followed from preseason practice to the banquet circuit. Furthermore, sports seasons have become expanded to the point that numerous major sports overlap. Finally, the lives of star athletes have become the object of increasing and more personal and critical public scrutiny as reporters and analysts of the contemporary sports scene seek to portray the "real" personalities of these athletes.

The apparent and actual changes in big-time amateur and professional sports and athletes over recent decades may be seen largely as reflections of tendencies toward increasing bureaucratization, commercialization, and professionalization.[16] "Bureaucratization" refers to the development of large-scale social units (or, "bureaucracies") with highly specialized divisions of labor, elaborate hierarchies of authority, and highly rationalized and formalized goal pursuits and regulatory controls. The large size or complex structure of bureaucracies such as universities, industrial corporations, metropolitan hospitals, and agencies of government often conjures up an image of impersonal relations with organization employees who seem to be excessively concerned about legalities and technical matters.

Bureaucracies become commercial enterprises when they are organized to generate financial revenues and profits. "Commercialization" refers to the business-like pursuit of financial gain in corporate bodies. Even though amateur athletes are not supposed to compete for money, we saw in the last chapter on intercollegiate athletics that some of the large sums of money involved in highly commercialized amateur sports may be used to recruit, subsidize, or otherwise use athletes for commercial purposes. Increasing commercialization of the structure of a sport, professional or amateur, is likely to increase the desire for financial reward among the competitors, organizers, and producers of the sport. In this chapter, "professionalization" refers to the willingness to accept financial or material compensation for one's performance. This pecuniary motivation among athletes and coaches is likely to be accompanied by the kind of professionalization of attitude referred to in the discussion of children and sport in an earlier chapter.[17] This latter concept implies an increasing concern about the demonstration of skill and winning and a diminishing concern about sportsmanship and fair play.

Pockets of relative amateurism remain in the Olympic realm, and commercialism and professionalism continue to be denounced by officials of the ruling bodies of many Olympic sports. Nevertheless, the corporate and individual pursuit of money and large-scale bureaucracy are dominant features of major Olympic sports as well as professional sports in the United States today. Precisely because these sports realms are highly organized and offer the prospect of direct or indirect financial gain and national or international fame, major Olympic and professional sports often are seen—especially by the less affluent and minorities—as important vehicles for achieving the American Dream. Thus, in a sense, major Olympic and professional sports in America have come to be seen as routes to the American Dream because they have evolved into the type of highly organized, commercialized, and professionalized enterprise Baron de Coubertin tried so hard to suppress. It is unlikely, though, that the Baron could have envisioned the *extent* to which bureaucracy, commercialism, and professionalism have marked the development of modern sports in the United States.

## A. *The Organization and Operation of Contemporary Professional Sports in the United States*

Pete Rose's unrestrained love for playing baseball did not cloud his assessment of the basic nature of professional sports or the society in which they are embedded today. He has said:

> Sports today is a business. Our whole society's a business. So sports just echoes the trend. Of course, the fans don't like that. They want ballgames to be an escape, a fantasy. But you have to be realistic...[18]

No single event can readily be identified as the beginning of the modern age of highly organized, commercialized sport in the United States.[19] The business of professional sports began to assume its contemporary form when the economy started to recover from the depression during the 1930s. Large-scale organization and sophisticated administrative planning began to characterize professional sports at the beginning of the 1950s, following the establishment of bureaucratic organization and administrative procedures in other sectors of American society.

Although professional sports leagues have not yet evolved to the point where they rival "Fortune 500" firms in their size or operations, the professional sports industry today mirrors many of the features of major economic corporations. The total 1977 gross revenues of the four major professional team sports in America—hockey, baseball, basketball, and football—of $640 million are rather meager in relation to Exxon's gross revenues that year of $48 billion.[20] However, like Exxon, professional sports enterprises buy equipment, rent or pay for building construction, make other capital investments, recruit personnel, pay salaries, negotiate with representatives of labor unions, engage in public relations and promotional activities, acquire "intelligence" about rivals, maintain an administrative hierarchy to make corporate decisions, rely on the latest technology in corporate planning and administration, and most basically, generate revenue for future operations.

Professional sports officials tend to be very reluctant to make public disclosures of team finances. However, it generally is believed that professional sports clubs have three main sources of revenue:

- gate receipts;
- the sale of television and radio broadcast rights; and
- income from ancillary enterprises such as concessions, parking, and the sale of game programs and souvenirs.[21]

One report[22] of the operating income of professional football teams in 1974 showed that 55% was from ticket sales, nearly 35% was from television and radio, and about 3.5% was from programs, concessions, and similar enterprises. One would guess that major professional individual sports such as golf, auto racing, tennis, horse racing, boxing, and bowling depend heavily on ticket sales and corporate or individual commercial sponsorship of events as well as revenue from selected broadcasts of popular events.

Broadcast revenues tend to be generated in professional team sports in two ways:

- individual clubs may negotiate their own contract with local radio and TV stations for the right to broadcast their games; and
- the league may negotiate with national networks for all clubs in its jurisdiction.[23]

Individual club contracts create significant income differences among teams because clubs differ in the size of their markets and in their local popularity. League contracts lead to a more equitable income distribution. In 1961, Congress passed legislation that allowed professional sports leagues to negotiate national broadcast rights for all their teams without being subject to antitrust laws. This new privilege meant that leagues were able to bargain for more lucrative TV and radio network contracts while offering fewer games for broadcast?[24]

There tend to be three major costs associated with ownership of a professional sports club:

- player compensation (salaries, bonuses, deferred payments and fringe benefits);
- game expenses (including rental of the arena and travel expenses); and
- general and administrative costs (including salaries of owners, executives, and concessionaires and costs of administering the daily business of the club).[25]

Compensation of players tends to be significantly more expensive than any other cost item in a professional sports club budget. In recent years, the cost of player compensation has escalated dramatically, and in many cases it is more than the combined amount of all other costs of club ownership.

The accounting report for professional sports should include money generated *through* them as well as in them. Major professional sports produce billions of dollars in advertising revenue for TV and radio and in business for the cities where their games are played. In addition, it has been estimated that $50 billion is gambled each year on sports.[26]

It was mentioned that Congress gave professional sports leagues an exemption from antitrust laws in regard to its negotiations for broadcast rights. In fact, this particular privilege represents just one example of the general exemption from antitrust legislation that professional sports leagues have traditionally enjoyed in the United States. A peculiarity of the business history of American professional sports leagues—in relation to other businesses in America—is that they have been explicitly or implicitly allowed by those who write and interpret the law to operate as a self-regulating monopoly or cartel *despite* substantial financial growth and success. That is, the individual firms or clubs within a particular league have been allowed to pool their resources and work in collusion on decisions of common interest such as rules, expansion, promotion, scheduling, player recruitment, and network broadcast packages.

The right to operate openly as a cartel is a legal privilege that is not shared by other American businesses. However, it has been viewed as a crucial element in the financial success of sports leagues. For example, National Football League commissioner Pete Rozelle acknowledged that all professional sports leagues were a "natural monopoly," but he also proposed that league members were business "partners" rather than competitors in the league venture and that the financial survival of the league depended on such an economic arrangement.[27] Rozelle made these comments in the context of a jury trial in which the Oakland Raiders and Los Angeles Coliseum claimed antitrust violations by the league in trying to block a move by the Raiders to the Coliseum.

The Sherman Antitrust Law, enacted in 1890, made illegal "every contract, combination in the form of trust or otherwise, or conspiracy in restraint of trade or commerce among the several states or with foreign nations."[28] There were a number of reasons to think at the time this law was passed that professional baseball would be found in violation of it. Among them were the facts that the baseball club owners operated as a cartel, conspired to depress player salaries, prevented players from switching teams to obtain a higher salary, and engaged in interstate commerce by collectively existing as a "combination" of twenty-four teams that played in eight different states. However, in 1922 the Supreme Court unanimously decided that baseball was exempt from regulation under the Sherman Antitrust Law because it involved "purely state affairs"—in offering local exhibitions—outside the federal jurisdiction over interstate commerce.[29] In the opinion written by Justice Oliver Wendell Holmes, the Supreme Court viewed the movement of players across state lines as "a mere incident, not the essential thing."

Although this decision has been a target of much criticism in legal and judicial circles, it has not been overruled. Despite some subsequent court rulings that have struck at certain restrictive or monopolistic practices in professional sports, baseball has remained exempt from antitrust regulation and other professional sports have remained relatively protected from such regulation. A major quandary for the makers and interpreters of the law has stemmed from a conflict between the principle of illegality of private restraints on free trade embodied in the Sherman Law and the practical value of joint action in sports leagues to achieve balanced, sustained, and geographically dispersed athletic competition.[30]

Without a clear and definitive judicial or legislative resolution of this quandary, professional sports club owners have enjoyed a special legal and economic status. By virtue of their special status, owners in professional sports leagues have traditionally been allowed to engage in the kinds of monopolistic practices that baseball owners enjoyed at the end of the last century. In recent years, though, economic competition from new or opposing leagues, ambitious owners with big checkbooks, the appearance of free agency, Congressional pressures, and legal action have combined to undercut the cartel-like operation of professional sports leagues. For example, the House Judiciary Subcommittee on Monopolies and Commercial Law was told by a Justice Department official that the antitrust laws should apply to professional sports, including baseball, as they do to every other unregulated sector of the economy. Abbott B. Lipsky, Jr., Deputy Assistant Attorney General in the Antitrust Division acknowledged that sports was a unique business and required "some consultation and cooperation among the teams in a given league in order for each to exist." However, he added that ". . . an admitted need for some cooperation does not necessarily justify any and all agreements among the teams in a league, and several types of league rules remain controversial."[31] Lipsky proposed that the "rule of reason" should be the main consideration in measuring alleged anticompetitive aspects of professional sports leagues against procompetitive arguments. He was the leadoff witness in three days of committee hearings covering a range of topics including league restraints on the purchase and sale of franchises, antitrust aspects of sports broadcasting, the player draft and free agency, and territorial restrictions on the movement of franchises.

A monopolistic structure in professional sports is a contradiction of the American Dream ideology because it reflects the existence of restraints or controls imposed on the pursuit of success in sports by aspiring owners and athletes. This ideology includes hard work, persistence, and open competition for advancement as major ingredients of the formula for success in American society. However, aspiring or ambitious owners who seek the economic, social, psychological, and other perceived benefits of sports club ownership may find that their desires to own a franchise, relocate it, or run it in their own way are frustrated by the cartel that dominates their sport. Al Davis' battle with fellow NFL owners and league Commissioner Pete Rozelle over his right to relocate his Raiders from Oakland to the more lucrative market of Los Angeles is illustrative in this regard. Athletes also have found their paths to the American Dream through professional sport blocked by restrictive practices by the owners or management in their sport. Even with free agency and the right to try to sell their services to the highest bidder, athletes have had to confront owners who could act collusively to limit their freedom of movement, make informal agreements about ceilings on their salaries, and move them from one club to another without their consent if they had accumulated only a few years of major league playing experience. The major league baseball strike of 1981 illustrates the persisting frustrations among players about their bargaining rights, even as their salaries soar and their economic security seems assured.

Thus, the traditional cartel-like organization and operation of professional team sports continue to pose obstacles for the pursuit of the American Dream through professional sport both for certain owners or would-be owners as well as for athletes. The different economic organization of professional individual sports such as golf, tennis, auto racing, and bowling might seem to allow a freer pursuit of personal success by athletes and investors. However, athletes usually must either be from a wealthy family or have a sponsor to be able to afford the training, equipment, and other expenses that make a career in these sports possible. In addition, there are ruling bodies in these sports that control who can participate in their events; who can invest in them; and how, when, and where they will be staged. In these respects, the organization and operation of professional individual sports seem to have more in common with Olympic sports than with professional team sports. Before considering in more detail the tax and profit incentives, the reserve and option clauses, the desire for wealth and economic freedom, free agency, public fame and pressure, and the other factors that fuel or frustrate the drive toward the American Dream through professional sports, the organization and operation of contemporary American Olympic sports will be considered.

### B. The Organization and Operation of Contemporary Olympic Sports in the United States

There may not be as much money involved in Olympic as professional sports and athletes in Olympic sports may not *openly* receive salaries or monetary prizes for their participation, but monetary considerations nevertheless have much to do with the organization and operation of contemporary Olympic sports. In view of the decline of the amateur ideal that was discussed earlier, this fact should not be surprising. During this century, the Modern Olympic Games seem to have evolved far from the noble founding principles of international brotherhood, joyful play, and participation as an end in itself. The Olympic Games are a highly commercialized enterprise dominated by international politics, by almost frantic efforts by nations to outdo each other on the athletic field and in the staging of the Games, and by athletes and coaches who seem intent on doing almost anything necessary to win.

The big business of the 1976 Montreal Olympics was called "the billion dollar game" by one observer,[32] and the escalation of costs during preparation for these Games illustrates the pattern of escalating costs and severe financial pressures at this highest level of international amateur sports. In 1968, two years before Montreal won the right to host the 1976 Summer Olympics, it was estimated that the cost would be $10-$15 million. This estimate was radically revised in 1973 to $310 million, but there still was no deficit projected. Costs were to include $250 million for the facilities, not including the Olympic Village (which was to be privately developed), and $32.5 million in operating expenses. Revenue was to be generated from the sale of Olympic coins, stamps, rights to the Olympic symbol, television broadcast rights, ticket sales, and a national lottery. By May 1976, two months before the Games opened, total revenue was $359.8 million. However, inflation, labor problems, corruption, and mismanagement had increased expenses to an estimated $1.4 *billion*, leaving an estimated deficit of about one billion dollars that has not been substantially reduced since then.[33]

If the 1976 Summer Games cost over one billion dollars, they were five times more expensive than the 1972 Games in Munich, over thirty times more expensive than the Rome Games of 1960, and over *150 times* more expensive than the Games in Los Angeles in 1932.[34] Among the reasons for the willingness of cities or national governments to stage Olympiads and other major international sports events might be the desire for prestige or political gain for the host city and nation and the organizers, projected revenues, *and* (overly) optimistic calculations of financial risks or costs. Despite the possibility of high costs, it appears that there are many governments and private groups and individuals who believe that the economic, social, or personal benefits from organizing, promoting, and staging big-time amateur sports spectacles justify the risks of investment. However, to remain financially viable, organizers of the Olympic Games and other major amateur sports competitions must conform to the kinds of organizational and financial practices that allow other businesses to remain in operation or they must seek special legal or economic privileges or subsidies. Special privileges and subsidies have contributed to the success of national sports teams in communist countries and countries—other than the U.S.—in the noncommunist world. Furthermore, as we have seen, special protection has been an important factor in the survival and growth of the professional team sports industry in the United States.

The overspending and mismanagement associated with the Montreal Olympics dramatically highlight the degree of financial and organizational difficulties that can arise in the Olympic sports if they are not run competently and responsibly. The *magnitude* of the Montreal Olympiad's financial and organizational problems may be exceptional in amateur sports, but the *kinds* of problems that arose in relation to the organizing effort are not. In the U.S., athletes, the press, and the sports public have complained for years about the poor organization—called "organized incompetence" by one writer[35]—and underfunding that have character- ized Olympic sports.

Blunders by American Olympic official during the 1972 Munich Olympics provided highly visible manifestations of the frustrations Ameri- can athletes have experienced under the Olympic system. A sprinter missed his trial because his coach used an incorrect schedule. The basketball team lost a gold medal to the Soviets after a highly controver- sial finish. A swimmer lost his gold medal because his use of asthma medicine before his event was ruled "doping." The top American pole vaulter lost the use of his pole because it was declared "illegal." In none of these cases was an effective appeal launched by U.S. Olympic officials. Furthermore, in a 1974 report, the Athletic Advisory Council of USOC observed that there may have been a "...significant lack of respect among competing athletes for the professional competence and judgment of medical personnel assigned to the U.S. teams..."[36]

Amateur athletes testifying before a Senate committee in 1973 told of the 1972 Pan American Games in Cali, Columbia, where athletes were crowded in dilapidated, bug-infested shacks without hot water, while officials stayed at the Intercontinental Hotel. They told of the 1972 Olympic track and field trials in Eugene, Oregon, where athletes paid for their own transportation and lodging and had little or no money left to pay for food. They also talked about competing against athletes from other countries who were subsidized by their governments as full-time athletes. They complained that too much of the money raised by the U.S. Olympic Committee went for administrative costs and staging the Games and too little supported preparation or development of the athletes to participate in them.[37]

Complaints about problems in amateur sports and concern about declining performance of U.S. athletes in international competition prompted the formation of the President's Commission on Olympic Sports in September 1975 under President Gerald Ford. It received an allocation of $596,000 to support its work, which was to be completed by January 1977. The composition of the Committee included U.S. Senators, Congressmen, Olympic athletes, executives in amateur sports, and others in sport. Its final report in January 1977 recommended a major reorganization of American amateur sports under the umbrella of a centralized sports coordinating body called the Central Sports Organization (CSO). This proposed reorganization was intended to meet three basic needs in the amateur sports world in the United States:

- a means of settling disputes among sports organizations over who gets international recognition as a national ruling body in particular sports domains;
- a means of providing equitable representation of all the administra-

tive bodies in a sport on a national governing body; and
- a central policy-making forum where directions and priorities could be established and fund-raising efforts could be coordinated for amateur sports.[38]

There is not yet a CSO in the U.S., although the AAU was reorganized (or renamed) as The Athletics Congress. The existing amateur athletic establishment with its established international affiliations poses a formidable obstacle to such extensive voluntary change in amateur athletics in the U.S. James Frey has proposed a self-described conservative estimate of 891,000 amateur sports organizations and affiliates in the U.S. that have memberships in the millions and generate income and expenses of approximately $1.25 billion.[39] The figures are conservative because they exclude media organizations, concessions, sporting goods dealers and manufacturers, hotels, restaurants, and other firms that help support amateur sports financially. The network includes USOC, TAC, intercollegiate athletic associations, physical education associations, school sports, the ruling federations and associations of individual amateur sports, and the assorted other associations that sanction, organize, and run amateur sports from the children's to the adult level.

According the Frey, the network linking the various organizations in the amateur sports realm in the U.S. includes loose, oligopolistic cartels—such as the NCAA and TAC—formed to create a scarcity of its product to increase demand but also to guarantee each participating organization a large enough share of the market and profit to satisfy it. As an example, he proposed that amateur and intercollegiate associations limit the locations and control the quality of their sponsored events in a manner similar to the way professional sports leagues restrict franchise locations and hold drafts to try to maintain athletic and economic balance among their teams.

Frey pointed out that cooperation within these amateur sports cartels did not necessarily mean cooperation between different cartels in the larger amateur sports network. In fact, disputes over jurisdiction of particular domains of amateur sports and competition for profits in the amateur athletics marketplace between different ruling bodies such as the NCAA, AAU (now TAC), USOC, and individual amateur sports federations in the U.S. were a major reason for the recommendation of the CSO by the Presidential Commission.

Frey predicted that efforts to centralize control of amateur sports in the U.S. would be strongly resisted because the member organizations of the cartels—such as the colleges in the NCAA and the sports federations in TAC and USOC—which are already sacrificing potential control and profits to their cartels, would be unlikely to accept further diffusion of their authority and profits to a nationalized body. Finding adequate resources to maintain existing operations is currently difficult for amateur sports organizations. If these organizations gave up additional resources to support a centralized sports organization, a decline in overall athletic performance in American amateur sports could result, which would be exactly the opposite of what the Presidential Commission hoped to encourage. As Frey suggested, either an elite class of athletes in selected sports would receive a disproportionate share of the limited resources allocated by a CSO or these resources would be diffused to such a wide extent that no organization would be able to give its athletes enough of the resources needed to stimulate winning world-class performances.

Although the President's Commission on Olympic Sports may not have appreciated the nature or extent of organizational and political obstacles to their proposed reorganization of amateur sports in the United States, they recognized that there were serious organizational and political problems in the amateur sports realm. They also recognized the financial difficulties in amateur athletics. They recommended a federal investment of $218 million for facilities and another $83 million annually for operating costs. The major financial difficulty in many amateur sports in the U.S. is that the governing bodies that control the sports have limited funds to support their athletes with coaching, training facilities and equipment, and travel money. It also is noteworthy that 75% of operating costs go to organization (administration, development, and facilities) and 25% support participation.[40] Many amateur federations rely on modest grants from USOC or TAC, operate with a part-time volunteer staff, and do not own their own facilities; and for some sports the governing body offers no organized program at all.[41]

In view of meager resources and a lack of overall coordination of the amateur sports network, it is not surprising that amateur sports organizations and ruling bodies battle with each other for control over their sports, govern them ineffectively, and create frustration or anger in their athletes. We have seen that even the highly commercialized realm of big-time college sports is not without financial or organizational problems. It would seem that except for elite athletes in the popular and highly commercialized "amateur" sports, the road to the American Dream through amateur sport is likely to be very narrow and bumpy, often leading to a dead end. Athletes' experiences along this road will be examined more closely after looking at the pursuit of the American Dream by participants in professional sports.

# The Pursuit of the American Dream in Professional and Olympic Sports in the United States

## 1. Professional Sports

## A. *Owners and Their American Sports Dream*

The American Dream pursued by owners has changed during the evolution of professional sports in the United States to reflect changes in the types of owners. The earliest professional sports teams were organized by players, and the teams were combined into leagues that failed largely because they were poorly financed and poorly managed.[42] The mistakes made by these pioneers in professional sports reflected their limited business and administrative expertise and entrepreneurial skills. However, the owners who came after them learned from past mistakes and combined a genuine love for the game with business acumen and entrepreneurial ability to place their sports on more solid financial and organization footing. In fact, they learned that a fruitful means of enhancing the financial survival of their sports was to establish the monopolistic practices that have become a key aspect of the peculiar business history of professional sports in the U.S.

The legendary early owners in professional sports matured with the growth of their sports. They were men such as George Halas in football, Eddie Gottlieb in basketball, and Clark Griffith, Connie Mack, and John McGraw in baseball.[43] These men were totally committed to their sports and involved themselves in all aspects of the operation of their franchises. They promoted their sports, made some money, and provided a stable basis on which their league could become established and grow.

The only business of these early owners was sport. After they had begun to establish their sports, they were joined by a new group of owners who were businessmen with substantial wealth acquired outside the sports domain. These new owners were able to gain public recognition for their other business interests and for themselves through their investment in sport. Brewery owners August Busch, Jr. of the St. Louis (baseball) Cardinals and Jacob Ruppert of the New York Yankees, and chewing gum magnate William Wrigley of the Chicago Cubs were prototypes of this new owner. Although initially there were fears that these industrialists would use their sports clubs primarily to sell their products, these men generally demonstrated a genuine devotion to their sports.

The recent boom era of professional sports in America began with the emergence of the National Basketball Association as a stable league in 1949 and the absorption by the National Football League of the three most successful All-American Conference teams.[44] In 1960, there began a period of expansion in professional sport in which existing leagues increased in size and new leagues were created, which usually either died or merged with established leagues. The number of professional sports teams has multiplied substantially since the early 1960s,[45] and the relocation of franchises has become commonplace.

During this recent expansion period in professional sports, the "sportsman owner" has faded, and another type has replaced him. The dominant type of owner in professional sports today is the corporate manager who views sport as a business investment. As Leonard has observed, "Frequently an absentee owner, the (modern owner's) concern often isn't for the town, team, or sport, but which team up for sale offers the best tax advantage."[46] Investors with earnings from other business investments to shelter have been attracted to professional sports by opportunities to take advantage of depreciation and capital gains tax laws, to run their club under an umbrella of protection from antitrust regulation, and to sell it at a substantial profit once their tax advantage has been used up.[47] The Tax Reform Act of 1976 restricted the owners' right to depreciate the value of their players on their tax statements, but the class of owners has continued to grow in the form of syndicates, shareholders, and conglomerates.[48]

There are remnants of earlier eras of sports ownership in professional sports today. For example, the O'Malley (Los Angeles Dodgers), Griffith (Minnesota Twins), and Rooney (Pittsburgh Steelers) families have had long and devoted relationships with their respective teams and sports. In addition, there are a few publicly owned professional sports teams, including the Green Bay Packers in football and the Milwaukee Bucks in basketball. There also are large corporations such as Gulf and Western (New York Knicks and Rangers) and CBS (New York Yankees) and investment syndicates such as in Cincinnati that have owned professional sports teams. The corporate owners tend to be faceless because they often are far removed geographically or in the corporate network from their sports "subsidiaries." The most prevalent type of owner today, the corporate executive with an interest in making money as well as winning championships, often is not so faceless. In fact, owners such as Ray Kroc (San Diego Padres) who owns the McDonald's fast-food chain, shipping magnate George Steinbrenner (New York Yankees), communications entrepreneur Ted Turner (Atlanta Hawks and Braves), and insurance man Charlie Finley (Oakland Athletics) have left enduring impressions on recent professional sports history through the force of their strong personalities and strong convictions about the operation of their clubs and sports.

Although many prospective owners appear to be attracted to professional sports by financial or tax incentives, many of the current owners can be heard complaining about the financial risks and burdens of ownership. There apparently has been some basis in their complaints, if reported financial figures from the major professional team sports are accurate. In 1974, only 2 of 26 pro football teams lost money, but 10 of 28 pro hockey teams, 12 of 24 major league baseball teams, and 22 of 27 pro basketball teams—involved at the time in a bidding war between leagues—lost money. By 1977-78, matters had improved overall. However, 4 of 28 NFL teams, 5 of 26 major league baseball teams, 10 of 18 NHL teams, and 9 of 22 NBA teams lost money.[49] Furthermore, of the major professional sports leagues in basketball, hockey, soccer, tennis, football, track, and lacrosse that were established since 1966, only the North

American Soccer League and Women's Professional Basketball League were survivors in 1980, and their survival was somewhat precarious[50] The failure of a sports league can be quite expensive for investors. It has been reported that the owners of the original franchises in the now-defunct World Football League lost $34,000,000[51]

Unless owners make a smart investment in a franchise with a good market potential and unless they run their team competently, franchise ownership will be a costly investment. Owner Brad Corbett of baseball's Texas Rangers has said, "It's no longer possible for someone to buy a team, delegate everything to other people and treat it like a hobby...Handled this way it can be an expensive hobby, and it's ultimately counterproductive, because the players feel the remoteness of an owner they never see and they react against it."[52]

Clearly, there are financial risks associated with owning a professional sports franchise, even though owning a team in an established league would appear to be a profitable investment for the majority of owners today. However, since the dominant type of owner in the current professional sports era was already quite wealthy before investing in a sports franchise, there are likely to be more important, or other, incentives than economic ones for ownership in most cases today. Clint Murchison, oil man and owner of the Dallas Cowboys, may have spoken for most or all of his wealthy colleagues in professional sports when he said, "You could make more money investing in government bonds. But football is more fun."[53] For many owners, the chance to mingle with players, take an active part in team strategy sessions, watch practices and games from the sideline, and become publicly associated with the accomplishments and stars of their team help fulfill lifelong fantasies as superfans and provide vicarious identification with the athletes responsible for their team's success.[54]

Though it may be tremendously exciting—especially with a winner—ownership of a professional sports franchise may not turn out to be the fantasyland owners envisioned. Since cartels control opportunities to enter established professional sports for potential investors, prospective owners must compete for the limited opportunities to take over an existing franchise or buy an expansion franchise. They may find that having enough money may not open the door if they do not meet the approval of the cartel controlling the sport they wish to enter. Even as part of the cartel, an owner may find that building or maintaining a winner, keeping players and coaches happy, and regularly filling the stadium can be difficult and frustrating. Furthermore, they may find themselves in contention with other owners and the league commissioner regarding the way they run their team or with arbitrators, lawyers, agents, and judges regarding disputes or contract negotiations with their coaches and players.

Having joined the league with the promise of privileges and protections afforded by its cartel-like structure, owners in recent years have discovered gaping cracks developing in the cartel. Combined with the financial risks of investment, the high salaries they feel they must pay players to achieve their sport's Holy Grail, "The Championship," and other frustrations and disappointments of running a professional sports franchise, the breakdown of the cartel may make owning a sports franchise somewhat less gratifying than originally anticipated. Unlike players, though, if owners decide that professional sport is not the fantasyland or gold mine they envisioned, they can withdraw, usually with a profit, and use their wealth, connections, and other assets to find fun, fulfillment, and a better financial return elsewhere. Being an owner today usually implies the possession of resources that allows many options for pursuing success and the American Dream. Being a professional athlete often implies that sport is perceived to be the best *or only* route to the American Dream.

## B. Athletes and Their American Sports Dream

### i. The Opportunity Structure

If the American Sports Dream of franchise owners is to achieve ego gratification, have fun, and make money, the American Sports Dream of athletes recently has been to become wealthy and financially secure. They have sought higher salaries, more economic freedom, and more control over their careers—along with public recognition in a number of cases—and they have used a variety of traditional labor and legal tactics to achieve these ends. A casual glance at the sports pages suggests that many athletes have achieved their American Sports Dream in recent years. We seem to read regularly about huge sums of money earned or won in the team and individual realms of professional sports. However, we should not be deceived about the road to success through professional sports for athletes or about the lives of the athletes who travel this road. Certainly, there *are* spectacular "rags to riches" stories in professional sports, and there are professional athletes who love what they do and could not imagine doing anything else—even when their optimistic hopes begin to fade. Nevertheless, for most athletes aspiring to success through professional sports, there will be frustration and failure because the American Sports Pyramid has very little room at the top. And for many of those who make it to the top, life as a professional athlete is likely to be brief and insecure.

The funnel-like opportunity structure of sports in the United States has been noted in past chapters. Statistics from 1972 indicated that the 400,000 high school baseball players each had a 1-in-4000 chance of becoming a major league rookie, and the 2500 college baseball players each had a 1-in-250 chance of making it to the major leagues. The statistics showed that in football, each of the 600,000 high school players had about a 1-in-3750 chance of becoming an NFL rookie, and each of the 40,000 college players had about a 1-in-250 chance of becoming a professional in that league. In basketball, each of the 600,000 high school players had a 1-in-10,000 chance of making it to the NBA or ABA, and each of the 17,000 college players had approximately a 1-in-280 chance of playing in one of these two leagues. In 1972, the average length of a career at the top level in professional baseball was 7-8 years, in professional football was 5 years, and in professional basketball was 5 years[55] These figures may have changed somewhat since the early 1970s, but the pyramidal structure of the American sports system remains virtually the same. For all but a tiny fraction of the young athletes in the U.S., a professional sports career is a pipe dream. For those who get a chance to wear the uniform of a team at the top professional level in his or her sport or compete in a professional tournament or race, achievement and success are likely to be elusive and fleeting.

## 1) Opportunities for Black Athletes

The disproportionate representation and outstanding record of achievement of blacks in the major professional sports of basketball, football, baseball, and boxing[56] seem to contradict the notion of sport as a limited and illusory mobility escalator for minorities. Instead, the pervasive involvement and considerable achievements of black athletes in these sports might suggest that professional sport is an accessible, "legitimate opportunity structure"[57] through which black males frequently achieve upward social mobility. Donald Ball called this view of opportunities for minorities in professional sport the "Jackie Robinson story."[58] Jackie Robinson's historic breakthrough in major league baseball after World War II marked the end of a period of over fifty years in which blacks were almost totally excluded from all major American professional sports except boxing[59] One could see this breakthrough as the begining of an era in professional sports in the U.S. in which blacks have come to experience unlimited opportunity and little or no discrimination or prejudice in their drive toward excellence and success.

Without diminishing the substantial progress of blacks and other minorities in professional sports over the past few decades, a close examination of professional sports today would seem to call for some qualification of the Jackie Robinson story. Donald Ball proposed the "Harry Edwards corrective" as a more restrained view of the experience of minorities in professional sport today. It acknowledges their improved opportunities while also pointing out the persistence of certain forms of racial discrimination[60] These forms of discrimination are more subtle than the overt forms that prevented blacks from competing at all in professional sports. Prominent examples that have been identified by sports participants and observers are *quotas* and *stacking*.

Quotas limit the number of minorities in a starting line-up or on a team roster. In this regard, former pro basketball star player and coach Bill Russell has told the story of a college basketball coach who played two blacks in his home arena, three during away games, and five when his team was behind[61] The obvious implication of this story is that an arbitrary limit is imposed on the number of blacks who can play—until victory threatens to slip away—perhaps because of a fear that the predominantly white audience of commercialized sports will not pay to see mostly black faces.

Stacking is positional segregation in a sport on the basis of race or some other objectively irrelevant ascribed status characteristic. The disproportionate assignment of blacks to noncentral positions—such as the outfield in baseball and receiver and cornerback in football—has been viewed as an insidious form of racial discrimination because it segregates blacks from positions with more visibility, more glamour, and more influence.[62] This segregation could limit income potential in sport and through outside commercial endorsements, limit public respect for black abilities—especially concerning intellect and leadership—and limit opportunities for positions of authority in coaching or management after retirement as a player.[63]

There is not yet agreement among sport scientists about the reasons for stacking, but sociological and social psychological explanations tend to be based on assumptions of racial stereotypes, fears, and prejudice. Stanley Eitzen and David Sanford reached the "inescapable" conclusion from their research that black athletes were systematically removed from positions of leadership as they moved from high school to college to the professional level.[64] This pattern of increased stacking and stacking in general could be explained by white coaches' stereotypical conceptions of blacks as less capable of leadership and rational, intelligent decision-making under pressure. In this conception, blacks are valued more for their physical gifts than for their intellectual or leadership capabilities.

Barry McPherson has proposed the alternative explanation that blacks may segregate themselves into the positions blacks traditionally have played through following the lead of their "idols."[65] However, this does not explain why blacks are increasingly switched out of central positions at higher levels of competition. Even if some self-selection occurs, it appears likely that it is an accommodation to a perceived pattern of stacking. For example, Gene Washington was a quarterback at Stanford through his sophomore year, and then switched to flanker. He became an all-pro wide receiver. He said about his switch, which he chose himself: "It was strictly a matter of economics. I knew a black quarterback would have little chance in pro ball unless he was absolutely superb."[66]

Along with quotas and stacking, racial discrimination concerning opportunities to enter and play at the major league level of professional baseball, football, and basketball and concerning pay levels has been found.[67] Blacks have had to outperform whites to reach the major league level of these sports and they have had to outperform whites during their major league careers to stay at that level. This means that blacks have had to be better than whites to receive an equal chance to become and remain a major leaguer. Regarding pay levels, some evidence has been uncovered for major league baseball showing that although black starters had higher average salaries than Latin or white starters, blacks tended to experience discrimination because they received less pay than whites for equivalent performance levels.

Arthur Ashe's achievements as a black tennis player brought him considerable wealth and public respect as an athlete and a person. His sports achievements and success are made more impressive because they were accomplished in the realm of tennis, a sport confined largely to the country clubs of affluent whites in the days when Ashe was learning to play. Since Arthur Ashe used sport as his path to success, it might seem curious that he has discouraged black youths from pursuing professional sports as their path to the American Dream. However, perhaps because of the great odds he had to overcome to become a black professional tennis star and because he recognized the value of attaining a good education while he pursued his sports career, Ashe has been especially sensitive to the uncertainties of depending exclusively on a professional sports career as the road to success.

Many black athletes have earned stardom and wealth in professional sports over the past few decades. However, it is sobering to consider Jay Coakley's estimates that fewer than 900 blacks were making their living in the three major professional team sports of baseball, basketball, and football in the late 1970s, and that black males in the 18 to 64 age range each had a 1-in-6000 chance of earning his living as a professional athlete *or coach*[68] Of course, the probability of becoming rich and famous is even slimmer. In this context, it is easy to understand why Arthur Ashe has advised black youths to spend two hours in the library for every hour spent on the athletic field[69]

## 2) Opportunities for Latin Athletes

Just as less affluent black—and white—youths in the U.S. have dreamed about professional sports as their road to fame and fortune, young Latin American males have dreamed about stardom in major league baseball. The phenomenal success of Mexican pitcher Fernando Valenzuela, both as a rookie and subsequently, with the Los Angeles Dodgers is the type of story that fuels the dream that one can rise above poverty and a limited education with athletic skills. Fernando's accomplishments and success have been a special inspiration to Latin youths[70] However, for young Latin American ball players, whose recruitment by major league scouts is relatively unregulated, the reality of trying to become a major leaguer may be even more cruel than for underprivileged American blacks and whites.

In a story for *Sports Illustrated,* Bill Brubaker documented the deceptive promises of major league stardom that lure many talented Latin American teenage ball players away from their homes and schools and into professional baseball in the United States[71] Unfortunately, most are not talented enough to make it in the major leagues. It has been estimated that 90% of *all* minor leaguers are released before they reach the major leagues. Only eleven Latins who signed before their 17th birthday were playing in the major leagues in 1981. Five of the eleven eventually finished high school. The young Latins who do not make it frequently return home to face unemployment or menial employment because they were encouraged to forsake a high school diploma or training for a nonbaseball job for the dream of becoming a major league baseball player. According to Brubaker, these experiences have prompted complaints in Latin baseball circles that have persisted for decades: complaints about the false hopes of stardom and misplaced priorities that major league scouts encourage; about the exploitation of poor young Latin American prospects by U.S. baseball organizations who offer Latins signing bonuses that are only a fraction of the amount offered to Americans of equal or lesser ability; about oversigning Latins, including many withoaut a chance even for doing well as a *minor* leaguer; about disparaging stereotypes of Latin ball players by U.S. baseball officials; about efforts to minimize the value of an education for Latin bal players; about a tendency to release Latins too quickly, before they are given a chance for social adjustment to life in the U.S.; and about signing of Latins not athletically or emotionally mature enough to emigrate to the U.S.

### 3) Opportunities for Female Athletes

Brubaker's study clearly reveals that a successful professional sports career in the U.S. is as much of a pipe dream for young Latin American athletes as it is for young black and white Americans. However, even though a professional sports career is unrealistic for most aspiring Latin and American *male* athletes, at least there *are* opportunities for some to achieve their dream. For females in the U.S., opportunities for a fulltime career as a professional athlete were practically *nonexistent* until the past decade. Furthermore, stereotypical conceptions of athletics as unfeminine discouraged many females from applying their athletic talents to a serious athletic career. Though she has learned to be comfortable with the image of a woman athlete, tennis star Chris Evert Lloyd recalled earlier years when she rejected an identity as an athlete to preserve her sense of femininity. She has said, "I was just *someone who played tennis matches.* I still thought of women athletes as freaks, and I used to hate myself, thinking I must not be a whole woman. The nail polish, the ruffles on my bloomers, the hair ribbons, not wearing socks—all of that was very important me, to compensate. I would not be the stereotyped jock . . ."[72]

Changing conceptions of women and women's roles and legal and political movements to reform the rights of women have contributed to a more favorable climate for women in sport and to more opportunities for females at all levels of sport. In earlier chapters, the recent boom in female athletic participation at the high school and college levels generated by Title IX was discussed. For female athletes at the professional level, an important event that gave increased visibility and recognition to them and their realm of sport was the challenge tennis match between Billie Jean King and Bobby Riggs in 1973. Riggs, a tennis star as a much younger man, had defeated a women's champion at the time, Margaret Court, in another challenge match earlier that year. Thus, King's clear-cut victory over Riggs before a nationwide television audience restored pride and respectability to women's sports and gave many athletic young females a role model. A measure of Billie Jean King's stature in women's sports and the public consciousness about women is the generality sensitive treatment she received in regard to her public acknowledgment in 1981 of a past lesbian affair with a former secretary.

Opportunities for women in professional sports have improved considerably over the past decade. In 1971, Billie Jean King became the first female athlete to win $100,000. The leading money winner on the men's tennis tour that year, Rod Laver, won $290,000 by playing in one-third as many tournaments. In 1972, Kathy Whitworth was the leading money winner on the women's professional golf tour with $65,063 in 29 tournaments. Jack Nicklaus, the top male golfer won $320,542 in 19 tournaments that year. In 1977, Chris Evert won $503,134, winnings that were bettered by only two males in professional tennis that year—Jimmy Connors, who won $922,657 and Guillermo Vilas, who won $800,642. In 1980, four women golfers earned over $200,000 in prize money. Ten male golfers won over $200,000 in 1980. In 1982, both Ivan Lendl and Martina Navratilova won over $1.1 million in tennis prize money.[73]

There are few opportunities in professional sport that have been as lucrative for women as the tennis and golf tours. Women have competed at the professional level in a variety of other sports, including basketball, bowling, and skiing; and after Tuesday Testa broke the sex barrier in February 1969 as a jockey at Santa Anita, women have competed with and against men in such professional sports as Indianapolis auto racing, drag racing, volleyball, and road racing as well as horse racing. However, it is noteworthy that the two major women's professional sports, tennis and golf, are characterized by what sport sociologist Nancy Theberge has called "structured uncertainty."[74]

Women who compete in these individual sports must adapt to variability and indeterminacy in tournament settings, their own performance, relationships with colleagues and audiences, life style, and probably most significantly, income. Unlike team sports in which contracts specify a salary for at least an entire season, as well as fringe benefits and pension plans for veterans, individual sports such as tennis and golf do not offer such financial security. Except for the relatively few women in these sports who have lucrative endorsement arrangements, income depends on performance from week to week in tournaments. Although there is a substantial amount of money available for the top few finishers in each tournament, the amount of prize money drops off markedly beneath these top few spots. The result of this structure of tournament prizes is that the stars do quite well financially, but many players do not earn enough to cover the costs of competing on the tour. For example, Theberge reported that in 1976, the cost of competing on the women's golf tour averaged $15,000 (for travel and lodging, tournament entry fees, and caddy fees). In 1976, players' winnings ranged from $25 to over $150,000. Only 42 players won $15,000 or more that year. Thus, the two major professional sports careers open to female athletes offer substantial uncertainty or insecurity for many of these women, and opportunities and rewards for female athletes in professional sports in general do not come close to approximating the opportunities and rewards for male athletes in professional sports.

The steep pyramidal structure of the American sports system offers a realistic hope of fame and fortune through professional sport to only a tiny fraction of the women, Latins, blacks, and whites who might hold such aspirations. Though most with such aspirations fall through the funnel before reaching the top of the pyramid, a number of athletes each year manage to reach the top and some become stars. For the relatively few who make it to the top of the ladder of achievement and success in sport as professional athletes, life can be richly rewarding psychologically, socially, and materially. However, investigation into golf and tennis has indicated that both male and female professional athletes in individual sports of these kinds may experience considerable uncertainty and insecurity. In addition, the short duration of the average career in the major professional team sports and the existence of certain forms of racial discrimination in professional sports have been noted. Thus, it should be apparent that reaching the top in professional sports is not always the achievable American Dream so many aspiring and fallen athletes and so many fans imagine it to be. In the next section, we will examine more closely some of the major dimensions of the life of a professional athlete to reveal more fully the substance and meaning of the American Dream in sport and the American Dream in general.

### ii. Life as a Professional Athlete: Realization of an American Dream

### 1) Money and the Modern Professional Athlete

For many of the professional athletes who climb from poverty or modest backgrounds through their career in sport, the biggest reward at the top of the American Sports Pyramid is money and the comfortable or extravagant life style it affords. Even in the mid-1960s, before the million dollar contracts and hundred thousand dollar tournament prizes, research showed that major league baseball players ranked money higher in importance than the fun, love, and challenge of the game and the prestige or esteem it conferred on them.[75]

A nationwide survey of self-described sports fans that was reported in the special Sports Illustrated series on "Money in Sports" in 1978 revealed that 87% of the fans believed there was too much emphasis on money in sports today.[76] This survey also showed that the majority of fans believed professional athletes were paid too much and were greedier and more self-centered than they used to be, and that the free-agent system was destroying the loyalty players felt toward their teams and fans. Nearly three times as many fans (43% vs. 17%) thought that athletes had less, rather than more, love for their games than five years earlier. It is noteworthy that despite these feelings, fans tended not to resent the players or lose interest in sports as a result of the excessive emphasis on money in sports and among athletes that they perceived. The *Sports Illustrated* survey indicated that the majority of fans forgot about the emphasis on money once the game began; said the publicity about big player salaries had no effect on their interest in sports; were not interested in the details of contract negotiations and player salaries; were bothered only a little or not at all about excessive player salaries; found it acceptable for players in individual sports to win hundreds of thousands of dollars a year in tournament prize money; believed that players had a right to renegotiate their contracts after a good season; and felt that players were smarter and more colorful than in the past, were as competitive as they used to be, had to work hard for their money, and were a good example for kids.

Even if the fans resented the money made by professional athletes, it is difficult to imagine the athletes ignoring or turning down the huge sums of money offered to them in or through sports today. The tournament winnings of top male and female professional golfers and tennis players already have been mentioned. In December 1980, Dave Winfield signed a ten-year contract with the New York Yankees for a reported $15 to $22 million (after inflation adjustments).[77] At the time, his contract made him the highest salaried professional athlete in American sports history. Los Angeles Lakers basketball star "Magic" Johnson, however, signed a long-term contract after the 1981 NBA season that reportedly surpassed the one signed by Winfield. Johnson's contract was to pay him $2,739.73 *per day* after taking effect in 1984.[78] As lucrative as Johnson's contract might be, it pales in comparison with the boxing earnings of Muhammad Ali. Ali reportedly earned over $10 million in the ring in both 1975 and 1976. Through 1978, he had earned nearly $49 million in boxing purses in his career, which included no fights between March 1967 and October 1970 as a result of his refusal to be drafted into the military for religious reasons.[79]

Huge salaries and winnings can be reported for a number of additional professional sports not yet mentioned, including auto racing, bowling, horse racing, hockey, skiing, and soccer. Even in the relatively minor professional sport of racquetball, the national champion, Marty Hogan, won $41,000 in 1977-78 and earned over $86,000 in 1980-81.[80] What seems as significant as the amount of money earned by professional athletes today is the rate at which salaries and winnings escalated in recent years to reach current levels. For example, in the major American team sports, average gross salaries increased between 1970 and 1980 from $29,303 to $143,756 in baseball, from $40,000 to $190,000 in basketball, from $25,000 to $108,000 in hockey, and from

$34,600 to $78,657 in football.[81] Except perhaps in football, these increases substantially exceeded the society-wide inflation rate during the 1970s.

What is also significant about athletes and money in professional sports today is the amount athletes now earn outside sports through endorsements and other business transactions to supplement their salaries and winnings. For example, in 1977, tennis star Bjorn Borg earned between $1.5 and $2 million for allowing his name to be associated with a variety of products ranging from cars to cereals, games, jeans, and towels. Whenever Borg set foot on a tennis court, he instantly became a human billboard. His headband advertising Tuborg beer earned him $50,000; the Scandinavian Airlines System patch on his shoulder was worth $25,000; and he received $200,000 for wearing Fila shorts, socks, and warmup suits, $100,000 for using Bancroft rackets, and $50,000 for wearing Tretorn tennis shoes. Fran Tarkenton, now retired from his career as a professional football quarterback, became a successful businessman during his playing career as the founder, owner, and board chairman of Behavioral Systems, Inc., an international management consulting firm. As the second highest paid pro football player in 1977, Tarkenton earned $350,000. He supplemented his football salary that year with income from Behavioral Systems, a television contract, and endorsements and promotional work for Delta air Lines, General Mills, AT&T, Puma, Eastman Kodak, and MSA, a computer software company. His estimated total income for 1977 was $1.2 million. Golfer Arnold Palmer, one of the first modern American professional athletes to use his appeal and financial success in sport to build a business empire, reportedly earned $55 million between 1955 and 1977 from his golf winnings and nonsports business interests. Some athletes, such as golfer Laura Baugh and soccer player Kyle Rote, Jr., have been able to use modest success and considerable publicity in professional sports as a springboard for much greater financial success outside their sport. For example, in 1977, Baugh earned $46,373 from golf and supplemented it with $300,000 in outside income. That same year, Rote supplemented his soccer salary of $20,000 with an outside income of $200,000.[82] Baugh benefited from a great deal of media attention that focused as much on her attractive looks as on her golf swing. Rote benefited from being a promising and good-looking young American in a foreigner's game as well as from being the son of a former star in pro football.

The incomes of star athletes and even *average* salary figures in professional sports can give a misleading impression of the financial rewards earned by *most* professional athletes today. To gain a more accurate impression of the financial success of the typical athlete in each of the assorted professional sports, it must be remembered that competitors in individual sports events are not guaranteed prize money; they must finish high enough in competition to be at a level where prize money is awarded. There are many athletes in individual sports who must perform well in a qualifying competition to be eligible for tournaments or races. If they do not perform well in the qualifiers *and* the regular tour events, they will not earn enough to cover their expenses and they may lose their sponsor as well as future chances to qualify for significant events.

In team sports, the Dave Winfields, "Magic" Johnsons, Earl Campbells, and Tony Espositos may earn 40 to 50 *times* the minimum salary in their sports. In 1977-78, the minimum salaries in the major professional sports ranged from $20,000 in football and $21,000 in baseball to $30,000 in basketball and hockey[83] The highly paid professional athletes may be worth their high salaries if they are exciting and colorful enough to attract large crowds to the stadium and large contracts for their sport from television executives[84] However, even marginal players may wonder if they are worth 40 to 50 times less than their superstar teammates, and they especially will wonder if they are worth substantially less than teammates who have signed lucrative contracts with the help of skillful agents but have not yet consistently proven themselves on the playing field. In cases where there are huge salary disparities or perceived inequities, money can be the source of significant player dissatisfaction and team dissension. In such a context, highly paid players are likely to feel relatively deprived if they see themselves as stars and believe lesser players are earning more than they are, while modestly paid players may deceive themselves about their playing ability and their financial worth and demand huge and unjustified salary increases.

The transformation of professional sports into corporate enterprises in pursuit of expanding markets and increased commercial gains readily explains a shifting concern among professional athletes from the game itself to the financial returns to be reaped from it. However, the increased commercialization and corporate growth in professional sports did not automatically or immediately create a substantially heightened pecuniary orientation or substantially higher income among professional athletes. Wilbert Leonard has proposed that the turning point in player salaries was in 1960 when the ambitious, young American Football League tried to outbid the more established National Football League for rookies and NFL veterans[85] This interleague bidding war and subsequent wars pitting the established leagues against the American Basketball Association, World Football League, and World Hockey Association provided athletes with new opportunities to sell their services in a competitive market situation. As rival leagues tried to outbid each other—at the expense of the survival of the younger leagues in certain cases—salaries of stars and general salary levels began a significant rise. Furthermore, word of large salary increases in one of the major professional sports tended to encourage demands for higher salaries in the other major sports.

There have been a number of other events and influences that have contributed to the current opportunities for wealth and financial security for professional athletes. In the mid-1960s, the star pitchers on the Los

Angeles Dodgers, Sandy Koufax and Don Drysdale, approached Dodger management together as a single entity rather than as possible competitors in their contract negotiations. They also relied on agent-lawyers to do their bargaining[86] The Koufax-Drysdale negotiations represented the beginning of a new phase in management-player contract negotiations that ultimately evolved into a regular reliance on agents and the negotiation of highly technical and lucrative contractual arrangements for athletes[87] The growing power and militance of players' associations or unions,[88] which produced strikes in baseball in 1972 and 1981, in football in 1974 and 1982, and in soccer in 1979, and court challenges to professional sports owners and league rules, added to the pressure on professional sports officials to increase financial compensation and economic freedom for athletes. However, the crucial event in the recent escalation of player compensation and enhancement of their economic freedom was the "Peter Seitz Revolution" in 1975.

### 2) The Peter Seitz Revolution and the Legal Status of Professional Athletes

In 1975, arbitrator Peter Seitz decided that the option clause in the contracts of pitchers Andy Messersmith and Dave McNally tied them to their teams for only one year. The effect of this decision was to invalidate baseball's reserve clause, which had tied players to their clubs for their entire careers or until their owners traded, sold, or released them. Freed from their monopsonistic relationship with owners in which they had been able to sell their services to only a single buyer, players were allowed to become free agents if they "played out their option"—i.e., played one year without a contract—and then could try to sell their services to the highest bidder among a number of owners who might want their services. In February 1976, a U.S. District Court Judge upheld the Seitz ruling, and the end of the 1976 season marked the beginning of the free agent era in baseball. Thus, Peter Seitz created for major league baseball players a legal status comparable to the legal status of basketball and football players, who were required to play one year beyond their contract at 90% of the previous year's salary to become eligible for free agent status.

The Seitz ruling also created a situation in which players of varying ability levels could try to test their value in an open market and in which players might think more about pacing themselves to avoid serious injuries that could shorten their careers or lessen their earning potential. Recognizing the potential for chaotic bidding that their new free agent rights could create, the Major League Players' Association agreed in 1976 to a four-year contract with the owners that limited the free-agent option to players with six years of major league experience. Clubs losing free agents would be compensated at most by an amateur draft choice.

The baseball compensation agreement was less restrictive than the "Rozelle Rule" in the NFL that allowed the commissioner to decide what was "fair compensation" for a lost free agent. The Rozelle Rule had a chilling effect on the signing of free agents because club owners were afraid they might lose more than they gained. Prior to the 1977-78 NFL season, the Rozelle Rule was dropped, and a codified set of rules was used to determine compensation, which could not include cash transfers between clubs. Instead, a number of college draft choices were to be awarded as compensation, with the number depending on the player's salary. In addition, if a player after four years decided to play out his option, he had to be paid 110% of his previous year's salary.

Pro basketball players, already the highest salaried athletes on the average, have enjoyed more economic freedom than professional baseball or football players. Their compensation rule, which was similar to the Rozelle Rule, was dropped in 1980. In addition, the option clause was removed from the standard player contract, allowing players to try to move to another team immediately after their contract expired rather than after an option year. Professional basketball owners were given a right of "first refusal," which allowed them to retain players on their club who became free agents if they were able to match the financial terms of contracts from other clubs with whom the player was negotiating.[89]

Free agency produced an unprecedented increase in salaries and loud complaints from owners about unreasonable and astronomical player salary demands. In 1981, the baseball owners tried to include additional restrictions on free agency in their new contract with the players' association, but the players resisted with a fifty-day strike that was longer than any earlier one in pro sports history.[90] However, the players had come a long way since Curt Flood had unsuccessfully challenged the reserve clause before the Supreme Court in 1972,[91] and they did not want to give up the economic freedom, bargaining power, and salary gains they had won subsequently. Furthermore, despite the owners' claims that free agency threatened the "competitive balance" and the financial survival of teams with less affluent owners, the competitive balance seemed to improve in baseball after free agency. In addition, since attendance and television contracts were rising to record levels during the late 1970s, there is reason to doubt that free agency was threatening the profitability of most major league clubs.[92]

Many professional athletes recognize and acknowledge that they are not intrinsically worth the hundreds of thousands or millions of dollars their contracts pay them. However, they also recognize that their legal rights, the market situation, the popularity and affluence of their sports, and the free-spending habits of wealthy and ambitious owners and sponsors give them opportunities for wealth and financial security that are almost impossible to refuse. In addition, they realize that owners have been willing to spend millions of dollars on players without proven star ability. Thus, even though the players do not want to bankrupt the sport that has given them an opportunity to achieve their American Dream, they do not want to pass up a chance to obtain a piece of the American Dream for themselves either. In an interview with *Sport* magazine in 1981, young baseball star Bob Horner who had had his own trials and tribulations with management in his brief major league career, expressed feelings about owners and big contracts in his sport that probably were shared by many other professional athletes.[93] It struck him as funny that owners who were signing players to multimillion dollar contracts were at the same time complaining about the inflation of player salaries. Horner felt that the players were sympathetic with other players who tried to take advantage of lucrative financial opportunities in their sport. Although he recognized that the salary escalation had to stop somewhere, he felt the players would not be the ones to stop the escalation. He said, "I guess what it all boils down to is win, win, win. If a guy's going to help you and he wants $10 million a year, who cares as long as he's going to help you win?"

### 3) Modern Professional Athletes as Heroes

The economic and legal changes in professional sports over the past two decades have enabled many athletes to realize an American Dream of mobility and an affluent life style. However, even if their success represents a visible and dramatic reminder of the continuing availability of the American Dream in American society, it has not necessarily earned them the unqualified and universal admiration and respect of fans. We have seen that the majority of fans believe professional athletes must work hard for their money and are a good example to kids, but it also has been revealed by the *Sports Illustrated* survey that fans tend to feel today's pro athletes are losing their love for their games, are more greedy and self-centered than in the past, and are spoiled and pampered. Therefore, while the quest for big salaries and large purses may be making many professional athletes rich, and may not dull the desire of most fans to follow their favorite sports, teams, and athletes, public awareness of the pecuniary and narcissistic orientations of professional athletes are likely to undermine any of the widespread and enduring public admiration and respect granted to traditional sports heroes in the past.

Heroes symbolize and convey the dominant social myths and values of a society, and they help integrate the members of a society by serving as a shared model of their ideals, aspirations, and dreams.[94] Through their idealized deeds and qualities, heroes help the members of a society rise above the mundane and routine aspects of their lives and they reaffirm what is perceived to be good about their society. Heroes are not merely objects of public attention; they inspire devotion or worship. Of course, in these terms, heroes are not real people; they are the creation of an adoring mass media and the public imagination. When people have a chance to look closely at the men and women who have been their heroes, they often are disheartened to discover they are human, with human frailties and weaknesses.

The close, frequent, and often critical media coverage of modern professional athletes typically humanizes them to the extent that they may be deprived of the capacity to appear heroic or admirable. They may become celebrities constantly in the spotlight because they excite public interest or curiosity with their colorful or unusual performances and life styles. Heroes generally are perceived as embodying more enduring and revered societal values, and they perform symbolic functions through their idealized actions and qualities. Historian Daniel Boorstin has proposed that celebrities are creatures of gossip, public opiniion, and the ephemeral images of the mass media, while heroes are created by folklore and the history books. He added that the repeated attention that makes heroes ultimately is the unmaking of celebrities[95] In the words of sports writer Roger Kahn, we need to "(t)ake everything, diffusion, tougher journalism and the rest, and go beyond, to know why the athlete, whom we idolized from great distance, is a callow hero (today). With his warts and shaky syntax, he is overwhelmingly available, playing too many sports for too many hours on too many television sets."[96]

Under close and constant public scrutiny on the field and off, today's professional athlete is not only humanized, but trivialized. The public loses its opportunity to imagine or romanticize, and instead is made cynical[97] Even hustling, dedicated, and enthusiastic stars such as Pete Rose lose some of their luster when the media concentrate on their materialism. When reporters probe every angle of an athlete's private life, heroic images are bound to crack. Star first baseman Steve Garvey of the Los Angeles Dodgers would seem to be almost a perfect embodiment of the dominant American sports creed: clean-cut, polite, handsome, smiling, dignified, willing to endure injuries, cool under stress and adversity, intelligent, religious, patriotic, loyal to his team, protective of his family[98] However, in the August 1980 issue of *Inside Sports*[99] Garvey and his wife found themselves the subjects of an article about their private lives that alleged marital difficulties and implied some artificiality or lack of sincerity in his public image. The Garveys filed an $11.2 million damage suit against the magazine's publisher, Newsweek, Inc., claiming that the article was "libelous, malicious, and contained quotes taken out of context," and that it had resulted in "physical and emotional harm" to their family. They said they expected a story that would be a favorable and positive treatment of "the special challenges of being married to a well-known athlete."

British journalist Henry Fairlie, a long-time observer of the United States, noticed and lamented that heroes had seemed to disappear from American society[100] Fairlie's analysis suggested that in addition to probing too much and too deeply into the lives and psyches of public figures, Americans had no heroes because they lacked shared values, they were unable to imagine selflessness in the current era of consumption and "grossly distorted individualism," and they seemed to pay more attention in the press to antiheroes than to traditional, and less controversial, "All-American" heroes. Indeed, when the press focuses on athletes in the traditional heroic mold such as Steve Garvey, it often seems to concentrate more on the controversial than the heroic.

The antiheroes symbolizing countercultural and individualistic themes, the outspoken, and the outrageous may receive more attention than athletes with more traditional and bland beliefs and behavior because the traditional types less accurately reflect the existing social and cultural climate. Press coverage can be seen as a reflection of the existing conditions in a society. In an American society experiencing social change, "grossly distorted individualism," and uncertainty about its future, antiheroes and celebrities are a more accurate barometer of the times than traditional "All-American" heroes. However, during times of change and uncertainty, the public would seem to have a special need for heroic figures—cast in a traditional *or* contemporary mold—to clarify and reaffirm the central values and myths that give meaning and a sense of stability and direction to their lives. Thus, ironically, it appears that today's press is conspiring with the conditions of society to try to deprive the American public of the heroes they need.

Despite the lamentations, hero worship among sports fans has not completely died. Research has shown that those who are younger and who are socially integrated in society are especially likely to have sports heroes.[101] There still are the Steve Garveys, even with a slight tarnishing of their image, to keep alive traditional values and to serve as heroes for traditionally-minded fans looking for symbols of stability and virtue. Furthermore, as society's values change, some of today's antiheroes and celebrities may become the next generation of "traditional" heroes.

Even if there is a dearth of traditional sports heroes and some cynicims among fans about the motives and behavior of contemporary professional athletes, fans still may envy or respect the mobility and financial success of the athletes. As long as there is an American Dream, upwardly mobile and rich athletes will symbolize a fulfillment of dreams held by the fans. Thus, nonheroic and wayward athletes may be excused by fans for their perceived greed or peculiarities in their life style off the field as long as they work hard and produce on the field *and* as long as their behavior on or off the field does not depart *too much* from conventional standards. For many fans, the sports world still is a fantasyland or means of escape, and they do not want to see real world problems or concerns of athletes disrupt their performances or ruin the fun. In the next chapter, more will be said about how contemporary athletes continue to perform heroic functions for fans and exert influence over them despite the decline of consensual or traditional "All-American" heroic types.

Fans and reporters often forget that many of the athletes from whom so much is expected are thrust on to the center stage under a constantly glaring spotlight as teenagers or young adults before they have had a chance to figure out their own identities or values or adjust to the sometimes suffocating attention focused on them. Their fantasies about the lives of professional athletes also might ignore other realities that make it difficult or impossible for the athletes to be embodiments of the dominant American sports creed. The fantasyland of sport that exists for fans is a world of work for professional athletes,[102] and this world of work is unlikely to live up to the fantasies or heroic myths.

## 4) Career Pressures on the Modern Professional Athlete

Senator Bill Bradley called his book about his experiences in professional basketball "Life on the Run."[103] His title was meant to convey the constant travel in his life as a professional athlete as well as the weariness, the sameness of the many hotel rooms and airport lounges, and the loneliness and sense of impermanence associated with the travel. He also wrote about the joys of friendship, teamwork, challenge, and accomplishment he experienced as a professional athlete. However, his enjoyment of these aspects of his athletic career was tempered by a number of problems and concerns that are common among professional athletes with "lives on the run." He was bothered by the invasions of his privacy by sports fans and the merely curious; by the obnoxious, taunting, and sometimes hostile behavior of spectators and fans; by the dangers and presumed obligations of fame that went with its potential benefits; by the exaggerated and artificial sense of self-importance that derived from celebrity status; by the pain of injuries; and by the uncertainty of retirement that could come suddenly and prematurely with injury.

Injuries are a source of concern or even anxiety among professional athletes who depend regularly on being able to push their bodies to high levels of exertion. Injuries are an occupational risk for all athletes.[104] For athletes in contact sports, there is a constant risk that the next injury will be career-ending. In sports such as boxing, there even are occasional cases of death resulting from the pounding sustained in the ring. A curious fact that emerged from a study about injuries in the NFL was that during the 1974 season, only 1.3% of the injuries resulted from illegal contact that produced a penalty.[105] This finding suggests an official tolerance or encouragement of violent, injury-inducing contact. Perhaps coaches allow or encourage violent contact in their drive to win through intimidation or domination. In their exhortations to players, coaches often associate the capacity to give or take violent contact with "masculinity." Perhaps league officials allow or encourage violent contact to attract fans and money to their sport on the premise that violent and dangerous sports sell. Whatever the reasons, rules or referees that allow a great deal of physical contact on the field contribute to a serious risk in the careers of many professional athletes. Furthermore, many retired professional athletes live with the accumulated scars, discomfort, and pain of their sports injuries for the remainder of their lives.

Despite its risks, the "controlled violence" of many professional sports generally is accepted by athletes as "part of the game" and even is relished by some. In fact, a number of professional athletes seem to be proud of their injuries and their ability to "play hurt" as marks of their virility or courage.[106] The ability of professional athletes to overcome, endure, or mask the pain of injuries in their careers often can be explained by the use of drugs. In fact, drug use has become a highly controversial aspect of modern professional sports.[107]

Two types of drugs are widely used in sports today. *Restorative* drugs are taken to alleviate illness, injury, pain, nervousness, and dissipation and include painkillers, tranquilizers, barbiturates, antiinflammants, enzymes, and muscle relaxers. The use of restorative drugs becomes controversial when it allows athletes to compete with an injury that could become much more serious under the continued stress of exertion or collision in competition. Athletes using restorative drugs temporarily may feel like their injury has gone because the pain has been masked, but the masking of pain only hides the fact that the injury has not gone away and could even be getting worse from continued stress.[108]

Basketball star Bill Walton accused the Portland Trail Blazers of misusing four pain-modifying drugs in treating one of his injuries, and he claimed that the use of one of them, Xylocaine, caused him to fracture a bone in his foot during a playoff game. Other professional athletes have suggested that their team doctors had misled them about the nature of their injuries so that they would continue playing.[109] Walton's case is particularly noteworthy, though, because he had a well-publicized philosophical aversion to drug use in general and an understanding of the risks of playing injured with the help of drugs. However, his resistance to drugs, which was consistent with the strong moral position publicly taken against drug use by most professional sports officials, made him the target of pressure and criticism. Coaches wanted him to play and team medical personnel were willing to administer the drugs that could make it possible. The press and fans wondered about his motivation and complained that he was a malingerer.

The injuries sustained when Walton eventually relented and decided to use drugs to help him play injured was part of a series of injuries that appeared to cause a premature end to his career. He has said, "... You hear time and again that you can't hurt it any worse. Somebody's got to come to you at some point and say, 'Hey, why don't you think about being champion *next* year.'... We learn to trust doctors. Sometimes we shouldn't."[110] Part of the problem of restorative drug use in professional sports is that the medical judgment of doctors or trainers may be compromised or clouded because they are paid by the team owners. Team owners and coaches often seem to feel, especially during close league races at the end of the season or playoffs, that players should try to contribute to the team effort now and heal in the off-season.

While there are controversial uses of restorative drugs in sport, the use of *additive* drugs generally is more controversial—and more illegal. Additive drugs such as amphetamines, methamphetamine ("speed"), and anabolic steroids are taken to induce better performances. They stimulate the central nervous system. In 1973, Dr. Arnold Mandell, a psychiatrist, served as an unpaid locker-room analyst for the San Diego Chargers of the NFL. He was alarmed to discover an extensive and dangerous level of amphetamine use—which he called a "plague"—by pro football players wanting to get an edge on their opponents. He said amphetamines were the "single factor that causes unnecessary violence in pro football today," and that doses were "enormous . . . as high as 150 milligrams."[111] Mandell's study indicated that amphetamines most frequently were taken to enhance performance by players in positions requiring fast reactions and reckless aggression and placing less emphasis on precise movements.[112]

Prolonged or excessive doses of amphetamines could cause ulcers, cerebral hemorrhage, paranoia, cardiovascular breakdown, deficiencies in nutrition, irritability, and aggressiveness.[113] Despite these serious potential side effects of amphetamines, the side effects of steroids have caused even more concern. In fact, one sports writer said that, "At a time of growing concern over the use of drugs in sport, steroids are the most prevalent and worrisome of all."[114] Steroids are fat-soluble organic compounds that are synthetic derivatives of the male hormone testosterone. In professional sports, athletes, such as linemen in football, have taken massive doses of several hundred milligrams a day to try to increase their muscle size, weight, and strength. The drug usually is administered by doctors in carefully controlled doses of only five milligrams a day for post-surgical treatment and to combat pituitary dwarfism. When used in massive doses, there are a number of serious risks: liver damage for both sexes; shrinkage of the genitals and impotence for males; and menstrual irregularities, an impaired reproductive capacity, and the development of male secondary sex characteristics such as a deepened voice and facial and chest hair for females.

Aging veterans trying to save a career, rookies and marginal players trying to establish one, and athletes feeling intense pressure from others or from inside themselves are among those most likely to use drugs to help them play or play better. Hal Connolly, hammer thrower and a veteran of several Olympic teams, explained why athletes will use highly suspicious or risky drugs even when there is no one telling them they must or should: "My experience tells me that an athlete will use any aid to improve his performance short of killing himself."[115] The irony is that prolonged, excessive, or inappropriate use of restorative or additive drugs could lead to diminished performance, injury, or a shortened career.

Athletes use a number of drugs off the field as well as on it. The social use of drugs such as amphetamines, marijuana, and cocaine along with the more socially approved—and legal—alcohol can be seen as a reflection of a drug-oriented culture in American society."[116] For professional athletes, entry into this culture may be facilitated or encouraged by their affluence. For some professional athletes, social drug use may be a response to the grind and pressures of their "life on the run."[117] However, social use may turn into alcoholism, drug abuse and dependence, causing a decline in an athlete's health and career.

Thus, drug use in professional sports intended to relieve insecurities, anxieties, or frustrations about personal lives or athletic performances ultimately can be self-defeating and self-destructive.

It is not difficult to imagine how a life on the run and in the public eye could cause serious insecurities, anxieties, and frustrations. There is constant pressure to achieve excellence and victory both from within and outside the athletic arena. This pressure is exacerbated by a life style during the long athletic season that is tiring and may offer little emotional security or support, and by a press and sports public with high and often unrealistic expectations.

Though heroic standards seldom seem to be applied to today's professional athletes, there continue to be high expectations for performance resulting from the lucrative contracts that have been signed in recent years. Public opinion can shift quickly, too. Even a superstar's pride and self-confidence can be shaken when a previously adoring public begins booing instead of cheering after an injury, illness, or personal problems diminish the athlete's performance.[118] Perhaps as a reflection of the times in sport and the larger society, a decline in performance by athletes or their inconsistent public behavior often is seen by the public as a result of drug use. In some cases, this may be true, but in others, injury, age, or psychological illness may be the cause.

John Lucas is one example of a professional athlete who had to endure public questioning of his character as he went through serious personal adjustment problems.[119] He was a professional basketball player who also had played professional tennis. He had been a model of good character, of reliability, as a professional athlete until changes in his role on his team combined with unsettling events in his personal life caused the sudden appearance of uncharacteristic impulsive behavior and poor judgment. His erratic actions were popularly attributed by fans, his team's management, and fellow players to drug abuse. After initially denying that his emotional problems were related to drugs, Lucas, himself, ultimately acknowledged that he had "a problem with cocaine." In a life largely made up of achievements and success, a sudden accumulation of adverse experiences had created a crisis of adjustment for John Lucas, which led him to drugs for relief.

Jack McCallum, who told the John Lucas story in a *Sports Illustrated* article, drew important general implications from it about the lives of professional athletes. He observed that the Lucas story revealed "... athletes are less than the superhuman creatures we so often perceive them to be and that they are subject to the same demons of grief, despair, and loneliness that ravage us all."[120] However, in the case of professional athletes, they must try to mature, cope, and adjust in front of a frequently critical and fickle press and sports public whose attention and expectations often help create or exacerbate the athletes' difficulties.

## 5) Retirement: Life after Sport

Even if life at the top of the American Sports Pyramid falls short of the idealized American Dream for professional athletes, these athletes frequently discover that they cannot match the psychological and material rewards of professional sport after their playing days are over. For most of their lives, they have derived their self-esteem and identity from being athletes, and they have tasted the fruits of being among the athletic elite, able to look down upon the many millions who aspire to or fantasize about life as a professional athlete. The adjustment to life after sport is difficult for many professional athletes because the taste of their former success lingers and because they have not adequately prepared themselves psychologically, financially, or occupationally for the change. In most professional sports, the end comes at a relatively young age, even for those fortunate enough to survive the first couple of years to become seasoned veterans. Thus, for many professional athletes, the most memorable and rewarding experiences of their lives will be over before they have reached their mid-30s.

Pat Jordan has written a sensitive and perceptive memoir about his failed attempt to become a major league pitcher.[121] His effort ended in obscurity in the minor leagues before he had a chance to throw a single pitch in a major league game. He was a "bonus baby" who failed to achieve his earlier promise. In retrospect as a successful sports writer, he wrote that baseball had left such a strong imprint on him that ten years after his baseball career ended, he thought of himself "not as a writer who once pitched, but as a pitcher who happens to be writing just now." Though he realized that he may have been deluding himself, he felt that baseball was the one experience in his life that would most accurately define him. He also felt that baseball had influenced him more than anything else ever would. Unfortunately, though, Jordan's baseball experience did not end "properly" or "neatly" for him. Instead, "(i)t just stopped, unfinished in my memory, fragmented, so many pieces missing . . . ," he said (p. 10).

The careers of professional athletes can end in a variety of specific ways, but most basically, they are ended by a voluntary or involuntary decision to retire.[122] In team sports, the decision usually is involuntary and is initiated by management. Many professional athletes who retire voluntarily delay the decision as long as possible because they fear their loss of identity and status or perhaps because they do not want to be seen as a "quitter." The accumulation of injuries or the recognition of a decline in skills with age might produce a rational decision to retire, but even such rational decisions seldom are made without ambivalence. The lost opportunity for big money may fuel this ambivalence in many cases and prolong careers beyond a graceful departure point. Pete Rose said in this regard that even if he discovered he could no longer hit, he probably would not quit if someone still was willing to pay him a million dollars a year to play.[123]

In individual sports such as golf, tennis, bowling, and skiing, professional athletes may decide voluntarily to retire because their declining performance is not earning them enough money to cover their expenses and provide for an acceptable standard of living. However, in boxing, the need for additional income might defer the retirement decision beyond the point when it is wise to hang up the gloves. In boxing, the decision to retire may be especially difficult because boxers traditionally have risen from poverty, achieved at least a modest degree of economic and social mobility as athletes, lived as extravagantly as their income permitted, and then skidded downward again after their boxing careers ended without the money, education, or occupational training to pursue comparable success in an alternative career.[124] The postponement of retirement from boxing can be tragic because it can result in permanent physical and mental damage that will cause incapacitation as well as downward mobility. For example, Kirson Weinberg and Henry Arond pointed out in their study of the occupational culture of boxers that:

> ...One estimate is that 60 percent of the boxers become mildly punch-drunk and 5 percent become severely punch-drunk... Many boxers persist in fighting when they have passed their prime and even when they have been injured. For example, one boxer, blind in one eye and barred from fighting in one state, was grateful to his manager for getting him matches in other states (pp. 451-452).

In general, it seems that professional athletes able to avoid serious injury tend to delay their retirement decision as long as possible. The decision is likely to be earlier and more wisely timed when athletes are college-educated and financially secure, recognize and accept their declining athletic skills, and can look forward to an attractive and rewarding alternative career for which they have prepared themselves.[125] Thus, the unwillingness to retire voluntarily in the face of inadequate or declining skills often will reflect a limited capacity to adjust to a life as a former athlete. However, the persistence of this reluctance is likely to cause involuntary retirement, which may make adjustment more difficult because it often is perceived as "failure."

In his analysis of failure in sport, Donald Ball wrote that, "For most players (all but the biggest stars) careers are short and the possibility of failure is always upon them; it is one of the constantly problematic facets of their occupational lives that they may face being failed at any time."[126] Professional athletes might reject the label of "failure" because they believe they have been unfairly treated and still are capable of playing at a major league level.[127] However, they are likely to be treated by others inside—and perhaps, outside—their professional sport as a failure when they drop or are sent down to the minor leagues or a comparable level of competition, they are released outright, or when they lose their playing privileges on their major tour circuit.

Ball proposed that reactions by others to a professional athlete's downward mobility or "failure" in his or her sport will vary according to the structure of the sport. In professional sports having a two-tiered hierarchy, such as hockey and baseball with their minor leagues, and tennis and golf with their satellite tours, those who fail at the major league level are "sent down" to compete at a lower level. At this lower level in their professional sport, the "failed" athletes remain visible to the public and their former peers. Thus, they assume second class status and constantly are reminded of their marginality in this sport. Ball suggested that athletes experiencing this kind of failure were likely to face degradation and embarrassment as a "deadman" or "nonperson." Other players, especially those uncertain or anxious about their own major league status, will be reluctant to associate with teammates who have been sent down or released. Former major league pitcher Jim Bouton described this reaction in relation to his own experience of being sent down to a minor league team:

> ...as I started throwing stuff into my bag, I could feel a wall, invisible but real, forming around me. I was suddenly an outsider, a different person, someone to be shunned, a leper![28]

In other professional sports there is not formal minor league structure. Players judged not to be good enough to play at the major league level in these sports are released outright. Thus, in these nonhierarchical professional sports, those who fail are removed from the public eye and do not suffer as much public embarrassment as "skidders" on public display in minor league competition. According to Ball, the absence of the "despised caste of the major leagues" is associated with a more sympathetic reaction from fellow athletes than in sports having such a caste system. Professional football players, for instance, realize that teammates released by their team will be out of the professional game in the U.S. unless they can arrange a contract or successful tryout with another team in the league. Thus, rather than being degraded or debased, failures in pro football are "cooled out." They are given sympathy, and rationalizations are offered to ease or disguise their failure. In addition, the absence of a minor league option reduces the opportunities to "hang on" and it becomes unrealistic, to keep alive false hopes of future stardom. Where opportunities are fewer, failure is more frequent and is likely to be more expected and less traumatic.

In addition to demotion to a lower level of competition and release, professional athletes may experience downward mobility in a "zigzag" form![129] Zigzag mobility masks impending failure by disguising it in the form of an apparent horizontal move, with the implied hope of future promotion. This type of mobility pattern occurs in the case of a fading star who is encouraged to become an assistant coach with his or her major league team or a player coach for a minor league affiliate.

Retired professional athletes have essentially two career choices after their retirement as athletes: to remain in sport in a lower status or to pursue a job or career outside sport. Studies of former major league baseball[130] and hockey[131] players have indicated that those who remained in their sport as coaches, managers, or scouts had less stable career patterns after their playing careers than those who moved into an occupation outside sport immediately after retiring as an athlete. Furthermore, those wanting to remain in sport have a menial status usually will find relatiely few openings.[132] Those who end their careers in the minor leagues in a downward slide may find they will continue sliding after termination of their athletic careers.[133]

Star professional athletes may be able to convert their sports fame into a good job opportunity at the end of their playing career. However, in the long run, stars and lesser athletes must be able to prove themselves on the job. Prior education and training are likely to be key factors determining how well athletes do in the long run on their jobs after they have ended their athletic careers.[134]

Those who retire voluntarily may adjust better to their sports retirement than those who end their playing careers as "failures" and are forced to retire. For those not prepared psychologically, financially, or occupationally for retirement, adjustment to another type of life can be traumatic. Anxiety about the future and the sudden loss of status and social identity may combine to create serious personality disturbances in former professional athletes. In fact, there are cases of such athletes who have been arrested for a variety of criminal offenses, become alcoholics and drug addicts, and committed suicide or attempted it.

Even the millionaire athletes are not immune from serious retirement problems. The case of former professional hockey player Derek Sanderson is a dramatic example.[135] In 1972, Sanderson was signed by the Philadelphia Blazers of the World Hockey Association to a five-year contract reportedly worth $2.65 million. At the time, his one-half million dollar per season salary made him the highest salaried American athlete, but after just eight games with the Blazers the team bought back his contract for $1 million. He had scored three goals for them. Sanderson then started a journey in which he played for six teams in the next six years. By 1978, he was out of hockey trying to recover from severe depression and the overuse of Valium, sleeping pills, and alcohol. Most of the nearly $2 million he had earned in his ten-year career was gone. By his own estimate, he had "blown" $600,000 of it. One million had gone to taxes, $100,000 to uncollectible loans to acquaintances, $100,000 to his agent, $32,000 for a car, $35,000 for one trip to Hawaii, $100,000 for his house, $45,000 for renovating an apartment, and many thousands more to maintain his extravagant life style.

Sanderson's dramatic case and the cases of numerous other professional athletes who have slid into bankruptcy and serious personal problems during and after their athletic careers demonstrate that the wealth and fame earned by athletes during their pro sports careers will not guarantee a successful and happy adjustment to athletic retirement. To enhance that adjustment, athletes need to be prepared for it and their preparation will be helped a great deal by responsible and sound personal, occupational, financial, and legal advice during their careers.

The pension plans and disability programs for retirees won by players' associations in a number of professional sports help ease the anxiety or uncertainty of the transition from sport. However, the completion of college, job training, and career counseling or planning before retirement are keys to avoiding a traumatic adjustment to life after sport. For black athletes, who have had few post-career management opportunities in sport, and for athletes from less affluent backgrounds, this preparation seems especially important to prevent a sharp downward slide after finishing their athletic careers. In general, the golden days of living out the American Dream as a professional athlete can end quickly and suddenly and, unless athletes are prepared for it, the Dream soon will become tarnished and turn into a nightmare of adjustment. In the words of Pat Jordan, who never fulfilled his American Dream as an athlete:

> I lost it all that spring. The delicate balance I had so assiduously created at Bradenton collapsed. Just like that. One moment it was a perfectly solid-looking structure—satisfactions, potential, success, talent—and the next it was nothing but rubble. The only thing left standing was a new and impenetrable frustration (p. 215).

## 2. Olympic Sports and the Pursuit of the American Dream

The chance to compete in an Olympics is won by a tiny proportion of the athletes in the Olympic sports, and the chance to win an Olympic medal comes only once every four years. Although there are many important national and international events in the various Olympic sports in the years between the Olympic Games, most of these events and their stars attract little public attention until just before the Olympic Trials. Thus, except in the major sports that are commercialized or suitable for televising, the careers and accomplishments of athletes in Olympic sports take place in relative obscurity. In most of the major sports, only the names of a few top performers are widely known. Recognition comes in Olympic years, but even record-setting gold medal performances in major Olympic sports may soon be forgotten by the public unless the athlete goes on to a career inside or outside sport that keeps him or her in the public eye.[136]

The limited amount of public exposure or recognition earned by most athletes in Olympic sports should not be seen as implying a lack of dedication to achievement among these athletes. At times, the desire to win a place on an Olympic team or a medal in Olympic competition can lead to the same kind of risky, potentially self-destructive behavior found in professional sports. For example, in 1979, a top American track and field coach estimated that 70% of all top-ranked U.S. track athletes, men and women, used steroids.[137] Part of the motivation to take such risks is the feeling among many athletes that the advanced scientific training, including drugs, and government support received by competitors from communist countries give them an unfair advantage. Thus, the risks are rationalized as a necessary element in the effort to remain competitive and win. Despite the Olympic Creed, winning is likely to be more important than merely participating among many of the top-ranked Olympians, even if there is no promise of financial compensation for a gold medal. The pressure on competitors in the Olympic arena is increased when victory is portrayed in nationalistic terms as contributing to the pride and glory of the whole nation.

The drive to excel in many Olympic sports can be very time-consuming and expensive.[138] In the United States, it is difficult or nearly impossible to achieve world-class stature in most Olympic sports without extensive training under expert coaches and without extensive experience in high-level national or international competition. Efforts by amateur sports officials to enforce a strict interpretation of the amateur code only serves to increase the strain on aspiring Olympic athletes without personal wealth, a college athletic scholarship, or the chance to receive money "under-the-table." For athletes being subsidized by under-the-table payments from commercial sponsors or manufacturers in their sport, circumventing amateur rules may cause anxiety about their amateur eligibility, a sense of hypocrisy, or a willingness to speak out against the rules.

In recent years, many Olympians have been willing to speak out about the aristocratic exclusiveness, hypocrisy, administrative ineffectiveness and unresponsiveness, and territorial conflict between ruling bodies in amateur sport that have frustrated them as competitors. In an earlier book, I called this movement of American athletes to reform Olympic sports "shamateur activism,"[139] with the term "shamateur" meant to imply the mirage of amateurism that characterizes so many Olympic sports.

Track and field athletes have been especially outspoken in recent years. Until 1981, a major target of criticism was the International Amateur Athletic Federation's (IAAF's) Rule 53, called the "contamination" rule, which not only prohibited athletes from accepting prize money but also forbad them from competing in the same meet as non-sanctioned athletes or ones accepting prize money. This rule, imposed on TAC by the IAAF, was a source of substantial criticism from track and field athletes because they viewed it as unrealistic and inconsistent with the commonly known practice of giving under-the-table money to top performers on the track and field circuit.[140] The emergence of the Association of Road Racing Athletes (ARRA), which was conceived in 1979 by a group of top U.S. road runners, and their oganization of a series of races with commercial sponsorship and prize money in 1981, put the athletes in direct confrontation with TAC and IAAF officials in regard to the contamination rule.[141]

This confrontation between the road runners and amateur sports officials reflected the athletes' desire to take control of their sport. When TAC officials stand firm on the existing amateur rules in the face of pressure from athletes to change them, they risk the loss of a number of established stars from the amateur ranks. However, if they give in to the athletes' demands, they could become embroiled in a conflict with international bodies such as the IAAF as well as the IOC. In the case of the confrontation over the contamination rule, TAC sought and obtained permission to rescind the rule in an IAAF meeting in Rome in late August 1981. As a result, amateurs were allowed to compete against professionals in track and field and road racing, and TAC began sanctioning prize money races on the ARRA circuit in the fall 1981.

Athletes in the more publicized and commercialized "major" Olympic sports such as alpine skiing, basketball, hockey, boxing, figure skating, and track and field would have much to gain from a loosening of amateur eligibility standards. Increased opportunities to use their athletic skills or athletic reputation to earn money from competition, sports-related jobs, or commercial endorsements would allow at least the top athletes in these sports to defray some or all of their personal athletic expenses such as training, equipment, coaching, and travel. Increased commercial opportunities also might allow a few of the stars of the major Olympic sports to build a financial foundation for the pursuit of their American Dream.

In a few of the major Olympic sports, the stars now can realistically dream about big money from converting their Olympic medals and fame into a professional sports career. In addition, under the existing amateur rules, there are "big name" athletes in major Olympic sports who earn money under the table while still "amateurs" and who convert their Olympic or amateur fame into lucrative commercial endorsements, jobs as television commentators, or careers in entertainment fields such as the ice shows, when their amateur careers are over. Prominent examples of Olympians without opportunities for pro sports careers who still were able to capitalize financially on their Olympic fame are figure skaters Peggy Fleming and Dorothy Hamill, swimmer Mark Spitz, and decathlete Bruce Jenner. Marathoner Bill Rodgers is probably the best example in the U.S. of an athlete who has been able to reap rich financial rewards from his "amateur" sports career without winning an Olympic gold medal. In 1980, he earned an estimated $250,000 from running, from his running store in Boston, and from promoting and selling running equipment.[142]

Far away from the national spotlight and big money in the amateur sports world are the athletes in the "minor" Olympic sports such as archery, shooting, field hockey, canoeing, yachting, fencing, and biathlon. They are closest to the Olympic ideal of amateurism because they are wealthy enough to afford to be amateurs or perhaps because not enough people are interested in their sport to create commercial possibilities in it. These athletes have little hope or desire for a special occupational opportunity or financial gain from their sports involvement. Unable or unwilling to use the Olympic Games or their amateur sports participation in general as a springboard to a greater American Dream, the athletes in these minor Olympic sports are likely to hold as their highest aspiration the chance to participate in the Olympics and test their skills against the best in their sport.[143] Unlike the more professionalized athletes in the more publicized and commercialized Olympic sports, retirement from serious competition for athletes in the minor sports will not cause a traumatic loss of public attention, because the public did not know them very well, or a significant decline in earning power, because there was little or no money to be made from their sport. Thus, the more amateur of the Olympic sports have certain advantages for their participants stemming from the *limited* opportunities they offer for rewards beyond victory or a medal in the sports arena.

# Television and the Future of Professional and Olympic Sports

Newspaper sports coverage, which began on a regular basis at the end of the nineteenth century, was a crucial factor in the early popular and commercial growth of sports in the United States. By the 1920s, radio broadcasts of sports events had begun, and the sports boom of this "golden age" and of later decades was significantly influenced by the growing popularity of radio. Professional sports leagues have derived direct financial benefits from radio through the sale of broadcast rights to their sports events.

Although the mass media of newspapers and radio have been key factors in the popular and commercial growth of sports by stimulating or holding fan interest and, in the case of radio, providing revenue, the *current* financial and organizational structure of professional sports, certain highly commercialized Olympic sports, and perhaps even the Olympic Games themselves are influenced mostly by television. Certainly in the past one or two decades, television revenue has had much to do with the profitability of professional sports franchises, the survival of new professional sports leagues, and the escalation of player salaries.

Sports enterprises make money from television by selling broadcast rights for their events. In 1961, the Sports Broadcasting Act gave the major professional sports of baseball, basketball, football, and hockey antitrust immunity for agreements within their leagues to pool and sell broadcast rights to sponsored telecasts of league games. This right to pool and sell broadcast rights enabled these pro sports leagues to eliminate competition between televised contests and to create instead the monopoly right to telecast "the only game in town" in their league in every TV community.[144] The networks have paid large sums of money for this right, and they, in turn, have sold shares in this right to sponsors wanting to present their advertising messages to television sports audiences. According to one expert on the economic and legal aspects of sports broadcasting, sponsors of network television sports programs are provided with a captive audience of predoinantly male viewers who generally are affluent enough to buy their products.[145] Furthermore, although season-long network television sponsorship can be quite expensive—or prohibitive for smaller firms—in relation to audience sizes, the cost per viewer of a one-minute message is almost negligible. In 1977, the cost of thirty-second commercials to sponsors of major events ranged from $12,500 for a Stanley Cup Playoff game in hockey to $70,000 for the All-Star game and $75,000 for a World Series game in baseball to $175,000 for the Super Bowl in football.[146]

As long as professional sports and the highly commercialized "amateur" ones—including especially the Olympics and college football—can attract large and relatively affluent television audiences, sponsors will continue to invest heavily in television sports and television networks will continue to pay large sums of money for broadcast rights. In the late 1970s, the most popular professional sports in the U.S. for television audiences were football, baseball, and basketball. The professional sports that followed them in popularity were tennis, hockey, boxing, golf, auto racing, soccer, and bowling, but these sports were much less popular among TV sports viewers than the three most popular ones.[147]

The differences in popularity are partially reflected in the figures cited for commercial advertising costs of major sports events. The importance of these differences to professional sports is reflected in the amount of revenue they were able to earn from national TV contracts. In 1977-78, professional football earned $60 million from national TV; their gross revenues were estimated to be $250 million. Baseball earned $23.2 million of its gross revenues of $230 million from TV, and basketball earned $10.5 millon of its gross revenues of $95 million from TV. Due to low audience ratings, the National Hockey League lost its American network TV contract in 1975, and by 1977-78, it was earning only $180,000 of its gross annual revenues of $65 million from national TV in the U.S. In 1974, the combined professional hockey leagues—with ten more teams than the NHL had in 1977-78—earned $11 million of its gross revenues of $90 million from national TV.

While the NHL was relying on a modest one-year deal with a string of independent stations in the 1977-78 season, the other major pro sports leagues in the U.S. were benefiting from four-year network contracts that paid the NBA $74 million or an estimated $880,000 annually to each NBA team, major league baseball $92.8 million or an estimated $970,000 annually per team, and the NFL $656 million or an estimated $5.8 million annually to each team. In 1982, the NFL signed a five-year network TV contract for over $2 billion, which gave each club $14.2 million annually; and the new United States Football League signed a two-year ABC TV contract for $22 million one year before it played its first game. These figures reveal very clearly the importance of television money to the financial success of professional sports franchises and leagues.[148] However, it should be added that the television money is essential to maintain the *existing* financial structure of professional sports, with their rapidly escalating player contracts and expanded league sizes.

Though their financial gains have been considerably more modest than those of the major professional team sports, other professional sports have benefited from television contracts. For example, the men's golf tour earned only $150,000 from TV in 1961, but TV revenues rose to $3 million in 1971 and $5 million in 1976.[149] Golf is the rare example of a sport able to generate network TV revenue despite relatively low ratings because its viewers tend to be affluent. For sports such as golf, tennis, and ski racing, television exposure can be more important than the revenue from television contracts because national television exposure can increase fan interest, the number of spectators at tour events, and the willingness of sponsors to invest in these events.

Big-time amateur sports also have benefited from TV revenue and exposure. For example, ABC paid the NCAA $29 million per year between 1978 and 1981 for the right to televise its college football games. The primary recipients of this money were the major football conferences at the Division I-A level. They received $533,000 for each national TV appearance, which was to be split among conference members, and $401,000 for each appearance on a regional telecast. Division II schools split $30,000 for regional telecasts and Division III schools split $15,000.[150] In 1976, ABC paid $62 million for the rights to televise the Winter and Summer Olympics, and if the United States had participated in the 1980 Summer Games, NBC would have paid the Soviets $85 million to televise their Olympics.[151]

The increasing largesse of national television networks, as well as revenue from independent stations and cable networks such as the Entertainment and Sports Programming Network (ESPN), have enabled some professional and Olympic sports to prosper and others to establish themselves and grow. There are a number of sports, including both highly commercialized amateur ones such as college football and basketball and professional ones, in which television exposure and revenue are the difference between solvency and financial collapse. For example, in professional sports, the failure of new leagues such as the American Basketball Association, the World Hockey Association, World Team Tennis, and the World Football League to establish popular franchises in major media markets such as New York, Los Angeles, Chicago, Philadelphia, and Boston prevented them from signing lucrative national television contracts, and probably was a major reason these leagues folded. Thus, it seems reasonable to assume that the more commercialized professional and Olympic sports become in the United States today, the more they will depend on television revenue and exposure for their growth or survival.

If professional and amateur sports increasingly base their growth or survival on television, that growth or survival eventually could become precarious. The former president of a WHA team warned that, "It is going to reach the limit where, say, a motor company finds that exorbitant advertising rates are no longer to its benefit. When advertisers quit, networks quit, and when networks quit, a league dependent on TV revenue will be jeopardized."[152] Hockey officials, having lost a national television contract, have a special appreciation of this delicate equation. The television-sport equation is made more delicate by the fact that sports programs offer unique sponsorship opportunities for a relatively small set of firms in a relatively small set of industries.[153]

While professional and Olympic sports generally have benefited from their relationship with television, they also have had to make concessions and modifications to accommodate the needs and desires of television executives. David Altheide and Robert Snow have argued that the relationship between television and sport serves to enhance the power of television and change the nature of sports.[154] Like professional sports, television is concerned with making a profit. However, the ways that sports and television make money are different. Television makes money by using its programs to draw viewers to commercial messages. Programs are "commercials for commercials" in this sense, according to Altheide and Snow. Programs attracting more viewers generate higher advertising rates from commercial sponsors, as long as the audience is affluent enough. In the case of television coverage of sports, the selection and scheduling of events is determined by audience ratings. Sports programs are fit into the time slots that are assumed to maximize their audiences, and sports that do not attract enough—or affluent enough—viewers in particular time slots are rescheduled or dropped. To attract and maintain the television investment upon which they have become dependent, sports must adapt themselves to the needs of television programmers and make themselves appealing to large television audiences.

The requirements of the television medium and television executives have led to a number of changes in the rules, staging, and scheduling of sports events. For example, in an effort to make their sports more suitable for television and more entertaining for a wider audience, baseball officials introduced a livelier ball, a larger strike zone, the designated hitter rule, and more colorful and stylish uniforms; football officials added "sudden-death" overtimes, longer kickoffs to encourage exciting runbacks, platooning of specialty players, and changes in penalties to help the offense; basketball reinstated the slam dunk and introduced the "24-second clock" to speed up the offensive action; golf changed from match play to medal play; and tennis introduced the tie-breaker to control the length of competition and added color to the balls and players' clothing.

Pro hockey and soccer have had problems adapting their games to commercial television because of their continuous action—with no predictable breaks for ads—and because of their low scoring. In addition, in hockey, there is the problem of following the course of the puck across the television screen. However, "instant replay" enables hockey viewers to see important action they may have missed when it happened, just as it recaptures important action—from a variety of camera angles—in other televised sports.

A number of the accommodations made by sports to television have compromised the quality of play, the comfort of paying spectators, or the integrity of the sport. For example, World Series games have been played at night—during "prime time"—despite bone-chilling October weather. A National League playoff game was played in a rainstorm. West Coast basketball playoff games have started in the morning for the benefit of the East Coast audience. Monday Night Football games have started at 9 p.m. for the benefit of the West Coast audience. In one case, Foxboro, Massachusetts, city officials complained that the 9 p.m. starting time contributed to violence in the stands and in the parking lot because a number of spectators used the long wait between the end of work and the beginning of the game to drink and get drunk. The city officials were unable to convince ABC or the NFL to switch the start of a Monday night Patriots game to an earlier time, despite threats to prohibit the game. When the Grand Slam of tennis was held in Boca Raton in 1978, the starting time was moved up one-half hour to accommodate TV, causing a near-riot among specators who discovered that the match was well into the second set by the time they reached their seats. The need to fit in a specified number of commercials in a game sometimes has caused interruptions in the flow of play during crucial points in the game. In one case, a soccer referee wore an electronic beeper on his shoulder so he could signal injury timeouts at the request of TV producers to allow one-minute commercial breaks. Finally, sports officials have discovered they must establish franchises in profitable TV market areas to be able to compete for television contracts.[155]

Research has shown that in the Olympic arena, television devotes more time to promoting their own programming, presenting commercials, and covering events peripheral to the sports competition than the competition itself.[156] At the 1976 Summer Games in Montreal, ABC-TV televised 90 hours of the Olympics, used 32 network commentators and 128 cameras, and relied on several hundred support personnel. They paid $25 million for the exclusive home-television rights and collected a reported $72,000 per minute for national commercials.

Despite the many hours of television coverage, the elaborate technology, and the substantial size of the crew of commentators and other network personnel, thirteen of the thirty-five scheduled Olympic sports received a *total* of three minutes and ten seconds of coverage, with most of that coverage consisting of a collection of film strips shown during the Sunday afternoon before the closing ceremonies. Boxing received the most coverage, five hours, but despite this extensive attention, two U.S. boxers were not seen, either live or on rerun, winning their gold medals. Overall, about one-quarter of the coverage was devoted to first-time showings of sports events, about one-sixth of the coverage consisted of commercial and network advertisements, and the remainder of the time, over three-fifths, was devoted to reruns, interviews, nonsports specials such as restaurant and museum visits, excerpts from a rock concert, a ride on the Metro, and seven and one-half minutes of credits to ABC-TV technicians during the closing ceremonies.

In general, then, ABC's perception of Olympic coverage was to emphasize the festive environment of the Games and their commercial messages more than the live action of the sports events. This is consistent with the aim of presenting the most appealing and profitable entertainment package possible, and a focus primarily on the details of Olympic sports events—especially minor ones—apparently was not seen by television producers as sufficiently entertaining or profitable.

Although they have made many concessions and modifications for the benefit of television, sports officials are not unaware of the dangers of too much reliance on TV. The history of professional boxing serves as a reminder of the dangers of excessive television coverage. A consequence of the extensive television coverage of boxing between 1946 and 1964, when the last Friday Night Fight of the Week was telecast, was that people lost interest in the small club boxing matches that provided new talent to the sport for exciting television matches. Overexposure also can lead to a decline in spectators at televised events since people might prefer the cheaper and more comfortable seat in their living room, where they can watch "instant replays" and other technical innovations meant to enliven the home telecast.

Professional football officials tried to initiate a black-out policy so local fans caould not watch home games on TV, but before the 1973 season the U.S. Congress decided to restrict the policy to games not sold out 72 hours prior to the start of the game. In a sense, professional football was a victim of its own popularity, to which television had made a large contribution. Congress felt it was in the public interest to provide local fans with television coverage of home games they could not or did not want to attend in person.

In general, officials of sports that have increasingly depended on television exposure for their popularity and television dollars for their commercial growth or survival are in a "Catch-22" situation. To continue to depend so heavily on television could risk the dangers of oversaturation of their audience and declining investments by commercial sponsors and in turn, by television itself. However, efforts to limit this dependence would deprive them of the revenue needed to sustain their existing financial structure and could invite further Congressional or legal intervention. Whatever the outcome of this dilemma, it should be evident that the kind of American Dream available to athletes thorough professional or commercialized amateur sports will be significantly affected by the future relationship between television and sport.

# Conclusion: An Assessment of the Myth and Reality of the American Dream for the American Sports Elite

The top rung of the ladder to the American Dream through sport is occupied by professional athletes and Olympians. For them, success can be spectacular, including national celebrity status and wealth for professional athletes and for Olympians, the glory of a gold medal, world-wide attention, and in some cases, lucrative post-Olympic careers or financial opportunities. However, the lure of the fantasized rewards for being a professional or Olympic athlete creates false hopes and misplaced dreams among athletes with no chance to join the American sports elite and causes frustration and disappointment even for many of those able to reach the top of the American Sports Pyramid.

In fact, opportunities to reach either of the twin peaks of the American Sports Pyramid are extremely slim. The walls of the Pyramid are greased, and the golden rings at the top are very difficult to grasp and even more difficult to hang on to for an extended period of time. Careers in professional sports tend to be quite brief, even for those able to survive the first couple of years. Ten years as a professional athlete is a long career. For amateur athletes, the chance to become part of an Olympic team is won by very few and comes only once every four years. There usually are many years of training and competition leading up to winning a place on an Olympic team. For the many Olympians who do not go on to professional sports, their Olympic thrill will have to be the joy of participation, since most Olympic athletes do not win medals and most receive very little attention from the roving television cameras and press. For the Olympic champions, the brief moments on the victory stand and even the days or weeks afterward to bask in the glory and national attention given to some gold medal winners may appear to slip away too quickly after the many years of preparation.

Dedication and hard work may be an important part of the success stories of those who become professional athletes and Olympians in the United States. However, athletes who accept the American Dream ideology and believe that their dedication and hard work will enable them to reach the top of the American Sports Pyramid are likely to be disappointed. There simply may not be enough room at the top for them. Dedication and hard work cannot completely compensate for insufficient talent. The top of the American Sports Pyramid tends to be occupied by athletes with unusual physical gifts. Dedication and hard work also may not compensate for being black, or poor, or female. Discrimination, prejudice, and a deprived background can pose significant obstacles to athletic achievement, recognition, and success even for those with great athletic potential.

Discrimination, prejudice, unequal opportunity, and the persistence of inequalities across generations in American society have closed or blocked many roads to the American Dream for minorities and the poor. The spectacular success of a number of black athletes and athletes with lower class backgrounds in professional and Olympic sports has encouraged the belief among minorities and in the lower classes that sport is their best chance to achieve the American Dream. As with whites and the more affluent, most minority and lower class athletes are likely to find that their climb up the American Sports Pyramid will end before they reach the top. However, in the case of minorities and the poor, the disappointment may be compounded because their singleminded commitment to sport may have left them without the education or skills needed to pursue success in other areas. Thus, the belief among minorities and the poor that sport is their only path to the American Dream becomes an unfortunate self-fulfilling prophecy when they sacrifice other potential roads to success for sport and then fail in sport.

Those diligent, talented, and lucky enough to make it to the top of their sport may be disillusioned by what they find there. In professional sports, the joys of competing with and against outstanding athletes and being compensated with fame and fortune may be offset by the pressures and frustrations of "life on the run" and conflicts with management about legal rights and financial compensation. Even wealthy franchise owners in professional sports may find that the fun of sports fades quickly with losing records, poor attendance, legal challenges, negotiations with agents and players' unions, lost tax privileges, a weakening cartel, the "Peter Seitz Revolution," free agents, rapidly escalating payrolls, and public criticism from players, fans, and the press.

In Olympic sports, the noble ideal of amateurism envisioned by Baron de Coubertin has been challenged by the realities of commercialism, professionalism, and international politics. In many Olympic sports, a strict enforcement of the amateur code would put world-class athletic stature and Olympic participation out of the reach of all but the wealthy in the United States. In fact, athletes in many Olympic sports accept subsidies such as athletic scholarships and under-the-table payments as support or compensation for their athletic participation. Even so, athletes in Olympic sports often do not receive enough financial assistance for training, equipment, coaching, and travel to enable them to compete at their best in Olympic-level competition at home or in international events. Congress and the federal government have begun to offer some subsidization to Olympic teams in recent years, but this support lags far behind the government support received by Olympic athletes in many other nations.

In addition to inadequate financial assistance, aspiring Olympians have had to deal with poor or unresponsive administration of their sports and conflicts between ruling bodies over territorial control in the amateur sports world. The top athletes in major Olympic sports with commercial opportunities have been allowed as "amateurs" to accept travel and expense money and time release payments for employment they miss while they are competing as Olympians. However, "amateur" athletes have had to take additional money for themselves from meet sponsors, equipment manufacturers, and others in under-the-table payments. These payments have caused guilt and anxiety about the loss of their amateur eligibility among athletes in Olympic sports. These feelings and complaints about the way their sports have been administered have caused a number of prominent Olympians to speak out against the amateur sports establishment and to try to reform the rules and control of their sports to reflect current realities of big-time amateur sports. Some athletes in road racing were able to exert enough pressure on TAC to cause it to seek and obtain permission at a meeting of the IAAF in 1981 to drop the contamination rule.

Both in professional and Olympic sports, the pressure to maintain a high level of performance and to win has driven athletes to seek an extra edge as competitors. Whether to enable them to perform with injuries, to establish themselves as newcomers, to save a fading career hurt by injury, age, or declining skills, or to remain competitive with athletes better supported and better trained in other countries, athletes in professional and Olympic sorts have resorted to drugs. Though the use of restorative drugs often is encouraged by management or coaches, restorative drug use ultimately could be as damaging to an athlete's career and health as the generally more controversial and risky additive drugs such as amphetamines and steroids.

The willingness of athletes to accept the risk of drug use along with the strains and pains of remaining a top-level professional or Olympic athlete is an indication of the tremendous drive to succeed at this level of sport, of the difficulty of remaining at this level, and of the importance of the money, glory, or self-fulfillment that can be earned by the best in America's biggest sports. The false hopes, disillusionment, physical pain, emotional strain, lack of privacy, public pressure and criticism, drug dependence, and even physical or mental debilitation are the potential costs of trying too hard to attain or hold on to an American Dream just beyond or slipping away from an athlete's grasp.

Perhaps the athletes in the minor Olympic sports experience the greatest fulfillment as American athletes, with the fewest costs. Their American Sports Dream is likely to be more modest than the Dreams of athletes in more publicized and commercialized sports. It is more likely to focus on the intrinsic rewards of joy and personal fulfillment and the medals that signify high achievement as athletes than on external rewards such as fame or money that might be generated from sports prominance. For these reasons, their departure from sports might be expected to be less traumatic and perhaps more graceful, than the retirement of major sport athletes, especially those who have become dependent on the fame or money they have received from sport and have no alternative means of gaining those rewards.

A major ingredient in the recent upsurge in the commercialization of American sports has been television. It has given national or international exposure to the top American athletes in professional and major Olympic sports. It has paid huge sums of money to the NCAA, Olympic Organizing Committees, and professional sports leagues and tours for the rights to televise their events. This money has been an important factor in the escalation of professional athletes' salaries, in the expansion of professional sports leagues and tours, and in the survival of leagues and franchises. The money has come from commercial sponsors who have paid increasingly expensive rates for television advertising. If the popularity of sports ever drops off or if advertisers decide they can get a better return on their investment dollar elsewhere, television will lose advertising revenue and will in turn reduce its financial commitment to sport. Thus, the increasing reliance on television to support its commercial growth in recent decades has tied the financial future of big-time sports in the United States to this medium. In today's American sports world, therefore, the kind of American Sports Dream available to athletes is determined by the exposure and investment of television.

Ultimately, television is dependent, too. It depends not only on the investment of commercial advertisers, but even more basically on the interest of the public. For sports, television cannot demand big money from advertisers unless they can promise large and relatively affluent audiences for sports events. Thus, the financial future of the highly commercialized televised sports in the United States ultimately depends on the fans.

This is somewhat ironic because the fans seem much more interested in who wins or loses on the field than in how much money is involved. If the commercial or pecuniary orientation of the people who run or play professional sports today becomes too pervasive or distracting for fans, there may be a decline in belief in the mythology of sport as fantasy or escape that has given sport a special appeal to many fans. Thus, sports organizers, owners, and athletes who become more consumed with the business of sport than with game on the field may find they are risking the support of fans who have made it possible for them to pursue their personal American Dreams through sport. Sport, the American Dream, and fans is a major focus of the next chapter.

# *Footnotes*

[1]These quotes about and by Pete Rose are from an article in *Inside Sports* magazine (February 28, 1981) by Nik Cohn, "Willie Mays, Pete Rose, and Lou Carnesecca: their brilliant careers."
[2]John Rickard Betts, "The technological revolution and the rise of sport, 1850-1900," *Mississippi Valley Historical Review,* XL (September 1953): 231-256. Reprinted in *Sport and American Society,* 3rd ed., ed. by George H. Sage (Reading, Mass.:

Addison-Wesley, 1980), pp. 58-80.

3David Q. Voigt, *America Through Baseball* (Chicago: Nelson-Hall, 1976), ch. 2.

4R. Terry Furst, "Social change and the commercialization of professional sports," *International Review of Sport Sociology,* 6 (1971): 153-173.

5Charles Bucher, *Foundations of Physical Education* (St. Louis: C.V. Mosby, 1968), p. 315.

6Peter C. McIntosh, *Sport in Society* (London: Watts, 1971), p. 177.

7Baron Pierre de Coubertin, "The meeting of the Olympic Games," *North American Review,* CLXX, (June 1900): 809.

8Cited by Howard Savage et al., *American College Athletics* (Boston: Merrymount Press, 1929).

9McIntosh, *Sport in Society,* p. 185.

10Cited in McIntosh, *Sport in Society,* p. 185. McIntosh also presents an amplification of the IOC standard of amateurism, Rule 26, as well as a 1961 restatement of it and an official interpretation of the practices it did not allow.

11This term will be used to refer generally to big-time amateur sports that are included in the Olympic Games. In the United States, these sports tend to be regulated by their own federations or associations and, more broadly, by The Athletic Congress (TAC), which replaced the AAU, the USOC, and at the college level by the NCAA, AIAW, and smaller associations.

12This point has been made by Harold J. Vander Zwaag in a discussion of some of the realities regarding the implementation of idealistic principles of amateurism ("Amateurism and the Olympic Games," *The Modern Olympics,* ed. by Peter J. Graham and Horst Ueberhorst (West Point: Leisure Press, 1976).

13Howard L. Nixon II, *Sport and Social Organization* (Indianapolis: Bobbs-Merrill, 1976), p. 55.

14Vander Zwaag, "Amateurism and the Olympic Games," p. 86.

15These changes have been noted in Nixon, *Sport and Social Organization,* ch. 6.

16Nixon, *Sport and Social Organization,* ch. 6.

17Harry Webb, "Professionalization of attitudes toward play among adolescents," *Sociology of Sport,* ed. by Gerald S. Kenyon (Chicago: Athletic Institute, 1969).

18Cohn, "Willie Mays, Pete Rose, and Lou Carnesecca...," p. 70.

19The general outline of this discussion of the "big business of sport" first appeared in Nixon, *Sport and Social Organization,* pp. 56-57.

20Cited in Ray Kennedy and Nancy Williamson, "Money in sports," *Sports Illustrated* (July 17, 1978), p. 34. Part I of a three-part series.

21John W. Loy, Barry D. McPherson, and Gerald Kenyon, *Sport and Social Systems* (Reading, Mass.: Addison-Wesley, 1978), p. 263. These authors offer (on pp. 263-279) a much more detailed analysis of the economics of professional sports than will be provided in this chapter. The collection of articles in Roger G. Noll's edited volume *Government and the Sports Business* (Washington, D.C.: Brookings Institution, 1974) provides additional detailed analyses of economic and regulatory aspects of professional sports.

22Henry G. Demmert, *The Economics of Professional Team Sports* (New York: Joint Council on Economic Education, 1976), p. 16.

23Wilbert M. Leonard II, *A Sociological Perspective of Sport* (Minneapolis: Burgess, 1980), pp. 251-252.

24Leonard, *A Sociological Perspective of Sport,* p. 252.

25Leonard, *A Sociological Perspective of Sport,* p. 238.

26Kennedy and Williamson, "Money in sports," Part I, p. 34.

27Rozelle's comments were reported in an Associated Press story, "Rozelle: 'NFL is a natural monopoly,'" which appeared in the *Burlington (Vermont) Free Press,* May 28, 1981.

[28]James A. Michener, *Sports in America* (New York: Random House, 1976), p. 386.

[29]Steven R. Rivkin, "Sports leagues and the federal antitrust laws," *Government and the Sports Business,* ed. by Roger G. Noll (Washington, D.C.: Brookings Institution, 1974), pp. 389-390.

[30]Rivkin, "Sports leagues and the federal antitrust laws," p. 388.

[31]Comments reported in an Associated Press story "Antitrust laws should apply to sports," which appeared in the *Burlington (Vermont) Free Press,* July 15, 1981.

[32]M. Auf der Maur, *The Billion-Dollar Game: Jean Drapeau and the 1976 Olympics* (Toronto: James Lorimer, 1976).

[33]These estimated costs, revenues, and deficit of the Montreal Olympics were reported in Loy, McPherson, and Kenyon, *Sport and Social Systems,* p. 280. It should be emphasized that they are estimates. The actual figures probably will never be public knowledge.

[34]Loy, McPherson, and Kenyon, *Sport and Social Systems,* p. 280. These authors presented estimated costs of $200 million for the Munich Olympics, $32 million for the Rome Olympics, and $6 million for the Los Angeles Olympics. Of course, inflation requires a recalculation of costs in 1976 dollars to provide more precise comparisons. Nevertheless, the pattern of dramatically escalating costs in recent Summer Olympiads would not be changed. Loy, McPherson, and Kenyon (p. 280) noted that the Winter Olympic Games also have become increasingly costly, though to a lesser extent than the Summer Games. For example, in 1960, the cost was $14 million; in 1964, $25 million; in 1968, $85 million. It might be added that in 1981, village officials in Lake Placid still were in search of funds to cover deficits incurred in staging their "modest" Winter Olympiad in 1980.

[35]Andy Meisler, "AAU and USOC: organized incompetence," *WomenSports* (August 1975), pp. 36-40. There are additional articles in this issue of *WomenSports* that report major aspects and problems of amateur athletics in the U.S.

[36]Cited in a *WomenSports* (August 1975) commentary by Elizabeth Koch, p. 37.

[37]Meisler, "AAU and USOC ..."

[38]These needs that were to be met by the CSO were presented by Kenny Moore in his *Sports Illustrated* article "Cure for an Olympian headache" (January 17, 1977). Other discussion of *The Final Report of the President's Commission on Olympic Sports 1975-1977* (Washington, D.C.: Government Printing Office, 1977) have appeared in James H. Frey's "The organization of American amateur sport: efficiency to entropy," *American Behavioral Scientist,* 21 (January/February 1978): 361-378, and in Benjamin Lowe's "Educational objectives for international sport studies," *Sport and International Relations,* ed. by Benjamin Lowe, David B. Kanin, and Andrew Strenk (Champaign, Ill.: Stipes, 1978). All three sources have been used to develop the discussion in this section about the CSO and President's Commission.

[39]Frey, "The organization of American amateur sport," p. 364.

[40]Frey, "the organization of American amateur sport," p. 369.

[41]*WomenSports,* "A short explanation of the gold standard" (August 1975), p. 43. On page 42 of this issue of *WomenSports,* the editors presented a summary of AAU finances based on the AAU financial statement for fiscal year 1973-74 (ending June 1974). This summary clearly reveals the relatively limited amount of AAU funds directly supporting specific athletic programs and athletes in their jurisdiction. The AAU had $1.5 million in its sports fund, of which $384,000 was donated by Chevrolet for the AAU Junior Olympics Program. This was a showcase program for young athletes that gave them a chance to advance to national competition. The AAU had no comparable programs for older competitors. Furthermore, continuing support for programs supported by single sponsors tend to be subject to the changing economic fortunes and largesse of the sponsors.

[42]Stephen K. Figler, *Sport and Play in American Life* (Philadelphia: Saunders, 1981), pp. 160-161.

[43]The changing patterns of professional sports club ownership have been discussed by Michener, *Sports in America,* p. 357, and by Leonard, *A Sociological Perspective of Sport,* p. 229. Jonathan Brower, in "Professional sports team ownership: fun, profit, and ideology of the power elite," *Journal of Sport and Social Issues,* 1 (1976): 16-51, has analyzed the motives, backgrounds, and prerogatives of contemporary owners.

[44]Figler, *Sport and Play in American Life,* p. 159.

[45]Figler, *Sport and Play in American Life,* p. 161, has presented a table showing the patterns of growth in professional sports since 1961, as well as a list of new leagues established since 1966.

[46]Leonard, *A Sociological Perspective of Sport,* p. 229.

[47]The financial and tax advantages of professional sports ownership have been discussed at much greater length elsewhere. For example, brief, relatively nontechnical discussions can be found in Michener, *Sports in America,* pp. 357-363, and in Leonard, *A Sociological Perspective of Sport,* pp. 229-236. More detailed and technical analyses can be found in Noll's edited volume *Government and the Sports Business*—especially in an article by Benjamin Okner, "Taxation and sports enterprises"—and in James Quirk's "Professional sport franchise values," *Proceedings of the Conference on the Economics of Professional Sport,* ed. by G. Burman (Washington, D.C.: National Football League Players' Association, 1974).

[48]A profile of contemporary sports club owners was presented by Ray Kennedy in a *Sports Illustrated* article "Who are these guys?" (January 31, 1977).

[49]These figures were reported in Leonard, *A Sociological Perspective of Sport,* p. 233. The 1974 statistics were taken from Demmert, *The Economics of Professional Team Sports,* p. 17, and the 1977-78 statistics were from Kennedy and Williamson, "Money in sports," Part I, p. 58.

[50]Reported in Figler, *Sport and Play in American Life,* p. 161.

[51]Michener, *Sports in America,* p. 365.

[52]Quoted in Kennedy, "Who are these guys?" p. 53.

[53]Quoted in Michener, *Sports in America,* p. 366.

[54]Brower, "Professional sports team ownership . . . ," drew this conclusion on the basis of comments made by owners about their motives for team ownership.

[55]These probabilities are based on statistics cited by D. Stanley Eitzen and George H. Sage, in *Sociology of American Sport* (Dubuque, Iowa: Wm. C. Brown, 1978), p. 226.

[56]The "black dominance" of these sports over the past few decades has been documented in a number of sources of sports statistics and records. Leonard, *A Sociological Perspective of Sport,* recently summarized this dominance on pages 139-141 and on pages 174-178.

[57]Richard A. Cloward and Lloyd E. Ohlin, *Delinquency and Opportunity* (Glencoe, Ill.: Free Press, 1960).

[58]Donald W. Ball, "Ascription and position: a comparative analysis of 'stacking' in professional football," *The Canadian Review of Sociology and Anthropology,* 10 (1973): 97-113.

[59]See, e.g., Jack Olsen's *The Black Athlete—A Shameful Story* (New York: Time, 1968), and Eitzen and Sage, *Sociology of American Sport,* pp. 235-239.

[60]Harry Edwards' *The Revolt of the Black Athlete* (New York: Free Press, 1969) inspired Ball to label this view "the Harry Edwards corrective." As a sociologist and activist, Edwards has spoken out for the rights of black athletes and against their exploitation.

[61]Reported in Figler, *Sport and Play in American Life,* pp. 244-245. Figler offers a good, brief, recent discussion of the phenomena of quotas and stacking (pp. 244-253). A recent summary of the assorted explanations of stacking as well as the excellence of black athletes is in Leonard, *A Sociological Perspective of Sport,* ch. 8. It should be

added that stacking is a well-documented phenomenon in baseball and football. However, its existence in other sports and the reasons for its existence in baseball and football are not yet agreed upon by sport sociologists.

[62]Figler, *Sport and Play in American Life,* pp. 248-249.

[63]A study for the NFL Players' Association by sociologist Jomills Henry Braddock II of Johns Hopkins University showed that race, *per se,* was more important than playing a "central," or leadership, position or than educational achievement and professional accomplishments in the choice of assistant and head coaches in the NFL. It also concluded that during the last seven years of the 1970s when expansion increased the number of NFL teams to 28, opportunities for blacks in coaching decreased. These results seem to reflect persisting discrimination and prejudice in professional sports regarding opportunities for authority, especially when they are combined with evidence of limited black coaching opportunities in other professional sports that blacks dominate on the playing field. Braddock's study was reported in a story in the *Burlington (Vermont) Free Press* on October 28, 1980.

[64]D. Stanley Eitzen and David C. Sanford, "The segregation of blacks by playing position in football: accident or design?" *Social Science Quarterly,* 55 (1975): 948-959.

[65]Barry D. McPherson, "The segregation by playing position hypothesis in sport: an alternative explanation," *Social Science Quarterly,* 55 (1975): 960-966.

[66]Quoted in Olsen, "The black athlete—a shameful story," *Sports Illustrated* (July 22, 1968), p. 29.

[67]For summaries of this evidence, see Eitzen and Sage, *Sociology of American Sport,* pp. 253-255; Leonard, *A Sociological Perspective of Sport,* pp. 181-183; Figler, *Sport and Play in American Life,* pp. 252-253.

[68]Jay J. Coakley, *Sport in Society* (St. Louis, C.V. Mosby, 1978), pp. 295-296.

[69]Arthur Ashe, "Send your children to the libraries: an open letter to black parents," *New York Times,* February 6, 1977, Section 5. Cited in Coakley, *Sport in Society,* p. 297.

[70]See Eddie Rivera's "Only in America, land of opportunity: go to sleep a pauper and wake up a millionare" in *Inside Sports* (June 30, 1981) about the ascendance of Fernando Valenzuela.

[71]Bill Brubaker, "Hey kid, wanna be a star?" *Sports Illustrated* (July 13, 1981).

[72]Quoted in a *Sports Illustrated* article "Love and love" (April 27, 1981) by Frank Deford.

[73]Most of these figures were taken from Leonard, *A Sociological Perspective of Sport,* p. 205, or from Ray Kennedy and Nancy Williamson, "Money in sports," Part II, *Sports Illustrated* (July 24, 1981).

[74]Nancy Theberge, "The world of women's professional golf: responses to structured uncertainty," *Play: Anthropological Perspectives,* ed. by Michael Salter (West Point: Leisure Press, 1978). Theberge offers an insightful sociological analysis of the structure and pressures of life on the Ladies Professional Golf Association (LPGA) tour. An interesting account of the "inside story" of women in pro tennis was presented by journalist Grace Lichtenstein in *A Long Way, Baby* (Greenwich, Conn.: Fawcett, 1974, 1975).

[75]Harold Charnofsky, "The major league professional baseball player: self-conceptions versus the popular image," *International Review of Sport Sociology,* 3 (1968): 39-53.

[76]Ray Kennedy and Nancy Williamson, "Money in sports," Part III, *Sports Illustrated* (July 31, 1981). The survey was conducted for *SI* by Yankelovich, Skelly, and White, a prominant national opinion research firm.

[77]See "The Winfield bonanza," a collection of three articles about the nature and implications of Winfield's contract, in *Sports Illustrated* (January 5, 1981).

[78]Reported in "Pro basketball" section of *Sports Illustrated* on July 13, 1981.

[79]Reported by Ed Schuyler, Jr. and Lee Mitgang in an Associated Press article that appeared in the *Burlington (Vermont) Free Press* on March 26, 1978.

[80]Salaries and winnings of the top earners in the major sports in 1977 and 1978 were

reported by Kennedy and Williamson, "Money in sports," Part II, and by H.L. Klein, "The golden age of salaries," *Inside Sports* (August 31, 1981). Salaries of assorted sports figures were compiled by Ellen Donato for a feature "Ballpark figures," which accompanied Klein's article.

[81]Salaries reported in Klein, "The golden age of salaries," p. 69.

[82]These financial statistics for Borg, Tarkenton, Palmer, Baugh, and Rote were reported in Kennedy and Williamson, "Money in sports," Part II.

[83]Kennedy and Williamson, "Money in sports," Part II.

[84]Michener, *Sports in America,* has discussed (on pages 367-374) the salaries of professional athletes and the income that stars and superstars may generate for their teams.

[85]Leonard, *A Sociological Perspective of Sport,* p. 238.

[86]The importance of this case in the history of management-player contract relations has been noted by Figler, *Sport and Play in American Life,* pp. 167-168.

[87]In *Pro Sports: The Contract Game* (New York: Charles Scribner's Sons, 1974), Sheldon Gallner used his legal training and expertise to explain professional sports contract negotiations and the role of agents and attorneys in these negotiations.

[88]Players' unions and labor relations in sports have been examined by James G. Scoville in "Labor relations in sports," *Government and the Sports Business,* ed. by Roger G. Noll (Washington, D.C.: Brookings Institution, 1974).

[89]See Leonard, *A Sociological Perspective of Sport,* pp. 244-248, for a statement of the Rozelle Rule and a discussion of the recent changes in the legal status of professional baseball, football, and basketball players.

[90]See Jim Kaplan's article about the 1981 baseball strike in "No games today," *Sports Illustrated* (June 22, 1981).

[91]Joseph Durso, in *The All-American Dollar: The Big Business of Sports* (Boston: Houghton Mifflin, 1971), ch. 7, presented a highly readable discussion of the major issues raised by the Curt Flood case. Durso's discussion preceded the U.S. Supreme Court decision, which was 5-3 against Flood but acknowledged the need for Congressional action to change the reserve system that Flood challenged.

[92]These veiws of the effects of free agency in baseball were shared by Jim Kaplan, "No games today." "The long-run effects of abolishing the baseball player reserve system" were examined by William L. Holahan in a technical economic analysis with this title, which appeared in *Sport in Sociocultural Process,* 3rd ed., ed. by Marie Hart and Susan Birrell (Dubuque, Iowa: Wm. C. Brown, 1981). Holahan concluded that if interteam monetary transfers are instituted, the abolition of the reserve system would not affect league balance, the survival of teams, team location, or trades.

[93]Stephen Steiner, "Sport interview: Bob Horner," *Sport* (August 1981).

[94]Discussions of the nature and functions of sports heroes in society can be found in a variety of sources, including the following recent ones: Richard C. Crepeau, "Sport, heroes and myth," *Journal of Sport and Social Issues,* 4 (Fall/Winter 1980): 23-31; Richard Lipsky, *How We Play the Game* (Boston: Beacon Press, 1981), ch. 5; and Unit III of *Sport Sociology: Contemporary Themes,* 2nd ed., ed. by Andrew Yiannakis et al. (Dubuque, Iowa: Kendall/Hunt, 1979)—which includes selections by Garry Smith on "The sport hero: an endangered species" and on ". . . sports hero worship;" by Randy Roberts on "Jack Dempsey: an American hero in the 1920s;" by Judith Davidson on "Heroines and heroics;" and by Niles Howard on "Playing the endorsement game."

[95]Daniel J. Boorstin, *The Image: A Guide to Pseudo-Events in America* (New York: Atheneum, 1975).

[96]Roger Kahn, "Where have all our heroes gone?" *Esquire* (October 1974).

[97]Crepeau, "Sport, heroes and myth."

[98]Crepeau, "Sport, heroes and myth," described Garvey as a "hero of myths past."

[99]Pat Jordan, "Trouble in Paradise," *Inside Sports* (August 31, 1980).

[100]Henry Failie, "Too rich for heroes," *Harpers* (November 1978), pp. 36-37. Discussed by Crepeau, "Sport, heroes and myth."

[101]Garry J. Smith, "An examination of the phenomenon of sports hero worship," *Canadian Journal of Applied Sport Sciences,* 1 (December 1976): 259-270. Reprinted in *Sports Sociology...,* 2nd ed., ed. by Andrew Yiannakis et al. (Dubuque, Iowa: Kendall/Hunt, 1979).

[102]Charnofsky's study of major league baseball players—"The major league professional baseball player..."—revealed that the ball players of the 1960s felt little connection with old-time baseball heroes and saw themselves as similar to the average working man in values, intelligence, and personality.

[103]Bill Bradley, *Life on the Run (New York: Quadrangle, 1976).*

[104]According to John Underwood, in *The Death of An American Game: The Crisis in Football* (Boston: Little, Brown, 1979), p. 27, a survey reported by the *New York Times* indicated a 100% casualty rate in an NFL season—with at least one injury per player. In his book, Underwood considers how excessive violence and injuries in football threaten the future of the sport. The general issue of violence in sports has been examined from a variety of perspectives in a collection of articles in the *Arena Review,* 5 (February 1981), ed. by Rick Horrow.

[105]From a Stanford Research Institute study that was cited by Underwood, in *The Death of An American Game...,* p. 177.

[106]This point was made by Allen Guttmann in From *Ritual to Record: The Nature of Modern Sports* (New York: Columbia University Press, 1978), p. 121. Guttmann also noted that the capacity to endure painful injuries was the subject of Frank Gifford's book *Gifford on Courage* (New York: Bantam, 1976), which told ten stories of "heroism in modern sports."

[107]Among the various examinations of drugs in sports are Bil Gilbert's "Three-part series on drugs in sport," *Sports Illustrated* (June 23, 30, July 7, 1969); Jack Scott's "It's not how you play the game, but what pill you take," *New York Times* (October 17, 1971); Arnold J. Mandell's "Pro football fumbles the drug scandal," *Psychology Today* (June 1975); Mandell's book *The Nightmare Season* (New York: Random House, 1976), in which he detailed the extensive use of amphetamines by professional football players; and Leonard's section on "Drugs in sport" in *A Sociological Perspective of Sport,* pp. 127-129.

[108]One of the drugs now used extensively by athletes to heal injuries quickly is DMSO. Hailed as a wonder drug by many athletes and some doctors, DMSO also has raised questions in the athletic and medical communities and in the Federal Drug Administration, who are not certain about its effectiveness or risks. See J.D. Reed, "A miracle! Or is it a mirage?" *Sports Illustrated* (April 20, 1981).

[109]See William Nack, "Playing hurt—the doctor's dilemma," *Sports Illustrated* (June 11, 1979).

[110]Quoted in Nack, "Playing hurt—the doctor's dilemma," p. 35.

[111]Quoted by Underwood in *The Death of An American Game.* See pages 71-79 for an extended discussion of Dr. Mandell's experience and observations. Underwood draws from Mandell's *Psychology Today* article and his book *The Nightmare Season.*

[112]The use of amphetamines in baseball was the subject of a *Sports Illustrated* "Scorecard" commentary by Jerry Kirshenbaum called "Uppers in baseball: a downer for the national pastime," which appeared in he July 21, 1980 issue.

[113]Leonard, *A Sociological Perspective of Sport,* p. 129.

[114]Jerry Kirshenbaum, "Steroids: the growing menace," *Sports Illustrated,* "Scorecard" section (November 12, 1979).

[115]Quoted in Gilbert, "Three-part series on drugs in sport," Part I, p. 70.

[116]Julius Erving made this point about drug use in sport and society in a *Sport* interview with Peter Vecsey in December 1980. Erving discussed the use of cocaine and other

drugs by NBA players, and argued that patterns of drug use in professional sports in general reflected patterns in the larger society. Erving himself was a strong opponent of drug use. Vecsey's interview was accompanied by highlighted stories about the athletic and social uses and consequences of drugs in pro sports. More recently, *Sports Illustrated* published a cover story in which a former NFL player alleged pervasive use of cocaine and other drugs by NFL players. (See, "'I'm not worth a damn,'" by Don Reese with John Underwood, in the June 14, 1982 issue of *Sports Illustrated*.) This story caused a public sensation and widespread concern. After some hesitation, NFL officials publicly acknowledged the seriousness of the problem. However, there was no immediate agreement between management and players about how to deal with it. Indeed, a controversy developed when the NFL management proposed checking players for drugs by urinanalyses. Representatives of the NFL Players Association reacted to this proposal as an invasion of privacy and as a challenge to the personal integrity of players. (See Douglas Looney, "A test with nothing but tough questions," *Sports Illustrated* (August 9, 1982).)

[117]In his *Newsweek* column on "Cocaine and basketball" on September 1, 1980, Pete Axthelm noted that some pros had asserted that cocaine relieved the travel grind.

[118]For example, Bruce Newman tells about professional basketball superstar David Thompson's effort to bounce back from a season of personal and physical difficulties. See "Flying high once more," *Sports Illustrated* (November 17, 1980).

[119]See Jack McCallum, "John Lucas: picking up the pieces," *Sports Illustrated* (June 8, 1981), and a "Scorecard" item in *Sports Illustrated* (February 1, 1982) about John Lucas, which was called "Toward rehabilitation."

[120]McCallum, "John Lucas...," p. 35.

[121]Pat Jordan, *A False Spring* (New York: Bantam, 1973).

[122]The discussion of retirement in the remainder of this section was based mainly on Barry D. McPherson's article "Retirement from professional sport: the process and problems of occupational and psychological adjustment" in *Sociological Symposium,* 30 (Spring 1980): 126-143. McPherson's bibliography is a comprehensive list of major theoretical and empirical studies and journalistic accounts of retirement from professional sport.

[123]Cohn, "Willie Mays, Pete Rose, and Lou Carnesecca...," p. 70.

[124]S. Kirson Weinberg and Henry Arond, "The occupational culture of the boxer," *Sport, Culture and Society,* ed. by John W. Loy and Gerald S. Kenyon (New York: Macmiollan, 1969).

[125]McPherson, "Retirement from professional sport..."

[126]Donald W. Ball, "Failure in sport," *American Sociological Review,* 41 (1976): 726-739. See also, Donald S. Harris and D. Stanley Eitzen, "The consequences of failure in sport," *Urban Life,* 7 (July 1978): 177-188.

[127]For example, Harris and Eitzen, "The consequences of failure in sport," point to the case of Bernie Parrish, who did not consider himself a failure when he was forced out of football for political reasons rather than poor performance. The story of Parrish's rebellion against the NFL establishment is told in his book *They Call It A Game* (New York: New American Library Signet, 1971).

[128]Jim Bouton, with Leonard Schecter (ed.), *Ball Four: My Life and Hard Times Throwing the Knuckleball in the Big Leagues* (New York: Dell, 1971), p. 106.

[129]F. Goldner, "Demotion in industrial management," *Organized Careers: A Source Book for Theory,* ed. by B. Glaser (Chicago: Aldine, 1968), pp. 267-279.

[130]Rudolf Haerle, "Career patterns and career contingencies of professional baseball players: an occupational analysis," *Sport and Social Order,* ed. by Donald W. Ball and John W. Loy (Reading, Mass.: Addison-Wesley, 1975).

[131]G. Roy, "The relationship between centrality and mobility: the case of the National Hockey League." M.Sc. Thesis, Department of Kinesiology, University of Waterloo, 1974.

[132]H. Blitz, "The drive to win: careers in professional sports," *Occupational Outlook Quarterly,* 17 (1973): 2-16.

[133]Michael Smith and Frederic Diamond, "Career mobility in professional hockey," *Canadian Sport: Sociological Perspectives,* ed. by Richard Gruneau and John Albinson (Don Mills, Ontario: Addison-Wesley, 1976).

[134]Haerle's research—"Career patterns and career contingencies of professional baseball players"—showed that professional sports fame was a more important predictor than educational attainment of *immediate* occupational attainment after retirement from sport, but that *in the long run,* the educational factor is much more important than fame as an athlete.

[135]Kennedy and Williamson, "Money in sports," Part II, special section on "Baubles, bangles and bankruptcy."

[136]See Dick Schaap's story of Bob Beamon, who set a remarkable record in the long jump, with a leap of twenty-nine feet two and one-half inches, at the 1968 Mexico City Olympics. The story is about Beamon's rise to glory and his subsequent disappearance from public sight. By 1976, USOC did not even have an address for him or know in what city he lived. Schaap's account of Beamon's rise and plunge is told in *The Perfect Jump* (New York: New American Library Signet, 1976).

[137]Kirshenbaum, "Steroids: the growing menace."

[138]Figure skater Dorothy Hamill, who won an Olympic gold medal in 1976, estimated that her family spent $15,000 on coaching, ice time, travel, and other skating expenses for her in 1974. See *WomenSports,* "Welcome to the amateur hour" (August 1975).

[139]Nixon, *Sport and Social Organization,* p. 66.

[140]Karen Allen, "Track and field athletes wrestle with amateurism," Gannet News Service story in the *Burlington (Vermont) Free Press* on July 14, 1981.

[141]See Kenny Moore, "Dawning of a new ARRA," *Sports Illustrated* (July 6, 1981), and "Track drops contamination rule," a "Sports Roundup" story in the *Burlington (Vermont) Free Press* on September 24, 1981.

[142]Allen, "Track and field athletes wrestle with amateurism." See also, a *Newsweek* article "The master of the marathon" in the April 21, 1980 issue about Bill Rodgers' athletic and financial achievements and success. The commercialization of Bruce Jenner has been examined in Barry McDermott's "Back to Bruce in a moment. First, this commercial," *Sports Illustrated* (September 26, 1977).

[143]See Lawrence Gluckman, "Olympic competition: viewpoints of Olympic athletes," *The Modern Olympics,* ed. by P.J. Graham and H. Ueberhorst (West Point: Leisure Press, 1976).

[144]Ira Horowitz, "Market entrenchment and the Sports Broadcasting Act," *American Behavioral Scientist,* 21 (January/February 1978): 415-430.

[145]Horowitz, "Market entrnechment and the Sports Broadcasting Act," p. 420.

[146]Statistics cited in *Broadcasting* article "Football price goes right out of the stadium" (August 7, 1978), pp. 36, 38-41.

[147]Statistics cited in Leonard, *A Sociological Perspective of Sport,* p. 277. From an Opinion Research Corporation national survey reported by Don Kowet in "TV sports: America speaks out," *TV Guide* (August 19, 1978).

[148]These figures were compiled from Demmert's *The Economics of Professional Team Sports;* the first part of the Kennedy and Williamson series on "Money in sports" in *Sports Illustrated;* a "Scorecard" item in *Sports Illustrated* (June 7, 1982) on the "Tube coup;" and a *Newsweek* article called "They're playing for keeps" about the NFL strike (September.20, 1982).

[149]Michener, *Sports in America,* p. 289.

[150]Cited in Figler, *Sport and Play in American Life,* p. 152.

[151]Leonard, *A Sociological Perspective of Sport,* pp. 272, 273. See William Oscar Johnson, "A contract with the Kremlin," *Sports Illustrated* (February 21, 1977) about

the network negotiations with the Soviets that led to the NBC contract.

[152]Quoted in Kennedy and Williamson, "Money in sports," Part I, p. 78.

[153]Horowitz, "Market entrnechment and the Sports Broadcasting Act," defends and expands on this point (pp. 427-428).

[154]David L. Altheide and Robert P. Snow, "Sports versus the mass media," *Urban Life,* 7 (July 1978): 189-204.

[155]See Leonard Shecter, *The Jocks* (Indianapolis: Bobbs-Merrill, 1969), ch. 2, for a discussion of the assorted ways television has influenced athletic contests, athletes, and their sports.

[156]Robert H. McCollum and David F. McCollum, "Analysis of ABC-TV coverage of the 21st Olympiad Games, Montreal," *Journal of Sport and Social Issues,* 4 (Spring/summer 1980): 25-33.

# 6

# Sport, the American Dream, and Leisure Participation

# *Introduction*

During the extended 1981 major league baseball strike, a group of Chicagoans that in 1979 had called itself *UMPS* (Union of Mortified Protesting Spectators) to protest the umpires' strike, reconstituted itself as *GRUMPS* (Grim Revival of the Union of Mortified Protesting Spectators).[1] Chicagoans were not alone in their protest against the baseball strike. In fact, in recent years, fans across the United States have criticized or questioned a number of things about baseball and the other major professional sports in their country. The 1978 *Sports Illustrated* survey cited in the previous chapter showed that a majority or near-majority of American sports fans believed that players had become greedier, more self-centered, and more spoiled; that owners were greedy, were in sports for publicity and recognition, and took unfair advantage of athletes; that agents should not represent players in contract negotiations and did not have a good influence on sports; that there were more personality conflicts in sports than in the past; and that there was more unnecessary violence on the field and more unruliness in the stands.[2] Furthermore, an Associated Press-NBC News poll conducted near the end of the 1981 baseball strike showed that 46% of the interviewees said they did not at all miss baseball, while only 15% said they missed it a great deal.[3]

Despite apparently widespread disenchantment with numerous aspects of professional sports, fans generally do not seem ready yet to give up their interest in sports. Indeed, according to the *Sports Illustrated* survey, a majority of fans would continue to attend games even if ticket prices were raised 25%. In addition, when fans were asked to compare current feelings with their feelings five years earlier, 38% said they had *more* interest in spectator sports (vs. 14% who said they had less); 45% said they got *more* fun out of watching sports (vs. 4% who said they got less); 30% said they were *more* loyal to their favorite teams (vs. 15% who said they were less); and 29% said they had *more* enthusiasm for star players (vs. 19% who said they had less). A steady diet of strikes, lawsuits, holdouts, walkouts, franchise relocations, and free agent team changes could alter the devotion of sports fans. However, a Seattle sports fan, Blake Eagle, probably spoke for many of the sports fans in the United States when he said, "Sport is my ballet, my opera... It is a major part of my life."[4]

Sport enters or fills the lives of fans in a variety of ways, from attendance at events to following it through the mass media. The estimated attendance at professional and college sports events in the U.S. in 1979 was over 320 million.[5] Included in this number were many who were regular spectators of a particular sport or team and many others who faithfully attended events in more than one sport. Much more numerous than regular spectators, though, are the tens of millions of fans who loyally follow their favorite sports, teams, and athletes on a daily basis through television, radio, newspapers, and magazines. We already have discussed the special significance of television in the recent commercial boom in spectator sports. Since 1975, the three major networks in the United States have televised more than 1200 hours of sports each year. A number of sports telecasts are regularly listed among the year's top-rated programs. For example, an estimated 100 million watch the World Series, 11.5 million watch Monday Night Football, 5 million watch a regular season NBA game, and 80 million or more watch the Super Bowl[6] The extent of the American public's interest in watching sports is indicated by the popularity of "pseudosports" events such as "Superstars," "Superteams," and "Celebrity Challenges," as well as the popularity of more conventional or "legitimate" televised sports events.

Beyond fans, there is another significant category of American adults whose lives are variously penetrated by sports or physical activity. They are not the professionals or professionalized in sport. We already have discussed them in prior chapters. They are the many millions who "play at" physical activity in their leisure time. We will call them "players" in this chapter, but this label does not necessarily imply that their leisure activities are restricted to the spontaneous, free, unregulated "play" that we defined at the beginning of this book. They are amateurs, but they may become very serious about their leisure participation in physical recreation, athletic games, or sport. They are, for example, casual, regular, or competitive runners, motorcyclists, bicyclists, tennis players, snow skiers, water skiers, swimmers, soccer players, rugby players, bowlers, golfers, basketball players, snowmobilers, softball players, sailors, and practitioners of karate or other martial arts. As leisure participants, they are—or are supposed to be—employed at something else. They may or may not be devoted fans of sport, but even if they are not, they may share the devoted fans' dedication to their leisure pastime. Together, players and fans are the main categories of leisure participants in sport to be considered in this chapter on sport, the American Dream, and leisure participation.

# *Leisure Participants and the American Dream: Sport as a Symbolic Refuge*

Leisure participation in sport or sport-like activities[7] becomes tied to the American Dream when fans and players begin to attribute special meaning or purposes to their sports involvement. When sport becomes the ballet and opera—and more—in the lives of fans and players, it may clarify basic values and affect personal identity issues and it may provide a feeling or illusion of success, fulfillment, or relief not found elsewhere in life. The capacity of sport to penetrate the lives of fans and players—just as it does for more professional sports participants—and to assume special importance for them helps explain why fans are tolerant of the problems, excesses, and distractions in the sports world and why players persist despite injuries, foul weather, and other forms of adversity.

Leisure participation in sport is most likely to be perceived by fans and players as having special significance in their lives when sport is seen as a fantasyland or refuge, free from the harsh realities of everyday life. When sport is seen in the romanticized or idealized terms conveyed by the dominant American sports creed, it becomes a world of traditional values and ideals untainted by the complexities, confusion, and corruption of "real life." These values and ideals are likely to become most meaningful and compelling when they are insulated from reality. Thus, fans and players caught up in lives with ambiguity, uncertainty, and contradictions may resist the intrusion of the "real world" into their leisure sanctuary of sport because they need this part of their lives to serve as a "symbolic refuge" or escape from their everyday problems, pressures, or concerns.[8] In apparent irony, the American Dream, which may be romanticized in the fantasy world of sport, might be a significant source of the life pressures that create the need for a refuge.

It appears that despite suggestions of diminishing resources, declining economic opportunities, and the need to limit aspirations in the 1980s, the American Dream remains alive for a large proportion of Americans. In a mid-1970s survey of Americans in the metropolitan labor force—including the unemployed[9]—Kay Scholzman and Sidney Verba found that a majority believed hard work was the most important factor in getting ahead and that a worker's child had at least some chance of getting ahead. The percentage believing in hard work ranged from 66% of those in the second-lowest occupational category in the study to 70% of those in the highest of the four occupational categories in the study. The percentage believing in mobility chances for the working class ranged from 62% of those in the lowest occupational category to 77% of those in the highest occupations. Scholzman and Verba also discovered that a substantial minority of Americans believed the chances for success were distributed fairly. The percentage believing in the fair distribution of chances for success ranged from 38% of those in the second-lowest occupational category to 46% of those in the next-highest—or third-highest—of the four occupational categories.

In general, Scholzman and Verba's data reveal that faith in the American Dream at the beginning of the last quarter of the twentieth century was not confined to the upwardly mobile and successful. More precisely, they found that faith in Horatio Alger and in individualistic notions of success was not strongly linked to the personal mobility experience or economic condition—including even unemployment—of Americans. Despite a tendency they found toward a declining commitment to the American Dream—especially concerning belief in fairness of opportunities—among younger Americans, the American Dream appeared to be still firmly entrenched in the American consciousness in the mid-1970s. This persisting, widespread, and deeply felt commitment is especially interesting, or curious, in view of Richard Lipsky's suggestion that this ideology never was totally compatible with the reality of a stratified society of social classes. Furthermore, with increased complexity and bureaucratization in American society, the gap between the ideology and the reality has widened.[10]

The persistence of this ideology in the context of an increasingly discrepant reality is made possible, in part, by the folklore and dreams dramatized in the symbolic arena of popular sports. The image-makers and promoters of popular commercialized American sports try to emphasize the good character of those who become stars; they try to create heroes even at a time when heroes seem to be in decline. More importantly for the persistence of the American Dream ideology, they emphasize the good character *and humble social origins* of their stars when they can, which offers dramatic proof of the openness of opportunity in American society and the success of those with the "proper" values. Thus, even as a "culture of narcissism"[11] seems to threaten traditional values of hard work and self-denial and corporate bureaucracy seems to undermine the traditional respect for rugged individualism, the world of sport continues to glorify the older values of the American Dream and the Protestant Ethic that spawned this Dream.

Continuing faith in the American Dream will tend to preserve the legitimacy of American capitalism and the dominant institutions in American society. However, this continuing faith is bound to create tension, anxiety, and frustration in a society where the realities of opportunity and success do not match the promise of the ideology. At some point, people must confront the reality of their progress up the American ladder of success, and when they do, many feel some type of emotional stress. A survey of *Psychology Today* readers found that when asked what emotions they remembered associating with money (or "success") at any time in the previous year, 71% recalled anxiety, 52% recalled depression, and 52% remembered anger. Though 51% also recalled happiness, a near-majority remembered feeling helplessness and over one-third recalled feeling resentment.[12]

The American Dream ideology encourages a syndrome of competitive striving and a sense of individual responsibility for success and failure. Strivers confront the realities of corporate hierarchies and social stratification and find their paths temporarily or permanently blocked. Those who want the good things in life without the competitive striving are likely to remain unfulfilled dreamers—unless they have been born into successful families. What is ultimately most frustrating about this striving in American society is that genuine success is frequently seen as reaching the top and "being #1." This emphasis on reaching the top and "winning" means that any lesser degree of achievement and success could create a sense of *relative* deprivation, as in the case of a one million dollar per year baseball player who is unhappy because a teammate is earning more money. The emphasis on being the best and winning represented to psychologist Karen Horney[13] a kind of neurosis of competitiveness, which she tied to the pursuit or power, prestige, and pleasure and we have associated with the push toward the American Dream's pot of gold.

The exacting competitive standards of achievement and success in American life in general allow few to experience genuine achievement and success, and for those who reach the top, there are likely to be continuing pressures to prove themselves. Thus, those caught up in the "neurotic competitiveness" of American society and driven by the American Dream often may feel unfulfilled, anxious, depressed, angry, or insecure. Feeling personally responsible for their fate, they might even begin to fear the process of striving or the prospect of failure. Sport contributes to this process by dramatizing individual and team victories in the face of seemingly insurmountable odds, by giving dramatic emphasis to the themes of the dominant American sports creed, and by reminding us of the modest beginnings of its greatest and richest stars. However, sport also can help alleviate the pressures and frustrations created by these dramatizations of victory, success, and the American Dream when it is perceived as a fantasyland or escape—as a "symbolic refuge."

Sport may cast its greatest spell over fans and players and provide them with the most pleasure and fulfillment when disbelief is suspended, illusion is created, and play is emphasized.[14] Fans often seem to have at least an intuitive appreciation of this idea. Dedicated fans lose themselves in total concentration and involvement in the action on the field or on their television, and they protest when the real world—in the form of strikes, contract disputes, and holdouts—disrupt their sports fantasies. Serious players talk of the "natural high" or "release" they experience when they are able to block out distractions and concentrate on pushing themselves to higher physical or competitive levels. However, despite efforts by fans and players to insulate their respective sports sanctuaries from the distractions and problems of the real world, harsh reality is always lurking, ready to intrude. Ironically, when it does intrude, it might be the result, in part, of fans and players becoming too immersed in their leisure worlds of sport and taking them too seriously.

Fans may pass the threshold of pleasure as fans when they depend too much on sport to serve as an escape and when they identify too closely with the teams or athletes they follow. The striving and competition for achievement, success, and the American Dream among teams and athletes in sport, with their emotional lows as well as highs, are not unlike what many fans seek to escape in their personal lives when they turn to sport. Becoming *too* immersed in sport could recreate and intensify for fans the frustrations and problems of their personal lives.

When players become obsessed with reaching increasingly higher levels in their sport, they are likely to try to reorder their lives to accommodate their growing obsession. In pursuing this obsession, they will experience a new set of demands and pressures that could prove to be as troublesome or disruptive as the ones they initially sought to relieve or escape through physical activity.

In general, then, leisure participation in sport for fans and players might serve as a symbolic refuge from the pursuit of American Dream in their personal lives. However, the image-makers and promoters of commercialized sports and the organizers of "recreational" sports often seem to give dramatic emphasis to dominant elements of the ideology of the American Dream and the importance of victory and success. Thus, as spectator sports become more commercialized and "recreational" sports become more organized and competitive, fans and players may be less likely to derive fun and escape from their leisure pastimes and instead become exposed to frustrations and pressures of the "real world" they wanted to avoid or forget.

The perceived capacity of sport to serve as a refuge from reality and the tendency for sport to mirror reality both must be recognized to understand the appeal and meaning of sport for fans and players. Major features of the involvement of fans and players in sport in the United States will be examined more closely in the remainder of this chapter.

# Fans

## The Emergence of the Modern Mass Sports Spectacle in the United States

The tremendous current popularity of spectator sports in the United States already was documented at the beginning of this chapter. This popularity did not suddenly occur within the last two or three decades. It has its roots in the commercial development of American sport in the nineteenth century. Discussion of this commercial development in previous chapters should have indicated that spectator sports already had become a significant element in American popular culture by the end of the nineteenth century.[15] Most fundamentally, the commercial growth of sport that we looked at in earlier chapters was made possible by a growing public interest in commercialized mass culture and entertainment.

Mass spectator sports emerged at the end of the nineteenth century in the United States in a context of conflicting and confusing social, cultural, and economic conditions largely produced by urbanization. The urban working classes felt inadequately integrated within the culture of their cities, and there were widespread perceptions of wage disparities and political inequities. The continuing series of economic crises, booms, and recessions heightened the frustrations, insecurities, and resentment of the masses. Before the nineteenth century ended, the discontent of the masses erupted into violent clashes between labor and big business and led to numerous occurrences of social unrest in the larger cities. Thus, the rise of commercialized sports at the end of the nineteenth century could be interpreted as part of a growing desire to find in mass culture an escape from the social, cultural, and economic conflicts and confusion of the period.

In words reminiscent of the analysis presented here of the American Dream and leisure sports participation in contemproary American society, Nicholas Petryszak asserted that after 1900, urban workers with their improved wages and increased leisure time "sought out substitute goals within which they might realize their long cherished ideals of individuality and opportunity... (They) sought to escape the disillusioning realities of American liberal society and seek instead the illusion of its ideals."[16] The sports spectacle, which had arisen as part of the commercialization of culture by business interests in an urbanizing and industrializing society, became at least a temporary means of escape and source of illusion for the unhappy and disillusioned by the beginning of the twentieth century. However, the world of illusion or fansasy created by sports spectacles for a restless and frustrated urban population in search of an escape also reaffirmed values and ideals of the Protestant Ethic and the American Dream, which complemented the processes of production and consumption associated with industrialization and capitalism.

In the early twentieth century, baseball bacame the "national pastime," and college football also achieved widespread spectator appeal. A number of other sports—such as tennis, golf, horse racing, auto racing, and boxing—were gaining national attention during this period. By the 1920s, spectator sports had grown to such proportions that fears began to be expressed about "spectatoritis," although it appears that active participation in physical recreation and leisure sports was increasing along with the growth of spectator interest in sports.[17] Sharing the limelight with entertainers, actors, musicians, and aviators, sports figures such as Babe Ruth, Jack Dempsey, Red Grange, Knute Rockne, Bill Tilden, Helen Wills, and Bobby Jones became national celebrities or even heroes. In regard to the 1920s, noted sports historian John Rickard Betts wrote, "In a decade dedicated largely to escapism, adventure, and general levity, sport gained the publicity which made it one of America's foremost social institutions."[18]

By the 1920s, spectator sports in the United States already had changed substantially from their beginnings as localized displays of loosely organized sports teams. Those with widespread or national appeal were characterized by increasing rationalization, bureaucratization, and corporate organization. These characteristics have become dominant features of mass spectator sports today. The sports spectacles presented to modern sports fans are produced by professional and amateur sports organizers who rationally calculate how they can attract the largest possible audiences to generate the largest possible profits. Modern fans watch athletes and teams who have taken advantage of the latest scientific and technical expertise and equipment, and they watch athletic contests in which as little as possible has been left to chance. Modern sports organizers and promoters try to make sure that the commercial product they are advertising delivers the entertainment value and experience fans want and expect.

A good illustration of the extent of evolution of the modern mass sports spectacle in the United States into an economic commodity is professional football's Super Bowl. According to Michael Real, who has written about the Super Bowl as a "mythic spectacle," it had become "the most lucrative annual spectacle in American mass culture" by the mid-1970s.[19] The 1974 game that he studied, Super Bowl VIII, attracted a live attendance of 71,882, a television audience of 70-95 million, and contingent of news people numbering over 1600. Commercial time was sold at a rate of $200,000 to $240,000 per minute, and the total advertising revenue earned by CBS from the game was over $4 million. The estimated amount of money spent in Houston, the host for Super Bowl VIII, by those there for the game was $12 million. The game generated over 3 million words of copy from the news people covering it.

Real noted that Super Bowl VIII itself was one-sided and boring. However, after the game, the one-sidedness prompted questions about whether the victorious Miami Dolphins were the greatest team in the history of pro football. Even without the post-game attempts to embellish the image of the game, the popularity of the spectacle was not likely to be threatened by a lack of excitement in the game. In fact, the game is only part of the spectacle, and fans probably are attracted at least as much to the spectacle and what it symbolizes as to the competition on the field. Indeed, with the extensive promotional build-up in the press and by NFL officials, the game becomes almost anticlimactic.

Although mass sports spectacles have become manufactured commodities or entertainment packages, they have not lost their capacity to provide escape or reaffirm cultural values and ideals. As "mythic spectacles," popular modern spectator sports events are ritualized mass cultural displays that provide opportunities to identify with cultural heroes (at least in terms of their exploits on the field) or with heroic action, become involved in activities that can be shared with others, and rediscover idealized values lost in the complexities and confusion of everyday life. It can be argued that sports spectacles have retained their general cultural and symbolic functions for spectators because the cultural, social, and psychological needs they met when they first became popular still are not fulfilled in everyday life for many people in American society. According to Petryszak, "The apparent growing number of sports spectacles today may point in fact, not to the public's increasing interest in sports, but to the growing inadequacy of North American culture and industry to provide the individual with a personal sense of fulfillment in his day-to-day life situation."[20]

# *TV and the Modern Sports Fan*

It should be evident from the previous chapter that a major influence shaping the symbolic drama and cultural experience of modern spectator sports is television. Important mass sports spectacles today usually are TV events. These spectacles are produced and packaged for television, and their largest audience consists of television viewers.

Television producers present sports spectacles meant to provide an entertaining diversion for their viewers. These spectacles also celebrate idealized values of American society. However, the primary motivation of the television producers of sport is to present programs that will gain the highest possible viewer ratings so the highest possible commercial advertising rates can be charged for them. In seeking the largest possible audiences, television sports producers try to take advantage of the elements of sport that are most entertaining. Thus, we see an emphasis on the drama, excitement, controlled violence, flamboyance, fast pace, courage, power, and gamesmanship in sport on television. To maximize the size of their audiences, television sports producers also try to make watching sports on TV as convenient as possible for viewers. As we observed previously, this can lead to inconveniences for spectators at the stadium and concessions from athletes, coaches, and sports executives in how they play their games.[21]

For the television viewer, sports programming has become extremely convenient in recent years. Even for those who live hundreds of miles from major league sports cities, it now is possible to watch 24 hours of televised sports every day, and the sports range from the popular ones such as football, baseball, basketball, hockey, horse racing, and auto racing to less popular ones such as lacrosse, polo, full-contact karate, weightlifting, the rodeo, and volleyball. The reason for this amazing potpourri of televised sports is not CBS, NBC, nor ABC; it is cable and pay television.

Taking advantage of advances in telecommunication "delivery systems" and an easing of FCC regulations, cable and/or satellite television networks such as ESPN and USA Network and superstations such as WTBS in Atlanta, WGN in Chicago, and WOR in New York have since the mid-1970s presented a significant challenge to the three major commercial networks' monopoly of American sports events.[22] The "Big Three" networks still control rights to the major sports events in America. However, by 1981, cable was in about 25% of the 80 million American TV homes, and that number was rising by about 250,000 subscribers per month. The proliferation and diversifiction of televised sports events for this substantial and growing segment of the American public that has been produced by cable networks and the superstations has lessened the influence of the Big Three networks on sports programming and audiences.

If sports events do not produce enough mass appeal for the major networks to justify their huge financial investment in them, then cable television can become "a viable competitor for the rights," according to Jim Spence, Senior Vice President of ABC Sports. In this regard, Van Gordon Sauter, former President of CBS Sports, has said:[23]

> Sports programming on prime time has decreased in recent years because the ratings haven't been high enough. The networks and advertisers view sport as an economic entity. Prices in prime time are staggering, and most sports simply don't produce enough return on the advertiser's dollar from a prime-time audience to make his commercials pay off. Only the NFL, the World Series, the Olympics, and a few other special events consistently generate audiences large enough to satisfy advertisers who prefer prime time.

A more competitive bidding situation for broadcast rights could keep the major commercialized sports rich and make some of the minor ones richer, and it could return more control over sports to sports executives. However, at least for the immediate future, cable networks are not likely to outbid the Big Three for major sports events because their much smaller audiences command much lower advertising rates that the major networks can charge. Indeed, ESPN, the all-day sports network, lost an estimated $75 million in its first 23 months. The key ingredients in the competitive bidding success of the cable systems will be their ability to expand their subscriber lists *and* get their subscribers to pau more for their cable use. Thus, if cable networks revolutionize television sports broadcasting and viewing, a major reason will be the willingness of sports fans to pay for television sports programs.

It should not be thought that the sports now seen on the Big Three networks are "free." The huge sums of money commercial sponsore pay to advertise their products on television sports programs are absorbed in the price consumers pay for these products[24] Thus, the American public—fans *and nonfans*—now pau indirectly for the televising of sports on the major networks. With the growth of pay cable television and the relinquishment or loss of sports broadcast rights by the Big Three, more sports fans may have to pay indirectly and directly for the sports they watch on TV.

If the ready availability of sports of all types on TV continues to attract subscribers, the result ultimately could be a drop in live attendance at sports events. If they earn enough money from television, sports may be able to survive this loss of paying customers. However, if athletes begin playing before diminishing crowds in the stadium, their motivation and enthusiasm may be adversely affected. In cable networks do not give sports contests that elaborate packaging, coverage, and extensive exposure that have been provided by the major networks, and if they cannot create or simulate the excitement of a sports drama played before a large and vocal crowd, televised sports programs and commercialized sports could begin to lose their spectacular character. If sports events become much less spectacular, they might also become less appealing and fulfilling for fans than other forms of mass culture. Thus, the possibility of a cable television "revolution" in American sports embodies future promise and danger both for fans and the sports in which television has helped them become so involved in the past few decades.

Rather than being influenced by the direct stimulation of others in the stadium, TV sports viewers react to and interpret what they see on the basis on how the action is presented to them. Research has shown that viewers of TV sports tend to be more attuned to the commentary of announcers than to the visual portion of the contest.[25] The amount and kind of dramatic commentary provided by announcers have a significant impact on what viewers see in a sports contest. Effective sports announcers can make a dull game seem exciting, and they can minimize the perceived excitement or importance of game action by not saying anything or anything exciting about it.

Not surprisingly, TV broadcasters whose ostensible job is to report the action on the field, have become entertainers whose job often becomes the translation of sports contests into mass entertainment. The best example of these modern TV sports entertainers may be the Monday Night Football broadcast teams led by Howard Cosell and Frank Gifford. These broadcasters have become well-known television personalities, and at times, their exchanges in the broadcast booth seem to take precedence over the action on the field. Their background reports, interviews, expert commentaries, special guests, personal embellishments, and selective treatment of the game action—guided by the producer in the control booth—create a distinctively focused viewing experience that makes watching a sports contest different from—and perhaps preferable to—attending it in person. Susan Birrell and John Loy have proposed in this regard that, "Television has trained America to focus on particular bits of action and ignore, or perhaps never come into meaningful contact with, a live event experience. Perhaps this explains why many disgruntled fans leave a live game complaining that they could have seen it better on television."[26]

## Social Class Variations in Spectator Preferences

The amount of television coverage of particular sports tends to reflect their relative popularity with TV viewers and the American sports public. However, American sports fans are not always of one mind about the sports they prefer to watch in person or on TV. Although there is a widely held belief that interest in sports transcends class and social boundaries in American society, this egalitarian belief is largely a myth. Social class is, in fact, an imporant differentiator of sports preferences for fans?[27]

## *Spectator Preferences of the Masses*

Although those from the lower social classes attend sports events less often than those from the more affluent classes, it appears that there is no significant difference between the masses and more elite classes in their frequency of sports consumption through the mass media such as TV and radio.[28] Furthermore, extensive television, radio, or newspaper coverage of sports such as professional football, basketball, baseball, hockey, and track have made them popular with fans with varied class backgrounds. However, there are certain spectator sports that seem to appeal mainly to the lower and working classes. Included among these mass spectator sports are bowling, pool, boxing, auto racing, arm wrestling, motocross racing, demolition derbies, and pseudo sports such as the roller derby and professional wrestling. Stanley Eitzen and George Sage have used the label "prole (for proletarian) sports" to refer to these kinds of sports and pseudosports, and they have proposed six possible reasons to explain their popularity among the working class.[29] First, the equipment and skills typically used in these sports tend to be basic ingredients of working class life, Second, prole sports tend to emphasize qualities such as physical prowess and manhood—or machismo—that are highly valued by the working class life. Third, there often are elements of danger and violence in prole sports that make them exciting and an emotional outlet for working class people. Fourth, working class fans frequently can identify with the stars of prole sports because these athletes seem to share a common ethnicity, language, or behavior with the fans. Fifth, prole sports typically exist outside the predominantly middle class environment of the school. Finally, Eitzen and Sage have proposed that prole sports often are individual—rather than team—sports, and individual sports seem to have a special appeal for working class spectators.

In general, Eitzen and Sage's analysis suggests that the sports with greatest appeal to working class spectators allow them to identify with athletes and teams expressing values such as individualism, strength, and power that they respect but cannot express adequately in their own jobs or lives. The power, violence, and destruction in their sports preferences might reflect the frustration or rage they feel as members of the more subordinate and economically deprived classes in American society. Another possible function of spectator sports is to redirect such frustration or rage away from their source in society into safer and more insulated channels such as the fantasy world of sport. This redirection or venting of potentially disruptive or rebellious energy in combination with the dramatization of the American Dream ideology in sports spectacles could contribute significantly to the maintenance of a social order characterized by assorted inequalities and inequities.

Since working and lower class people are less educated and less integrated into formal educational systems than middle and upper class people, it is not surprising that their spectator preferences tend to be for sports that are not school related. It might be more surprising that the spectator sports with special appeal to the working and lower classes are individual rather that team sports since people in these classes seem more interested in *playing* team sports.[30] However, the great popularity of a number of individual sports with working and lower class spectators suggests that individualism—combined with some other prominent characteristics— is important to the masses as well as the more elite in American society. In fact, the masses seem interested in watching *and competing in* a number of individual sports such as boxing, wrestling, and auto, motorcycle, and snowmobile racing as well as aggressive and contact team sports such as football, hockey, and basketball. Probably more significant than the individual or team aspect of their sports is the common capacity of these sports to represent important values and meet important needs in their class situation. Furthermore, the limited economic resources associated with working and lower class status pose a major constraint upon the sports—whether individual or team—that the masses can play. Spectator preferences, especially in regard to TV, are not as economically constrained.

### Spectator Preferences of the Elite and Striving

Among the most prominent sports with special appeal to more affluent middle class spectators are tennis, golf, sailing, and skiing. The spectator sports of the very rich include polo, yachting, and sports car racing. Horse racing is the "sport of kings" because its earliest patrons were aristocratic and its current owners and breeders are generally upper class. However, as a spectator sport, it has widespread popularity in American society. In many cases the distinctive spectator sports preferences of the rich and upwardly mobile reflect interests cultivated during their prep school or college experiences or associated with exclusive private clubs. Not surprisingly, these classes are more likely than lower classes to follow college sports, in contrast to the tendency for professional sports interests to cut across social class lines.

Perhaps more interesting than the nature of the sports preferences of affluent spectators is how they spend their money as sports spectators and consumers. In his classic study the *Theory of the Leisure Class,* Thorstein Veblen proposed that a strong desire for esteem or honor existed among those with sufficient wealth to escape the normal struggle for survival[31] That is, having accomplished a part of the American Dream, the affluent become relatively more concerned with goals of social prominence and recognition. Since wealth in a capitalistic or materialistic society is a mark of success, it can create respect or envy and be a source of social recognition. According to Veblen, the wealthy try to *display* their wealth through *conspicuous consumption* and *conspicuous leisure* to gain the esteem, honor, or social recognition they desire.

We might argue with Veblen about whether the established upper class or the more insecure nouveaux riches and upwardly mobile are more inclined toward conspicuous status display. However, it should be evident that leisure participation in sport—as a spectator or player—offers a number of opportunities for such status striving and display.[32] Indeed, some owners have acknowledged, and most fans believe, that owners purchase sports franchises at least partly to satisfy needs for publicity and recognition. As spectators, the upwardly moblie and wealthy can conspicuously consume by attending as many of the major and more expensive national and international sports events as possible and by buying the most expensive tickets to these events. They can fly to these events, drive or be driven in fancy cars to the stadium, wear expensive jewelry and furs, and watch the game from exclusive seating reserved for the most distinguished spectators.

Wealthy spectators also might be able to buy a special box at the stadium of a local or favorite team. Texas Stadium, the home of the Dallas Cowboys of the NFL, offers this possibility. Stadium boxes there are 16 by 16 foot rooms that cost $50,000 in the early 1970s. For this price, purchasers were given the right to buy a dozen seats for every game at $10 per ticket. They also could decorate their box with luxurious furnishings. Stadium boxes and high-priced season tickets usually entitled their holders to membership in an exclusive stadium club, which is likely to be frequented by famous sports personalities and other prominent people. A wealthy oil baroness who was a Texas Stadium box holder commented about her privileged vantage point in the following way: "This is really the only way to watch football. . . Our chauffeur brings us out several hours before game time. We have dinner at the Texas Club, here on the Inner Circle level. There are cocktails served in our box. Afterwards, they show the highlights on closed circuit television and we sip champagne while the parking lot clears."[33]

It may not be possible for a sports spectator to display as much extravagance at home as at the arena. However, it still is possible to host lavish parties to watch live or personally taped sports events on modern wall-size television screens. So both at home and at the stadium, sports fans and putative sports fans can try to impress others with their conspicuous spending. In doing so, they might earn the respect, recognition, or envy they have sought and found so elusive in other parts of their lives. They also may see watching sports as an escape from the "rat race" and status striving that dominates the rest of their lives, but the search for status through conspicuous sports consumption plunges them back into the midst of the strivings they ostensibly wanted to avoid.

## *Fan Violence: Catharsis or Newly Inspired Aggression?*

The mass appeal of sports with "controlled violence" and the opportunity they offer to vent frustration or hostility have been noted. However, in recent years, the controlled violence in spectator sports has become uncontrolled at times both on the field and in the stands, and there is some doubt about whether watching violence in sports is the emotional release often assumed by defenders and observers of sport[34]

Physical contact in sport is not necessarily violent if it does not cause injury or is not meant to hurt an opponent. However, as athletes are encouraged or allowed to become more aggressive in a sport or in a contest, it becomes more likely that contact will become violent and move outside the boundaries of the rules. Of course, liberal rules, or a liberal enforcement of the rules involving contact, will contribute to a violent climate in a sport. When the importance of winning is heightened in this climate by commercialism, mass media attention, and competition for player status, violence is more likely. The use of drugs by athletes to make them more aggressive, the urging of extreme "aggressiveness" by coaches either to enhance winning or to win over fans perceived to enjoy violence, and poor or inconsistent officiating further increase the likelihood of violence on the field. If violence on the field reaches a fever pitch or is allowed by game officials to get out of hand, it may encourage spectators in the stands to become violent as well.

The sports arena often is seen as a place where fans can safely give vent to their pent-up frustrations, anger or hostility[35] For example, fans may harass opposing players and coaches, scream at referees, "ride" members of the home team who do not seem to be performing up to par, or hang coaches in effigy as a demonstration of their dissatisfaction with a team's performance. Verbal abuse might upset a player's or team's concentration, and it might hurt the pride of an athlete or coach. However, physically violent acts such as throwing objects at athletes, coaches, and referees or fighting with other spectators can have more enduring and injurious effects. Furthermore, when the collective expression of violence by spectators is not effectively brought under control by stadium authorities or the local police, it may escalate to a point where it is more violent than the action on the field in even the most aggressive contact sports. Where the loyalties of spectators are distinguished by racial or national identities or social class, extremely tense games or unexpected outcomes can arouse especially ugly incidents of fan violence.

In countries outside the United States, soccer contests have been the scene of extremely violent collective behavior of fans. For example, on May 24, 1964, a disputed referee's decision in a game between Peru and Argentina set off violent clashes among spectators that resulted in 293 deaths, and in 1969, a soccer game between El Salvador and Honduras was the precipitant of a war between these countries[36] In a number of cases, fan violence may be incidental to the action on the field, which often had been the case in the notorious "soccer hooliganism" in Britain of the past two decades. This violence has involved rioting in the stadium and on the way to or from the soccer match, property damage, and personal injury, and its regularity and seriousness have made it a nagging problem of social control for British authorities.[37]

Fan violence in or around American sports arenas generally has not reached the level or extent of these examples from other countries. However, fan violence in the United States has been quite violent and destructive. For example, during the third game of the 1973 playoffs between the New York Mets and the Cincinnati Reds, fans reacted to a fight between New York's Bud Harrelson and Cincinnati's Pete Rose by throwing things on the field; the debris caused a delay in the game. In 1974, New York boxing fans, unhappy about the loss by Puerto Rican Pedro Soto to Mike Quarry, reacted by ripping out seats, tearing down ceiling panels, and pulling toilets from their moorings in Felt Forum where the bout was held. In a 1975 NFL playoff game in Minnesota, a game official was knocked unconscious by a whiskey bottle thrown by a Viking fan. In another NFL game, a Minnesota player, Chuck Foreman, was the victim of a snowball thrown by a spectator in Buffalo; the snowball caused an injury to Foreman's eye. Horses and jockeys in the Kentucky Derby in recent years have been targets of paper cups and beer cans thrown by fans. In 1976, a smokebomb was thrown onto the track. In 1977, the final out in the Yankees' World Series victory over the Dodgers was followed by a rush of thousands of fans onto the field in Yankee Stadium where they did considerable damage to the field and caused several injuries. There were nearly forty arrests. The Dodgers had taken the precaution of landing their team plane at a private field to avoid a confrontation with wild Yankee fans.

At times, promotional stunts have been the cause of fan violence. For example, on June 4, 1974, "Beer Night" (10 cents per cup) attracted over 25,000 spectators to a baseball game in Cleveland. The resulting inebriation led to the closing of the visiting Texas team's bull pen to protect the players from fire crackers and beer cans hurled by Cleveland fans. It also led to a number of delays in the game from streakers on the field and other forms of disruption. Fans even climbed on top of the Texas dugout threatening the players' lives, and eventually the chief umpire had to forfeit the game to Texas because he could not restore order. In 1979, the second game of a scheduled double-header between the Chicago White Sox and Detroit Tigers in Chicago had to be canceled when 7000 fans charged onto the field before the second game. The resulting riot, which probably was stimulated by an advertised anti-disco music demolition derby that was to occur between games, involved a number of small fires and the destruction of the batting cage. Police believed that many of the thirty-nine people they arrested for disorderly behavior were intoxicated.

The number of instances of rowdy fan behavior at baseball games might seem surprising because baseball can give the impression of being a relatively slowly paced and calm sport. Nevertheless, researchers observing spectator behavior during forty major league baseball games in a recent season found that fights in the stands were fairly frequent and appeared to happen in a predictable manner.[38] In nineteen of the forty games studied, thirty-nine spectator fights were observed. These fights were most likely to occur on Fridays or Saturdays, at night, in the warmest summer months, in the less expensive seats, during the late innings, and after offensive rallies in which at least one run was scored. Socioeconomic considerations were suggested by the location of these fights. Taken together, these findings suggest that the heat of the air, the crowd, or the game will provoke rowdy behavior predominantly among working class fans looking for a chance to "let off steam" after a day or week of frustrating and tiring work.

Although the intensity or violence of the action in a baseball game may not match sports with more continuous action or more contact, aggressive plays, menacing gestures, emotional reactions to umpires'decisions, and fights on the baseball field could stimulate violent outbursts by spectators. Any arena where a large crowd is massed to observe a competition with the potential of excitement, tension, and the expression of hostility could become the setting for antisocial or violent outbursts from spectators. If fans enter the arena with hostile feelings and/or with a strong need or deisre for their team to win, and they observe a contest that is tense, violent, and poorly officiated, actual or perceived hostility on the field could provide a salient model for fan behavior. If alcohol of some other element such as the anonymity of the crowd situation has lowered fans' inhibitions, fans would seem likely to try to translate the model of violence into actual violence. In fans enter the arena looking forward to violent action on the field and looking for a chance to vent their own hostile impulses, the possibility of fan violence would seem even more likely. In the latter case, mass sports spectators' antisocial feelings, and the competition on the field may be salient only insofar as it offers models or opportunitnes for the expression of these feelings.[39]

"Controlled violence" in sports frequently is defended as an important "safety valve" for the release of pent-up hostile or antisocial feelings that inevitably build up in a competitive situation or reflect an innate human impulse toward aggression. In this *sport as catharsis* view, sport is seen as a safety valve because it contains expressions of antisocial feelings and aggression within the sports arena and keeps them from spilling over into other parts of society where they would be more disruptive. It is assumed that the release of hostile impulses in the sports arena will allow fans (and athletes) to leave the arena feeling relieved of such antisocial inclinations. If this view is correct, then even violent collective outbursts by fans that do not result in serious injury or damage might be justified or rationalized. For if it is thought that aggressive or antisocial impulses eventually must be given vent somewhere in society in some form, then their expression as collective outbursts by spectators in the sports arena could be seen as more desirable than other expressions of these impulses in other settings. At least in the sports arena, authorities have a chance to try to contain and channel these outbursts and control them before they get out of hand.

However, the sports as catharsis argument had been a target of much criticism by sport sociologists and psychologists in recent years.[40] Proponents of this argument seem to minimize or overlook the frequency of incidents of fan violence, the high level of hostility sometimes expressed by them and the number of occasions when collective outbursts by fans get out of hand. More fundamentally, critics of the catharsis argument point out that there is little evidence showing that violent displays by fans provide relief from hostile impulses and make fans less inclined toward violent or antisocial behavior outside the sports arena. In fact, research recently has shown that watching violent or intensely aggressive sports tends to inspire new and higher levels of hostility in fans.[41] Fans who watch noncontact and nonaggressive sports such as swimming and gymnastics are not likely to feel more hostile as a result of watching these sports, while fans who watch violent contact sports such as ice hockey and football and even psuedosports with apparent violence such as professional wrestling tend to develop more hostile or aggressive feelings as spectators.

It may be that the expression of hostility or violence by fans is only "innate" to the extent violence is built into the cultural fabric of the sports to which they are exposed and is prevalent in the society in which they are socialized. Violent sports are not necessarily a safety valve for society—i.e., an alternative to other forms of more disruptive violence in society such as war, rioting in the streets, or violent crime. They may instead mirror the overall pattern of violence in society and even contribute to it by providing models of violent expression. In this latter regard, a study showed that 74% of hostile outbursts by ice hockey fans were preceded by extraordinary displays of violence on the ice.[42]

The reason violence remains in sport may have less to do with its perceived cathartic or safety valve function than with its perceived popularity among fans. In highly commercialized sports, officials seem reluctant to change anything that might make their sports less exciting because less excitement could mean fewer fans. Thus, if the prospect of highly aggressive play, crashing physical contact, or violence is equated with excitement by sports officials, promoters, or producers, the risk of serious physical injury to the players or the incitement of violence among spectators is likely to be accepted or rationalized. Complaints from athletes, fans or sports critics about excessive sports violence are likely to be ignored or rejected if violence on the field or in the stands does not significantly dampen fan interest. Fans can be expected to tolerate or enjoy violence in sports as long as it is part of an overall cultural pattern in their society. In American society, violence is lamented but also taken for granted. Highly aggressive behavior often is seen as part of the drive to success, and vicarious participation in imaginary or fictive violence in popular culture provides pleasure, excitement, or release. Outbursts of fan violence in American sports can be expected as long as there are regular or spectacular displays of violence to arouse emotionally vulnerable fans or encourage impressionable ones.

# The Decline of Traditional Sports Heroes: Some Added Considerations

Even though contact and the prospect of violence may attract fans to a number of sports in America, violent athletes are not necessarily heroes or stars in these sports. Some may be stars; some may be journeymen relying on their ability to give and take physical punishment to sustain professional careers; and many may be portrayed as lacking in the personal qualities worthy of public admiration. In fact, as we observed in the last chapter, the close, frequent, and critical scrutiny of the stars of the major contemporary sports in America has left fans with very few traditional "All-American" sports heroes. Even those few with traditional heroic qualities are unlikely to escape the probing of a critical press, and those who do may fail to capture the national imagination in the manner of a Jack Dempsey, Babe Ruth, or Joe DiMaggio. Of course, the public image of these great sports heroes of the past was polished or protected by the much more worshipful press of their day.

Today's sports heroes may seem less exemplary to fans than the heroes of the past, but modern sports stars have not lost their capacity to thrill fans with displays of their marvelous athletic skills in the sports arena. In the arena, modern athletes perform as actors in mythic spectacles. In this setting, they can continue to perform the traditional heroic function of transporting fans from their mundane everyday lives into a fantasyland of illusion and escape. Be identifying with the stars of these sports spectacles, fans can vicariously experience achievements and success that may have evaded them in "real life' Thus, while modern athletes may be losing their credibility and impact as traditional heroes because they have become too familiar or too human in their roles outside the sports arena, as performers in sports spectacles, they remain capable of exciting or transporting fans with heroic deeds.

Superstar athletes with pecuniary motives, narcissistic life styles, contentious views of management, and unpopular or unconventional attitudes might represent split personalities to fans. In general, the images of contemporary athletes are much more complex than the images of past sports heroes, and it can be more confusing for fans today looking for uncomplicated heroes to figure out how to react to the stars of their favorite sports. In fact, society now is more complex than it was, and the complex inmages of modern athletes are a reflection of this.

However, despite this modern complexity, striving for the American Dream and material consumption are pervasive social and cultural patterns that cut across diverse segments of contemporary American society. In the commercialized realms of modern American sports, the American Dream and the promise of material success it promises also are widely shared by athletes, despite their many other differences.

By virtue of their own diversity, modern athletes in popular mass sports *collectively* have the capactiy to appeal to diverse segments of the American sports public. Even if they do not meet traditional heroic criteria, the diverse collection of well-paid stars in modern big-money sports can symbolize, popularize, and sell the ideologies of the American Dream and consumption to a broad cross-section of American sports fans.

Advertisers take advantage of the celebrity or quasi-heroic status of a diverse array of modern sports stars to sell their products. These stars have become idols of consumption, and according to Lipsky, this commercialization of athletes is a natural outgrowth of the development of a consumer ideology in American society.[43] Thus we see prominent sports personalitites as diverse as Mickey Mantle, Muhammad Ali, Don Meredith, Pele, Billie Jean King, "Mean Joe" Green, Sugar Ray Leonard, O.J. Simpson, Chris Evert Lloyd, Jim Palmer, and Joe Namath endorsing products ranging from soda to iced tea, beer, popcorn makers, American Express cards, rental cars, and underwear.

There may be very few athletes today who conform to the traditional All-American hero model or who engender the degree and scope of admiration or devotion granted to sports heroes earlier in this century. However, today's sports stars are not devoid of heroic qualities, and collectively they have the capacity to exert substantial influence over fans. Modern sports heroes can offer fans the chance for vicarious success, fulfillment, and escape through their feats in the sports arena. As idols of affluence and consumption outside the sports arena, they provide fans with models of success in an era of mass consumption. Fans may question their credibility in endorsing products, but prominent athletes still help to encourage or reinforce a pervasive pattern of mass consumption among fans.

Even though traditional heroic types have declined in sport, we must be careful not to underestimate the possible influence of modern stars on fans. It must be remembered that despite the assorted distractions and criticisms caused by big money in sports today, the interest of fans in watching sports, their loyalty to their favorite teams, and their enthusiasm for star players have been rising in recent years. Furthermore, the majority of American sports fans still believe that pro athletes are a good example for kids.[44] With the continuing mass appeal of sports, today's sports celebrities and quasi-heroes seem to possess the same capacity to provide escape and a reinforcement of values that has been ascribed to traditional sports heroes.

Richard Crepeau has suggested that the wider selection of hero types today may be offering in many cases—such as Pete Rose—"old myths in new models."[45] For fans, the persistence of these old myths may be an important aspect of the appeal of mass sports spectacles to them. It seems unlikely that sports spectacles could be as popular as they are today if athletes lacked the capacity to symbolize these myths and perform at least quasi-heroic functions for sports fans, The considerable, and rising, popularity of mass sports spectacles today indicates that the decline of *traditional* sports heroes or widespread consensus about heroes has not meant the death of heroes or heroic functions, fans probably will search elsewhere for heroes who can provide them with vicarious fulfillment of their dreams or a temporary escape from the pressures of striving for them. As society becomes more complex and the mass media become more critical or demanding of heroes, this search is likely to become more confusing and less satisfying.

## F.A.N.S. as a Social Movement

In view of the self-interested actions of owners, organizers, and athletes in the most popular of today's big money sports, the ability of these sports and their stars to maintain or enhance their hold on fans might seem curious. However, it appears that fans generally have ignored or glossed over the distractions and abuses of their loyalty and support. There was one prominent effort recently to organize fans as a national movement to protect their rights as consumers. The fate of this effort revealed the tolerance or apathy of sports fans—or the deeper symbolic meaning of sports spectacles and their "heroes" in fans' lives.

In the summer of 1977, consumer advocate Ralph Nader initiated a campaign to defend the rights of sports fans. The resulting consumer movement was called F.A.N.S.—Fight to Advance the Nation's Sports."[46] Led by Nader and executive director Peter Gruenstein, F.A.N.S. tried to draw attention to and rectify a number of perceived abuses of fans' rights stemming from the commercialization and "corporatizing" of spectator sports. They proposed a "bill of rights" for fans that focused on matters such as their lack of representation in the governance of the sports they watch and pay to see; the limited public information about the operation of professional and amateur spectator sports; the unreasonably high ticket prices; the expensive and poorly prepared food sold at sports stadiums; the monopolistic and special tax privileges enjoyed by sports franchise owners; and the limited concern about spectators' interests shown by those who televise sports events.

Despite national publicity and a tour of the talk show circuit by Gruenstein, F.A.N.S. aroused little interest among fans and died about a year after it was formed. In promoting his organization, Greunstein has said, "We're in the Stone Age of consumerism in sports... There's little recognition of fans as consumers and little understanding of the business of sports."[47] The outcome of F.A.N.S. suggests that fans do not view themselves as consumers and are not interested in plunging themselves into a movement that would politicize their sports participation and further remove their sports world from the fantasyland that provides them with much-valued escape or enjoyment. They might complain about indigestible and overpriced hot dogs, greedy owners and athletes, annoying holdouts and strikes, and expensive tickets. However, as long as the rewards of watching sports compensate for the distractions, fans are likely to continue to ignore efforts to defend their rights.

# Leisure Players

## From Play to Sport: From Fun to Obsession

Sports arenas packed with spectators and tens of millions of televisions regularly tuned to sports events have led to concern about *spectatoritis,* which implies that people watch sports instead of playing at them. However, sports spectatorship has not grown at the expense of active participation; active participation has grown along with spectatorship in this century.[48] During the past decade, there seemed to be considerably more attention focused on the boom in *active* leisure participation in sports and physical recreation than on spectators or spectatoritis.[49]

Many of the physical activities that enjoyed a burst of new interest in the past decade lacked the competitiveness or organization of sport. These activities were pursued to reduce waistlines, enlarge muscles, relax minds, and present challenges. In being more playlike than sportlike, the pleasure in these activities came from doing them rather than from winning. In recreational forms of such popular activities as jogging, alpine and Nordic skiing, hang gliding, backpacking, rock climbing, surfing, roller skating, swimming, water skiing, snowmobiling, sailing, white water boating, bicycling, orienteering, and the Oriental martial arts, there is no winning other that your own improvement or mastering the activity.

When people genuinely play at physical activity without thinking of external constraints, pressures, prizes, or of the need to win, playing can be physically refreshing, mentally relaxing, and fun. However, when the elements of organization, regulation, competitiveness, external reward, and winning begin to slip into leisure playing, it escalates to a higher level of seriousness that may transform the play into sport and the fun into an obsession.

A Gallup poll conducted in 1978 found that nearly half (47%) of all Amricans participated in physical exercise on a daily basis. Although the strenuousness of these daily exercise habits undoubtedly varied a great deal, it is significant that the percentage of daily exercisers in 1978 was double the percentage in 1961.[50] At the beginning of the 1960s, the physical fitness of the American population was poor enough to cause President-elect Kennedy to write an article for *Sports Illustrated* about the "soft American."[51]

The recent boom in physical activity should have allayed a substantial amount of the earlier concern about the physical deterioration of Americans. However, the transformation of casual or playlike leisure-time physical activities into intensely serious sports may be robbing these activities of many of the qualities that originally motivated participation in them. The evolution of joggers into serious distance runners is a popular phenomenon of the past decade that illustrates the nature and implications of this transformation.

The explosion in interest in jogging and running can be seen in the growth in circulation of *Runners World,* the major magazine read by running enthusiasts. In 1966, it began as a small newsletter published by Bob Anderson. By July 1978, the newsletter had become a smartly designed, full color magazine with a national circulation of 250,000. In May 1980, circulation was up to 475,000 per month. In addition, in its first year in print in 1977, Jim Fixx's *The Complete Book of Running* sold 400,000 copies[52]

Interest in serious distance running has grown to the point where the most prestigious marathons in places such as Boston, New York, and Honolulu attract thousands of runners who want to challenge their 26 mile 385 yard courses. In 1980, Boston had to impose qualifying standards to restrict participation to "serious" runners. Men under 40 had to have finished a marathon in the previous year in an AAU-accepted time of less than 2 hours and 50 minutes. Men over 40 neded a time better than 3:10, and women needed a best time of at least 3:20. These qualifying standards restricted the 1980 Boston Marathon participants to approximately 6000. Though this event was well-established as the premier American marathon in the early 1970s, it then drew only a few hundred entrants who had no qualifying standards to meet, and it was run in a relatively casual and unstructured manner[53]

Relatively few people who jog or run compete even in one of the small-scale marathons in their local area. However, a large number compete at least occasionally in organized races of more modest lengths. Many of these runners view their leisure involvement in running as a serious commitment. However, these people did not step into running shoes and immediately become serious competitors. According to Jeffery Nash, those who become serious competitive distance runners may go through distinct stages of socialization in which their identity changes as they become more serious about running[54]

In Nash's conceptual framework, the establishment of a self-identity as a serious competitive runner often begins with being a casual, part-time jogger. Joggers differ from runners more in terms of their commitment than their speed or pace. Their reasons for jogging are likely to include the desire for better health, a longer life, relaxation, a sense of freedom from the mundane, and a greater awareness of their physical capabilities. Weight control may be the most common reason people begin to jog. Joggers may have a sporadic schedule of participation, and they make no special effort to rearrange their lives to accommodate jogging. In Nash's words, "Joggers say that they are not so much concerned with running per se as with exercise or something to be gained *from* running." Thus, jogging is seen as a means to an end, and joggers are not motivated by the intrinsic pleasure of the physical activity itself. Jogging is not an important aspect of a person's sense of who he or she is or what is important to the person.

When joggers trade in their tennis shoes or basketball sneakers for track shoes and invest in clothing designed for runners, they may be turned into what Nash has called a "regular runner' Many joggers do not go through this transition, and for those who remain joggers, their playing at this activity will remain instrumentally motivated, casual, and part-time. Those who become regular runners will become more serious about their commitment to running and begin to associate part of their identity with running. They are identifiable not only by their attire, but also by their regular schedule of running, which may require some rearrangement of their daily routines. They may share similar kinds of motives for running with joggers, but regular runners place much more emphasis on these motives than casual joggers. Regular runners also may begin to appreciate the intrinsic value of running.

Since running usually is a solitary activity, regular runners might occasionally participate in organized "Fun Runs" for companionship. These Fun Runs might stimulate an interest in entering races. Regular runners initially may enter races for social reasons, to satisfy their curiosity, or merely to have fun, but this involvement in organized competition could mark the beginning of their transformation into serious competitive distance runners.

Though they still are leisure-time "players" in the sense we defined this term earlier in this chapter, serious competitive distance runners are intensely devoted to running and rearrange their lives to accommodate their increasingly demanding schedules of training and competition. They see intrinsic or even spiritual meaning in their running, but they also are driven by a need to improve their performance and win. Most significantly, from Nash's perspective, those who have reached the level of commitment to running attained by serious distance runners tend to express their self-identity through their running. They are the most completely outfitted in running gear and related merchandise such as dog repellant, belt radios, and timers, and they are the most enthusiastic readers of publications for runners. For the most committed of these leisure-time runners, running is likely to have become their central life focus. Though they may have responsible jobs and families, even these things may become secondary to training and competing in running. They develop sophisticated and lengthy training routines that may cover over 100 miles and many hours each week; they require special diets; they look for regular opportunities to compete in races; and their interaction with others often is influenced by their interest in running.

Noted doctor-runner George Sheehan, who has lectured and written extensively about the practical and spiritual benefits of running, has defined what it means to have a self-identity as a runner:[55]

> I am a runner. Years ago that statement would have meant little more to me than an accidental choice of sport, a leisure-time activity selected for reasons as superficial as the activity itself.

> Now I know better, The runner... runs because he has to. Because in being a runner, in moving through pain and fatigue and suffering, in imposing stress upon stress, in eliminating all but the necessities of life, he is fulfilling himself and becoming the person he is.

For Dr. Sheehan, running became "a self-renewing complusion," but it was a compulsion he enjoyed. The more he ran, the more he wanted to run. Though he enjoyed the competitive challenge of races, the hour he reserved for running each day was a time of play, personal rediscovery, and joy. For many, though, their exercise or sports compulsion becomes an addiction.

Addiction to physical exercise has been called a "positive addiction" in contrast to "negative addictions" to substances such as alcohol and other drugs[56] Positive addictions are supposed to be psychologically and physiologically supportive. Running, which has been called the "heroin of all the positive addiction activities," is said to produce the sense of euphoria or "high" that is associated with some negatively addicting, mind-altering drugs when it is pursued strenuously for extended periods of time[57] However, as in the case of negative addictions, addictions to running and other physical activities imply a growing psychological and physiological dependency. When addicted players try to reduce their involvement, they may experience withdrawl symptoms ranging from feelings of irritability to tension, guilt, anxiety, and bloatedness[58]

Ironically, the addictive commitment of leisure players to their physical activity often is the outgrowth of their initial desire to improve their health or sense of well-being or merely to have fun. However, the compulsive need for more miles or hours of training can lead to overtraining and risks of injury and impaired health. In addition, highly dedicated leisure players may find that they are sacrificing their family and marital partner to pursue their leisure obsession. For example, a recent study by James Robbins and Paul Joseph showed that running commitment was associated with marital disagreements, which were caused or exacerbated by the runner's commitment[59]

The extent or degree of negative addiction among leisure participants in sport should not be exaggerated; and even if a significant number of highly committed players are addicted to their leisure activity, their addiction should not literally be equated with heroin addiction. There *are* risks of excessive or addictive commitment to playing at physical activity, just as there are risks from excess in other types of activity. Both the benefits and risks of a serious leisure commitment to running or other physical activities must be considered to understand how casual playing at these activities turns into serious commitment and a transformed self-identity.

According to Robbins and Joseph's research, the occupational aspirations of committed runners do not seem to suffer from their reordering of life priorities to facilitate their running. Running may surpass the importance of work for these players, but it is not because work has become less important, rather running has become more gratifying.

Thus, serious playing may not diminish work or career goals, and it may provide renewal or relief from striving when players derive fun or a "high" from their leisure participation. However, when serious commitment involves a compulsion to win, the benefits of leisure sports may be offset by a reinforcement of frustrations, pressures, and anxieties players want to leave behind when they play at their leisure activities.

Participation in sports as leisure players necessarily involves competition, and the competitiveness and need to win in popular spectator sports and in American society in general often make it difficult not be become serious about winning. When players derive a large part of their identity from their leisure sports participation and see themselves as "athletes," and when competition for these players offers the chance for public recognition and other rewards, the need to win may become the dominant aspect of participation.

When 1960 Olmypic swimmer Lance Larson had a chance to compete in Masters swimming meets as a 41 year old dentist, he renewed his youthful commitment to his sport and found himslef bettering records he had achieved over twenty years earlier[60] For him and the other former champions who were attracted to the big regional and national competitions, the meets meant more than the official Masters' ethos that stressed physical fitness, recreation, and camaraderie. In Larson's words: "I think it's the competition that motivates me more than anything else. . . I enjoy winning. Probably also the recognition that goes along with it. It's sort of like being on stage again, sort of an ego trip." Another Masters participant, 1956 Olympian Carin Cone Vanderbush, expressed her feelings about winning even more strongly when she said, "We all want to succeed. I don't like to come in second to anyone, not even a man."

For serious players who need to win in leisure sports, having a successful career or a happy marriage and family life can take some of the sting out of their "playing." For those serious players without career success or a supportive family, the failure to satisfy a compulsion to win can be doubly frustrating. Thus, a few find victory and success as players in the highly competitive realms of leisure sports. However, the chance for refreshment, fulfillment, or escape for most players is likely to come from resisting inner, peer, and commercial pressures to transform their playing into an addiction and their fun into a compulsion to win. When players lack success or contentment in other parts of their lives, they may be especially vulnerable to these pressures. If they become addicted or compulsive, fulfillment, success, and contentment are likely to be as elusive or fleeting in their leisure as it is in the rest of their lives.

# Social Class Variations in Player Preferences

## Mass Sports Participation

The increasing affluence of the average American and the proliferation of public recreational facilities after World War II have combined to produce an increasing "democratization" of leisure sports opportunities in the United States.[61] Sports such as tennis, golf, and swimming, which once were restricted to the affluent members of socially exclusive private clubs, now are available to less affluent members of American society through community recreational facilities and programs. However, despite the leveling of social class distinctions in opportunities to play at physical recreation and sports, patterns of active leisure sports participation still are marked by social class differences.

The general kinds of social class differences in spectator preferences described earlier in this chapter tend to reappear in patterns of active participation in sports. In contrast to the more affluent classes, however, working and lower class Americans frequently find that the sports they like to watch are not readily accessible to them as players. Equipment and private facilities may be too expensive. Community recreational facilities may be crowded or unavailable. A rigid work schedule or the need to have a second job could make it difficult or impossible to find enough leisure time for regular active participation. For these reasons, leagues organized by community recreation departments, churches, local businesses, unions, and employers for sports such as bowling, basketball, volleyball, and softball often are popular with the working class.[62] Without these opportunities, active leisure sports participation is likely to be very limited for the less affluent members of the working class and in particular, the poor and unemployed.

Along with the economic and practical reasons that make sponsored league competition popular with the masses, there seem to be symbolic reasons for the mass appeal of certain kinds of leisure sports. Sports such as weightlifting, arm wrestling, boxing, wrestling, the martial arts, drag racing, auto racing, motorcycle racing, and snowmobile racing, which are popular with working and lower class spectators, also tend to attract interest in *active* leisure participation among the members of these classes. For the members of these classes who can afford the money or time to participate actively in these kinds of sports, the symbolic meaning and functions of this leisure sports participation may be the same as the meaning and functions of watching these sports for people of their status in American society. Sports symbolizing strength, physical dominance, and power provide the masses with a chance to play at roles in which they can be what their jobs or society do not allow them to be. They can rise above their status as a cog in an assembly line or a number in an unemployment line; they can be assertive and dominant instead of subordinate; and they can temporarily forget about being deprived of many of the "good things" that are supposed to be available to all who try hard enough for them in American society.

For the achievers and winners in the "power" sports, the rewards of playing may be sweet and satisfying compensation for indignities, frustrations, or deprivations experienced elsewhere in their lives. For all those players—and spectators—from the lower echelons of society who find in sport rewards that have eluded them elsewhere in their lives, leisure sports particiption may be a major source of pleasure or fulfillment. In the eyes of some sports observers, the enjoyment and real or vicarious fulfillment derived from leisure sports participation by the masses should not be viewed in positive terms. According to Marxist sports critic Paul Hoch, the functioning of sport in this manner ultimately serves the interests of the dominant or ruling class and works against the interests of the less privileged. Taking off from Karl Marx, he argued that sport had replaced religion as the "opiate of the masses" in modern capitalist societies[63] By this, he meant that sport provided a temporary "high" or distraction for the masses and distorted their perspective by inducing them to look for joy and fulfillment through "false" channels. Thus, for Hoch, leisure sports participation was not simply a welcome relief or escape for the masses. Instead, he saw it as a "tool of exploitation" by the ruling class, who encouraged mass sports participation as a way of defusing, redirecting, or muting mass alienation or discontent that might have been directed against the power structure and the established order of society that gave the ruling class its privilege and authority.

There are many who would challenge the argument that a ruling class in American society creates and manipulates leisure sports opportunities for the masses to pacify them and distract them from their "real" class interests of revolution and social change. It is true that employers organize recreational programs for their workers. However, it is unlikely that they are acting as part of a capitalist class conspiracy against workers or that they expect or are able to drain all their workers' job dissatisfaction or alienation through these programs. In addition, there is a danger that unhappy workers will become unhappier if they experience further frustration and failure as leisure sports players. Evidence cited earlier about violence and sport also suggests that the leisure involvement of the masses in sports with aggression and the chance for violence might encourage them to be *more* surly, disruptive, or destructive.

Watching and playing at sports may not be a substitute for the American Dream for the masses. However, many of the choices of sports by the masses seem to reflect a desire for vicarious power, success, and escape as well as entertainment. To the extent that the masses actually perceive leisure sports participation as a means of relief, release, escape, or fulfillment, it may function as the symbolic fantasyland described earlier in this chapter. *In this sense,* watching and playing at sports may be an opiate of the masses after all. Leisure sports participation by the masses may not be as consciously exploited or manipulated by dominant class interests as Hoch asserted; nevertheless, watching and playing at sports may be significant ways that the masses adapt to their exclusion from the American Dream. In addition, by providing real or vicarious opportunities to pursue competitive success and express dominant societal values and modes of striving, leisure sports participation may help to reinforce mass acceptance of the American Dream that they have been denied.

## Elite Sports Participation

The sports with special appeal to upwardly mobile and successful Americans as leisure players probably are most clearly distinguished from leisure sports with mass appeal by their lack of physical contact. The white collar world is characterized by mental and physical discipline, and the leisure sports choices of upper-income groups tend to have this character. In addition, the striving and successful in American society tend to prefer leisure athletic activities that can be pursued on an individual basis rather than with teams; that involve precise, disciplined movements; and that are expensive or socially exclusive. Their leisure recreation may not be competitive, and it may not be very physically strenuous.[64] However, the recent popularity of competitive distance running and swimming with upper-income players indicates that the casual and noncompetitive motives of these players may change as they become more involved in their leisure pastimes. Along with running and swimming, the leisure activities with special appeal to the more affluent in American society include tennis and the other court games, golf, sailing, alpine and Nordic skiing, polo, yachting, bicycling, backpacking, hiking, and mountain climbing.

Unlike the masses, the upwardly mobile and successful in American society can readily find evidence of the American Dream in their jobs, careers, life styles, and position in society. Nevertheless, relief and escape may be on the minds of more privileged leisure players as well as working and lower class players. However, in the case of the more privileged, there is likely to be a desire for relief and escape from the pressures of a world in which they are making it or have already made it. If the strivers and achievers of the upper social strata begin to derive more enjoyment or satisfaction from their leisure activities than from their careers, they may find themselves becoming as serious and committed as players as they had been in their careers. If they become too serious or committed, they could become compulsive or addicted and lose the desire or chance for fun and satisfaction, which were their original reasons for playing.

In general, winning and losing are unlikely to be as important to upper-income as lower-income players. The contrast in perspectives between the more affluent is revealed in the comments of a young basketball player from the Bedford Stuyvesant area of Brooklyn who said, "When I play, I play to win, and I'll do almost anything to win. You got to recognize, I ain't winning anywhere else."[65] These comments may reflect the obsession with winning of a lower class youth looking at sports as his only ticket to success. However, the idea of being a loser in life may be shared by his elders who look at the leisure sports of their adulthood as their single chance to salvage some self-respect and recognition. For the upwardly mobile and successful who play at leisure sports, money, a rising or successful career, and a comfortable or extravagant life style still will be there whether they win or lose on the athletic field.

Relatively more important than winning, *per se,* for upper-income players is likely to be the demonstration of form, style, or "class." As in the case of spectator sports, active participation in leisure sports may be seen by upper-income and especially upwardly mobile players as an opportunity to garner status recognition and polish their image. Thus, they may pay special attention to sportsmanship, proper form in executing the skills and movements of their sports, and fashionable style in outfitting themselves for participation. Knowing the nuances of rules and observing them in competition, taking private lessons, using expensive equipment and clothing, and participating in exclusive clubs and events all can be seen as aspects of the conspicuous demonstration of status or "class" in leisure sports. The need to win and the desire to gain status recognition may come together for upper-income players at the higher levels of competition in their leisure sports, as in the case of Masters swimming.

Along with certifying the high social standing or class of their members, exclusive private clubs contribute to the persistence of social class differences in the larger society. In his study of golf and social inequality, James Davidson argued that private clubs help maintain the privileged status of their members in society in a variety of ways.[66] For example, their discriminatory admission policies often exclude the less affluent, nonwhite, and nonProtestant or nonChristian members of society, and they foster socioeconomic, racial, and religious homogeneity among club members. Frequent interaction in athletic and social activities within this closed circle of the club reinforces social prejudices about out-groups and reassures members of their own special merit in society. Clubs also increase the chances that offspring will marry into families of similar class status and that they will develop sports skills that will enable them to interact in club circles and with the high-born later in life. Many clubs also automatically transfer membership to the children of members if they fulfill residency and other similar requirements. Furthermore, clubs provide easy access to others in similar or functionally-related occupations, and they offer a casual setting for the transaction of business.

In addition to contributing to the perpetuation fo social differences between their members and others in society, exclusive private clubs perpetuate social differences between their own members—in particular, between men and women. Walter Zelman has noted that, "The American sports world has always been a predominantly male world. But it is less so among the rich and more so among the poor."[67] The sports in which women have been more accepted—such as tennis, golf, swimming, and skiing—traditionally have been sports of the elite and more affluent classes. Most lower-income women have been relatively unfamiliar with them, and have been unable to afford them. Their sports world has been a very narrow one, limited to a few sports such as bowling.

Even though women of the middle and upper classes have had more leisure sports opportunities than women of the working and lower classes, their opportunities in exclusive private clubs have tended to reflect and reaffirm the different and subordinate position they have traditionally occupied with respect to men in the larger society. For example, in the private golf clubs that Davidson studied, women played golf less frequently than men, had poorer tee times, usually did not play with men, were responsible for organizing children's activities at the club, and tended to be excluded from important economic and political decisions about the club's survival.

To the extent that private clubs remain socially and economically exclusive and limit access to certain sports and high-quality facilities to players with high status in society, they will be antithetical to the ideals of open and equal opportunity, which are supposed to be dominant values of American society and the institution of sport. In fact, the survival of exclusive private clubs mirrors the persistence of entrenched social class inequalities in American society as well as leisure sports. A rise in the general standard of living and an expansion of public recreational facilities have caused some leveling of social class distinctions in leisure sports participation during this century. However, the more affluent still have easier and better access to the physical recreation or sports they want to pursue. They do not have to fight the crowds wanting to use public facilities, and they often can avoid conflicts over access to recreational space that have pitted tennis players against each other, soccer players against football players, surfers against swimmers, racquetball players against handball players, cross country skiers against snowmobilers, fishermen against water skiers, and bicyclists, joggers, and roller skaters against each other in recent years.[68] Unlike the masses, the more affluent may be able to go where space and facilities are less crowded, purchase time in private facilities or join private clubs, or even buy their own facilities or space such as tennis courts, swimming pools, private beach rights, or land for riding horses, jogging, or cross country skiing. That is, by virtue of their privileged status, more affluent players are likely to enjoy the luxury of choice in what types of sports they play at and how, when, and where they play at them, which is not available to the masses.

# Fans, Players, and the American Dream: Catharsis, Therapy, or Frustration?

Striving for the American Dream, trying to hold on to it, and living without any chance to capture even a piece of it, all create life pressures, tensions, and desires that could lead to leisure participation in sport as a fan or player. For many of the fans and players in American society, their leisure sports world may be a symbolic refuge that has special meaning and functions beyond fun and entertainment. As a symbolic refuge, the sports world may help fans and players cope more effectively with life in the shadow of the American Dream. However, we have seen in this chapter that leisure sports participation may create pressures, tensions, frustrations, or other problems of its own for fans and players who expect or need more from it than casual fun or entertainment.

Psychiatrist Henry Kellerman has said that"... sports can be cathartic, but never therapeutic."[69] Kellerman was explicitly referring to fans, and he meant that being a fan allowed people to act out their frustrations and fantasies on a symbloic level but it did not help them achieve real solutions to their life problems and disappointments. After fans turn off the television or leave the stadium, their fantasy world begins to evaporate and the burens of reality again press in upon them. To the extent that spectator sports encourage fans to be passive participants in life and to respond to problems through escape, dreaming, or vicarious experiences, Kellerman may be right about the effect of watching sports on fans. However, if leisure sports participation can clear the mind or relieve the tensions that produce or exacerbate life's problems, it may have the capacity to be therapeutic as well as cathartic.

Active participation as a player seems more likely than passive participation as a spectator to have the dual capacity of catharsis and therapy. A regular run, swim, or workout at the gym or on the athletic field or a vacation spent hiking, white water canoeing, or sailing could provide the temporary escape needed to relieve tensions and put problems in a fruitful perspective so that resolving or coping with them will be easier. On the other hand, if players become preoccupied with their leisure pastime, develop an addiction to it, or become obsessed with self-improvement or winning they are likely to find "playing" much less relaxing and fun, and its effects on them may be more harmful than therapeutic. Thus, the capacity of leisure sports participation to provide catharsis and therapy or to create frustrations and problems of its own is likely to depend of the *type of involvement* (passive as a fan or active as a leisure player), the *motives for involvement* (better health, relaxation, fun, or more symbolic purposes such as vicarious release and fulfillment or status recognition), and the *level of seriousness and commitment*.

We have seen in this chapter that the social class of fans and players can have a significant influence on their sports preferences and opportunities and on what they expect to derive from their leisure sports participation, Research also has shown that the tendency to favor active participation over watching sports in adulthood is more likely in the upper than lower strata.[70] Active playing is likely to continue into the middle-aged years for the more affluent, and it may actually increase during these years for people who have "made it" in their careers and can afford more time and money for leisure. In contrast, active leisure participation of the masses drops off to an almost negligible level by middle age.

The tendencies for the economic and social elite to be active players rather than merely spectators and for the masses to be spectators reflect the different statuses and roles of the elite and masses in society. The strivers and achievers in American society might use their leisure time for increased physical and mental fitness; they might seek new thrills in skiing, sailing, or white water boating; they might seek solitude in jogging, backpacking, or Nordic skiing; they might seek the challenge or temporary escape of a vigorous competitive game of handball, racquetball, or tennis; or they might seek a higher level of self-awareness in leisure activities that test their physical and mental limits such as distance running or swimming, rock climbing, and mountaineering.

The main attraction of sport for the masses may be the vicarious or fantasy experiences it provides for them in their role as fans. As a fantasyland, the mass sports spectacle may distract spectators from their deprivations and frustrations and help them tolerate or adjust to their status in society. The violence of mass sports spectacles also might encourage spectators to express their own hostility. In either case, though, we see the capacity of mass sports spectacles to act on a symbolic level to influence those who watch them. From the perspective of American society in general, these spectacles of sport and their heroes or quasi-heroes have their most significant impact when they offer escape and when they keep alive the dominant values of an American Dream that is likely to be an elusive or fleeting reality in the lives of most spectators.

# *Footnotes*

[1]John Papanek (ed.), "Raiders of the lost season," *Sports Illustrated,* "Scorecard" section (August 3, 1981).

[2]Ray Kennedy and Nancy Williamson, "Money in sports," *Sports Illustrated* (July 31, 1978). Part III of a three-part series.

[3]Reported in Papanek, "Raiders of the lost season."

[4]Quoted in Kennedy and Williamson, "Money in sports," Part III, p. 50.

[5]Stephen K. Figler, *Sport and Play in American Life* (Philadelphia: Saunders, 1981), p. 299.

[6]These estimates of television audiences were reported in John W. Loy, Barry D. McPherson, and Gerald Kenyon, *Sport and Social Systems* (Reading, Mass.: Addison-

Wesley, 1978), p. 311. These authors also present estimates of the extent of other forms of sports consumption by fans.

[7]In this chapter, "sport" may refer to "sportlike" activities such as physical recreation and athletic games when used in relation to leisure players.

[8]The functioning of sport as a "symbolic refuge" also is discussed by Richard Lipsky in "the athleticization of politics: the political implications of sports symbolism," *Journal of Sport and Social Issues,* 3 (Fall/Winter 1979): 28-37, and in *How We Play The Game: Why Sports Dominate American Life* (Boston: Beacon Press, 1981); and by Howard L. Nixon II, "Idealized functions of sport: religious and political socialization through sport," *Journal of Sport and Social Issues,* 6 (Spring/Summer 1982): 1-11.

[9]Kay Lehman Schlozman and Sidney Verba, *Injury to Insult* (Cambridge: Harvard University Press, 1979).

[10]Lipsky, *How We Play The Game,* p. 123.

[11]Christopher Lasch, *The Culture of Narcissism* (New York: Warner, 1979).

[12]Carin Rubinstein, "Money &," *Psychology Today* (May 1981). This survey generated 20,000 responses to the questionnaire printed in the December 1980 issue of the magazine. The survey uncovered two significant clusters of beliefs about the elements that were very important in the pursuit of success (which was interpreted as "making a lot of money"). In the dominant cluster were the following elements (ranked in order of their relative importance): ambition; hard work; brains and talent; education; and patience and frugality. In the other cluster, which reflected cynicism rather than faith concerning the American Dream, were the following elements (ranked according to their relative importance): risk taking; connections; luck; greed; and dishonesty. The dominance of the former cluster indicates that the predominantly middle class readers of *Psychology Today* were more likely to have faith in the American Dream than to be cynical about it.

[13]See Karen Horney, *The Neurotic Personality of Our Time* (New York: Norton, 1937) and *Neurosis and Human Growth* (New York: Norton, 1950). Lipsky, in *How We Play The Game,* cites Horney's ideas in his fifth chapter and comments on them in a footnote (p. 166, #123).

[14]Lasch, *The Culture of Narcissism,* p. 197.

[15]The major source for the discussion in this section was Nicholas Petryszak, "Spectator sports as an aspect of popular culture—an historical view," *Journal of Sport Behavior,* 1 (February 1978): 14-27. Petryszak provides a more extensive analysis of the historical development of spectator sports than we are presenting in this section.

[16]Petryszak, "Spectator sports as an aspect of popular culture . . . ," pp. 18-19.

[17]Geoffrey Godbey and John Robinson, "The American sports fan: 'spectatoritis' revisited," *Review of Sport & Leisure,* 4 (Summer 1979): 1-11.

[18]John Rickards Betts, *America's Sporting Heritage 1850-1950* (Reading, Mass.: Addison-Wesley, 1974), p. 250. Betts presents a detailed historical account of the growth of American sport between 1850 and 1950.

[19]Michael Real, "Super Bowl: mythic spectacle," *Journal of Communication,* 25 (Winter 1975): 31-43.

[20]Petryszak, "Spectator sports as an aspect of popular culture . . . ," pp. 25-26.

[21]See David L. Altheide and Robert P. Snow, "Sports versus the mass media," *Urban Life,* 7 (July 1978): 189-204.

[22]See William Oscar Johnson's two-part series in *Sports Illustrated* (August 10, 17, 1981) on "The TV revolution" for a more extensive treatment of the nature and implications of cable and satellite television systems on televised sports.

[23]Spence and Sauter were quoted in Johnson, "The TV revolution," Part I, p. 62.

[24]Ira Horowitz, "Sports broadcasting." In *Government and The Sports Business,* ed. by Roger G. Noll (Washington, D.C.: The Brookings Institutions 1974), p. 321.

[25]Paul Comisky, jennings Bryant, and Dolf Zillman, "Commentary as a substitute for action,"*Journal of Communication,* 27 (1977): 150-153.

[26]Susan Birrell and John W. Loy, Jr., "Media sport: hot and cool," *International Review of Sport Sociology,* 14/1 (1979): 5-19, p. 13.

[27]See, e.g., D. Stanley Eitzen and George H. Sage, *Sociology of American Sport* (Dubuque, Iowa: Wm. C. Brown, 1978), ch. 8, on "Sport, social stratification, and social mobility;" and Wilbert M. Leonard II, *A Sociological Perspective of Sport* (Minneapolis: Burgess, 1980), ch. 7, on "Sport and social stratification." These chapters in Eitzen and Sage and in Leonard were the major sources for the discussions of mass and elite spectator sports preferences presented here.

[28]Barry D. McPherson, "Sports consumption and the economics of consumerism." In *Sport and Social Order,* ed. by Donald W. Ball and John W. Loy (Reading, Mass.: Addison-Wesley, 1975).

[29]Eitzen and Sage, *Sociology of American Sport,* p. 216.

[30]*Ibid.*

[31]Thorstein Veblen, *Theory of the Leisure Class* (New York: Macmillan, 1899)

[32]Howard L. Nixon II, *Sport and Social Organization* (Indianapolis: Bobbs-Merrill, 1976), pp. 34-35.

[33]Quoted in Wells Twombly, "Life in football's half-Astrodome," *San Francisco Sunday Examiner & Chronicle* (January 2, 1972), p. 4C. Cited in Eitzen and Sage, *Sociology of American Sport,* p. 218.

[34]See the *Arena Review,* 5 (February 1981), for an entire issue devoted to varied perspectives on "violence in sport." The articles in this issue look at violence in sport from legal, legislative, historical, psychiatric, psychological, and sociological viewpoints.

[35]See Nixon, *Sport and Social Organization,* pp. 25-27, for a discussion of collective violence by fans, which served as a basis for some of the ideas expressed here.

[36]See Leonard, *A Sociological Perspective of Sport,* ch. 13, and Figler, *Sport and Play in American Life,* ch. 7, for additional examples and analyses of fan violence and violence in general, in sports.

[37]See, e.g., Ian Taylor, "Soccer consciousness and soccer hooliganism." In *Images of Deviance,* ed. by Stanley Cohen (Middlesex, England: Penguin, 1971), and "'Football mad': a speculative sociology of football hooliganism." In *Sport: Readings From a Scoiological Perspective,* ed. by Eric Dunning (Toronto: University of Toronto Press, 1972).

[38]Cameron K. Dewar, "Specatator fights at professional baseball games," *Review of Sport & Leisure,* 4 (Summer 1979): 12-25.

[39]See Michael D. Smith, "Sport and collective violence." In *Sport and Social Order,* ed. by Donald W. Ball and John W. Loy (Reading, Mass.: Addison-Wesley, 1975), for a more extensive and systematic treatment of the possible reasons and meanings for collective violence in sport.

[40]See, e.g., Eitzen and Sage, *Sociology of American Sport,* pp. 69-71, for a concise discussion of this issue; and Jay J. Coakley, *Sport in Society: issues and controversies* (St. Louis: C.V. Mosby, 1978), ch. 4, for a lengthier treatment.

[41]A recent study by Robert L. Arms, Gordon W. Russell, and Mark L. Sandilands, "Effects on the hostility of spectators of viewing aggressive sports," *Social Psychology Quarterly,* 42 (1979): 275-279, is an example of the research supporting this anticatharsis argument.

[42]Michael D. Smith, "Precipitants of crowd violence," *Sociological Inquiry,* 48 (1978): 121-131.

[43]Lipsky, *How We Play The Game,* p. 117.

[44]Findings of the *Sports Illustrated* survey reported in Kennedy and Williamson, "Money in sports," Part III.

[45]Richard Crepeau, "Sport, heroes and myth," *Journal of Sport and Social Issues,* 4 (Fall/Winter 1980): 23-31, p. 30.

[46]See Ralph Nader and Peter Gruenstein, "Blessed are the fans, for they shall inherit $12 bleacher seats, indigestible hot dogs, $2 bottles of beer and 100 overpaid superstars," *Playboy* (Spring 1978). See also brief accounts of this movement in Figler, *Sport and Play in American Life,* pp. 172-173, and in Leonard, *A Sociological Perspective of Sport,* pp. 301-303.

[47]Quoted in Kennedy and Williamson, "Money in sports," Part III, p. 41.

[48]Thomas M. Kando, *Leisure and Popular Culture in Transition* (St. Louis: C.V. Mosby, 1975), p. 212.

[49]See Figler's chapter on "Trends and the future of play, sport, and athletics" in *Sport and Play in American Life* for an additional discussion of a number of the important ideas in this section.

[50]L. Jennings, "Future fun, tomorrow's sports and games," *The Futurist,* (December 1979): 417-431.

[51]This article appeared in *Sports Illustrated* on December 26, 1960.

[52]These figures were cited by Figler, in *Sport and Play in American Life,* in his discussion of "The marathon metamorphosis," p. 301.

[53]*Ibid.*

[54]Jeffrey E. Nash, "The short and the long of it: legitimizing motives for running." In *Sociology: A Descriptive Approach,* ed. by Jeffrey E. Nash and James P. Spradley (Chicago: Rand McNally, 1976).

[55]Dr. George A. Sheehan, "On the run but in no hurry," p. 82. First of two excerpts from his book *Running and Being* (New York: Simon & Schuster, 1978) that appeared in *Sports Illustrated* (April 17, 24, 1978).

[56]See, e.g., William Glasser, *Positive Addiction* (New York: Harper and Row, 1976); William P. Morgan, "The mind of the marathoner," *Psychology Today* (April 1978); and Michael L. Sachs and David Pargman, "Running addiction: a depth interview examination," *Journal of Sport Behavior,* 2 (August 1979): 143-155.

[57]William Glasser, "The positive addiction equipment," *Starting Line* (March 1978). Cited in Sachs and Pargman, "Running addiction . . . ," p. 146.

[58]Sachs and Pargman, "Running addiction . . ." See also William P. Morgan, "Running into addiction," *The Runner,* 1 (1979): 73-76, and "Negative addiction in runners," *The Physician and Sports Medicine,* 7 (1979): 57-70.

[59]James M. Robbins and Paul Joseph, "Commitment to running: implications for the family and work," *Sociological Symposium,* 30 (Spring 1980): 87-108.

[60]Sol Stern, "At 41, Lance Larson swims faster than when he was 18 and setting U.S. records," *Sports Illustrated* (July 27, 1981).

[61]Nixon, *Sport and Social Organization,* pp. 35-36.

[62]Eitzen and Sage, *Sociology of American Sport,* p. 211.

[63]Paul Hoch, *Rip Off The Big Game* (New York: Anchor Books, 1972). Marx had argued that *religion* was the opiate of the masses in capitalist societies because it diverted the attention of the poor and oppressed from their worldly deprivation and oppression and focused it instead on the rewards of the after-life. In having this narcotic effect of dulling the senses and providng a false sense of well-being, religion was assumed to defuse or redirect revolutionary feelings that might have been directed toward the dominant capitalist class and the system of inequalities it maintained. See Thomas W. Martin and Kenneth J. Berry, "Competitive sport in post-industrial society: the case of the motocross racer," *Journal of Popular Culture,* 8 (Summer 1974): 107-120, for an interesting analysis of the functioning of motocross racing as an opiate or mechanism of vicarious relief and satisfaction for its otherwise alienated working class male participants.

[64]Walter A. Zelman, "The sports people play," *Parks and Recreation Magazine,* 11 (February 1976): 27-39. Reprinted in *Sport and American Society: Selected Readings,* ed. by George H. Sage (Reading, Mass.: Addison-Wesley, 1980), 3rd. ed.

[65]Quoted by Zelman, "The sports people play," in *Sport and American Society . . . ,* p. 233.

[66]James D. Davidson, "Social differentiation and sports participation: the case of golf," *Journal of Sport Behavior,* 2 (November 1979): 171-210.

[67]Zelman, "The sports people play," in *Sport and American Society . . . ,* p. 235.

[68]Jay J. Coakley, in "Participation trends in physical activity and sport: implications for the sociology of sport," *Review of Sport & Leisure,* 4 (Winter 1979): 30-47, has explored possible implications and policies for leisure participation in sport and physical recreation tied to excessive demands for limited recreational space and facilities.

[69]Quoted in Lipsky, *How We Play The Game,* p. 127.

[70]See, e.g., Harold M. Hodges, *Social Stratification* (Cambridge, Mass.: Schenkman, 1964), p. 166; Zelman, "The sports people play;" Leonard, *A Sociological Perspective of Sport,* pp. 146-147.

# 7

# Sport and the American Dream: Assessment and Conclusions

SPORT AND THE AMERICAN DREAM

# Sport and Dominant American Values

There is a pervasive syndrome of intense and, at times, desperate or neurotic, competitive striving in American society. It is a syndrome that has developed from a belief in the American Dream and the associated desire *or need* to be—or at least appear to be—*successful*. Although success may have as many specific interpretations as there are social and cultural groups in American society, it usually means being rich, famous, or powerful at some level of the society. It also means being able to look down on others who have been outperformed, worn down, outclassed, or surpassed in some way in the race to succeed.

Competitive striving, achievement, mobility, and success are major elements of the dominant American Dream ideology in American society. A former athletic director at the University of Southern California indicated the relevance of sport to the American Dream when he said, "Athletes develop dedication and a desire to excel in competition, and a realization that success requires hard work ..."[1] In fact, sport can be seen as part of the basic institutional fabric of American society, and its dominant ideology can be seen as a mirror of dominant value themes in the larger society. When sport is experienced as a mass spectacle, it may become a kind of fantasyland in which major societal values and myths are given dramatic emphasis or attain special symbolic significance. When it is seen in idealized or romanticized terms, sport may appear to symbolize widespread and equal opportunity to climb the ladder of success through hard work and competitive achievement. That is, it may appear to be a symbolic embodiment of the promise of the American Dream.

# Symbolic Emphases and Functions of Sport in American Society

Those who are serious about their sports involvement—either as fans or as more active participants—can find in sport a reaffirmation of central values, aspirations, and myths of the larger society that can give meaning and direction to their own lives. Sport may not necessarily be fun for those who work at it seriously. In fact, the spontaneity and freedom associated with fun are found more often in the realms of play, recreation, and games than in sports. However, for serious sports participants, sport is likely to have a deeper meaning or purpose than the chance to have fun.

In functioning as a fantasyland that romanticizes the ideals of the

American Dream, the sports world at its various levels keeps alive hopes of success for the striving or ambitious, provides relief from the pressures of striving for fans, and helps to sustain faith in the American Dream among the striving *and* those with little chance to succeed. Those who rise above their humble social origins to succeed in sport seem to represent dramatic proof of the opportunities for mobility and success open to all in American sport and society. These "rags-to-riches" stories also seem to be a clear refutation of the cynics and critics who point to contradictions between the ideology of the American Dream and the realities of a corporate, class society and of discrimination in America.

By mirroring or reinforcing the American Dream, sport legitimizes competitive striving while it also provides the less successful with a continuing source of hope or meaning within the dominant value system and structure of American society. By attributing failure to lack of effort or other deficiencies of personal character, coaches and others with influence in sport may cause individuals to blame themselves for failure that actually may stem more from biases or obstacles in the social system. By encouraging the untalented to persevere in their quest to succeed, those who control and promote sport may be nurturing misguided or unrealistic hopes. By placing an exaggerated emphasis on winning, the coaches, promoters, and image-makers of sport may be encouraging a quest for success that goes beyond the rules, the law, or the limits of morality. The rewards of victory or success may become more important than the process or means of striving for them, which could lead to a perversion of the dominant American sports creed and the idealized pursuit of the American Dream. In fact, at all levels of sport that were examined in this book, the greater emphasis on winning and success associated with more professionalization and commercialization tended to produce a greater temptation to win "by any means" or to cheat. Thus, the pressure to strive for victory and the American Dream in sport may lead to a perversion of the process of achievement for the sake of trying to assure victory and success. This intense competitive striving in sport is a mirror of the drive to succeed elsewhere in American society.

# *Sport and Social Control*

To suggest that sport reflects or reaffirms the dominant ideology of society or offers an escape from pressures or disappointments created by that ideology does not necessarily imply that sport is deliberately and skillfully manipulated by a dominant or ruling class to serve its class interests. Sport may mirror and reinforce values and beliefs that legitimize the status, privileges, and power of the successful. However, it does not necessarily induce a "false consciousness" about the harsh realities of life in American society or mindless acceptance of subordinate status, setbacks, or failure in the pursuit of the American Dream.

Frank Parkin has suggested that an "aspirational" perspective accepts the existence of class and status hierarchies, but assumes there will be opportunities for the talented and industrious to climb the hierarchies, whereas a "deferential" perspective accepts the class system as fixed and unchanging? The acceptance of the American Dream induced by sport may be more voluntary and aspirational than mindless, manipulated, and deferential because sport may make the pressures of striving and the frustrations of setbacks and failure seem a natural and just part of life in an "affluent society."

It may be argued that sport lacks the social influence of the more central societal institutions. It also may be argued that the reflection and reinforcement of status inequalities and the inducement of aspirational perspectives by sport are not really necessary to preserve the social order. Nevertheless, Loy, McPherson, and Kenyon have proposed in conjunction with these arguments that sport has significance on a symbolic level in dramatizing and ritualizing the problematics of achieving respectability in an American society obsessed with status rank, advancement, and success[3] It captures a number of apparent contradictions and potential sources of tension in American society—such as individualism and group loyalty, cooperation and competition, equality of opportunity and inequality of rank and rewards, winning and losing, and success and failure; and it makes them seem to fit together. In dramatically emphasizing these pervasive and opposing themes as part of an apparently coherent cultural system, sport enables its followers to understand and adjust to life in American society. In offering a simplified or romanticized picture of life in America, sport also may become a world in which idealized societal values seem more compelling and provide relatively unambiguous meaning and direction. Thus, in being a symbolic refuge, sport may *subtly* exert social control and influence personal identities, aspirations, and adjustment.

# Television and the Popular Appeal of Sport

The capacity of sport to influence fans, athletes, and other participants depends on its popular appeal. Sport is likely to have special popular appear as long as it symbolizes the promise of the American Dream and offers a chance to escape into a dreamland in which idealized values, images, and heroes seem to predominate. Television has played a key role in recent years in perpetuating an idealized image of mass sports by producing them as "mythic spectacles." Ironically, though, television has been a major force behind the commercial boom in sports in recent years that has transformed the major sports into businesses and their athletes into businessmen with little in common with the idealized and romanticized images that underlie the mass appeal of these sports.

In fact, television executives are likely to promote sports in whatever form they think appeals to their viewers who can buy their advertisers' products. As businessmen themselves, television executives are committed less to the integrity and survival of sports for their own sake than to the use of sports to make money for the corporations that employ them[4] Television could diminish the popular appeal of the sports it has made popular and rich by giving the public too much of them. A decline in television investment would quickly follow this drop in popularity, as TV executives look elsewhere for other vehicles to win viewer ratings. Television also could diminish the popular appeal of the sports and athletes it televises by creating so much interest in corporate and financial gains within sport than fans no longer can find the fantasy world that gave sport its special appeal. In either case, television would contribute to a reduced role of sport as a symbolic refuge for fans as it unintentionally diminished its popular appeal.

# *Reality Confronts Fantasy in Sport*

The capacity of sport to inspire commitment or devotion among fans, athletes, and other participants is assumed here to depend on its capacity to function as an escape or fantasyland in which idealized values, aspirations, and imagery predominate. However, despite the best efforts of organizers, producers, and promoters of sport, reality may intrude into the fantasyland, and this intrusion may rob sport of its fantasylike qualities. For athletes, coaches, owners, and others actively involved in sport, there are likely to be problems, pressure, and disillusionment that severely test the romantic assumptions about sport they learned during their innocence. The losers and failures are especially unlikely to ignore or deny their problems, pressures, and disappointments.

Fans usually will find it easier to slip into and out of the sports fantasyland without being bothered or burdened by sport's less enchanting features. However, more, and more critical, coverage of sports today have made it increasingly difficult for fans to ignore the parallels between their imperfect society and the world of sport. Even if fans are able to hold off or suspend reality, excessive identification with fantasy heroes or too much devotion to their favorite teams can lead to their own pitfalls. Heroes lose. Home teams lose. When they do, serious fans who most want to find escape or vicarious fulfillment in their sports watching are likely to be most vulnerable to emotional letdowns that remind them of the frustrations of their everyday lives or exacerbate the pressures they wanted to escape.

We have seen in the previous chapters that in Little League, high school, college, Olympic, professional, and even adult leisure sports, the reality of competitive striving often fails to live up to the promise or moral standards of the dominant American sports creed or the success ideology of the larger society. Children, adolescents, and adults frequently try too hard to win, cheat, hurt their opponents, are frustrated or devastated by failure, and voluntarily or involuntarily leave sport. There are fewer and fewer opportunities to compete, much less succeed, in sport as athletes try to move up the American Sports Pyramid. The American sports system is a very steep pyramid with very little room at the top and with few who remain there as athletes for an extended period of time.

Even the world of adult leisure sports has become more elitist in recent years as it has become more organized and competitive. In a number of these sports, only the affluent and talented have regular chances to compete where they want. This development is contrary to the trend of democratization that generally has characterized leisure sports participation during this century.

In the world of highly organized sports from Little Leaguism to the highest professional and commercial levels, meritocratic and egalitarian principles are supposed to imply an opening up of participation opportunities to the talented and hard-working, whatever their social background or other ascribed characteristics. However, we have seen that opportunities continue to be blocked in a variety of ways for minorities, the less affluent, and women. The tragedy for the less privileged who pin their hopes for success entirely on a sports career is that they will have nothing to cushion their sports failure and no alternative legitimate or societally approved means—such as education or job training—to achieve respectability, mobility, and success.

Those who succeed in sport—whether as Little Leaguers, as high school or college athletes, as Olympians, as professionals, or perhaps even as serious competitive leisure players—may be extravagantly rewarded with popularity, respect, money, and hero worship. However, life for the serious and professionalized at all levels of American sport is not likely to be a fantasyland; it will be work. Sport *has* been a path to success and to an assortment of American Dreams for its champions and stars, but few of the champions and stars of the lower levels of sport are able to achieve a career at the top of the American Sports Pyramid. Most of the tiny fraction of aspirants who make it to the top find that their career as a professional or Olympic-level athlete is relatively brief. Many find their lives filled with unexpected pressures and demands. The pressures on American sports stars may not be greater than those experienced by the successful in other realms of American society. However, these pressures may be felt more intensely by sports stars because these stars are likely to be much younger and subjected to much more public scrutiny and criticism than the stars of industry, the professions, politics, and other realms of American life.

# *Sport in a Changing Society: Integrating Traditional Values with the Modern "Money Mania"*

Despite the intrusion of reality on several fronts, the institution of American sport continues to symbolize for many Americans a world of idealized traditional values, aspirations, and images. However, the sports world also reflects the changing character of American culture and society. Thus, modern sport has become corporate, highly commercialized, and rational-legal; and modern athletes have become concerned about their public image, legal rights, financial security, and commercial possibilities. These characteristics of modern sports and athletes have become incorporated into the modern sports fantasyland to some extent. In the words of Richard Lipsky, the more traditional Protestant Ethic values have merged with the new money mania to make modern sports stars "idols of consumption."[5] For example, shortly after the 1980 Olympics, the heroic image of hockey goalie Jim Craig and his warm relationship with his father were combined in a television advertising campaign for Coca-Cola.

The desire for money in American sport certainly is not new. Indeed, the modern commercialization of sport in the United States is rooted in the nineteenth century. However, the opening up of opportunities for quick and spectacular financial success to large numbers of athletes, coaches, investors, promoters, organizers, and others across a wide spectrum of sports is a fairly recent development of the past decade or so. Of course, in relation to the vast numbers who aspire to an American Dream of financial success through sport, only a tiny elite at the top ranks of the sports world currently enjoys the rich fruits of the recent commercial boom in sport. Nevertheless, their success symbolizes and dramatizes the spectacular possibilities of competitive striving in sport in America. These possibilities have led to much talk of money to be earned in sport today. For example, former Marquette University basketball coach Al McGuire remarked at a public banquet that he had learned three things in life he always tried to pass along to his player: "The first is to make as much money as you can. I forget the other two."[6]

McGuire's remark drew applause as well as laughter, reflecting the fans' willingness to accept or tolerate the pecuniary motives—and even greed—in modern sports. However, fans may become much less accepting or tolerant of financial aspirations and pecuniary motives when they lead to distractions from the action on the field of play where their fantasies are constructed—or worse, to interruptions in the schedule of their sports fantasies. The unsympathetic response by fans to the

1981 baseball strike and 1982 football strike illustrates the limits of their tolerance.

# Sport, Success, and Fulfillment

The functioning of modern sports as a fantasyland or symbolic refuge depends on how fans and other sports participants perceive and experience sport. Sport is likely to function as a symbolic refuge only to the extent that its image-makers, promoters, and heroes deflect attention from the contradictions and corruption of ideals in the real world of sport that threaten to invade the "refuge," undermine the credibility of its creed, and deprive it of its symbolic functions or influence[7] For athletes driven toward increasing professionalization and an obsession with winning or personal success, sport will not be an escape. For those who feel the pressures of competitive striving most intensely in sport, the American Dream may become an American Nightmare. Sport may be a fantasyland for many, but it cannot genuinely fulfill the dreams of success of those who merely watch nor those without the talent or opportunity to outcompete their opponents.

Sport does not *create* talent in those who aspire to success through it. It offers a chance to display talent for those already possessing it and willing to work to develop it[8] For minorities, the poor, and women, even the possession of natural talent and the willingness to work to develop it may not be sufficient to become stars—or perhaps even participants—in sport.

The American Dream and dominant American sports creed both seem to promise that virtuous striving within culturally approved channels will be richly rewarded. However, losing and setbacks are much more common experiences than winning and success in sport and elsewhere in American society. When a convoluted logic of competitive striving makes defeat or even second place a cause of deeply felt disappointment, self-doubt, or shame, competition no longer will be a stimulating challenge but will be a grim mission and losing will become unacceptable—something to be avoided or escaped by any means, including cheating and self-destructive drug use.

Sport may be least likely to produce an obsessive or neurotic drive to win and succeed when it is least tied to the dominant ideology and structure of the larger society. However, our definition of sport as *institutionalized* physical competition implies a link between sport and the larger society. Thus, physical competition may most escape the constraints, pressures, and obsessions of success-oriented striving when it is most playlike *and least sportlike.* The "New Games"[9] of recent years have offered an alternative to conventional sports for leisure players. They have de-emphasized structure and competition for the sake of unrestrained physical expression and fun. However, the New Games are not likely to replace mass sports spectacles nor highly organized and competitive sports in general. As long as Americans continue to transform their play into sport and their fun into obsessions with winning and individual success, sport will survive and the syndrome of competitive striving will survive along with it. As long as the American Dream continues to fire American aspirations and sport continues to be popular, sport is likely to remain a fertile source of fantasies and dreams that will become a reality for a few but will be fleeting or totally elusive for most.

# *Footnotes*

[1]Quoted in Harry Edwards, *Sociology of Sport* (Homewood, Ill.: Dorsey, 1973), p. 71.

[2]Frank Parkin, *Class Inequality and Political Order* (London: Paladin, 1972), pp. 85-86.

[3]John W. Loy, Barry D. McPherson, and Gerald Kenyon, *Sport and Social Systems* (Reading, Mass.: Addison-Wesley, 1978), pp. 413-414.

[4]In August 1981, television was in the middle of a dispute between the NCAA and the College Football Association (CFA), an NCAA splinter group of 61 major football schools wanting more control over big-time college football. In defiance of the NCAA, the CFA voted to approve conditionally a $180 million contract allowing NBC to televise football games of member schools for four years, beginning in 1982. The NCAA earlier had negotiated (but not yet finalized) a four-year, $263.5 million deal with CBS and ABC. The power struggle between the CFA and NCAA could have led to the NCAA disciplining or even expelling CFA schools remaining committed to their own television package. However, without its most prestigious members, the NCAA could not remain the powerful force in college athletics it had been for at least the prior few decades. In this struggle, the threat of a conflicting TV contract ultimately enabled the CFA to pressure the NCAA into a special meeting for all its members to consider a reorganization plan that would give the big-time football schools the contriol over their programs and financial relief for them that they have long desired. According to John Underwood, in a *Sports Illustrated* article ("To-do over what to do," September 21, 1981) about this matter, the stance of the television networks thorughout this battle between the rebellious CFA and the NCAA was to do whatever best served their business interests.

[5]Richard Lipsky, *How We Play the Game* (Boston: Beacon Press, 1981), p. 151.

[6]Quoted in Norman Cousins, "A sense of values," *Greeley (Colorado) Tribune* (October 1977); and cited also by George H. Sage, "Sport and American socieity: the quest for success." In *Sport and American Society: Selected Readings,* ed. by George H. Sage (Reading, Mass.: Addison-Wesley, 1980), 3rd ed., p. 118.

[7]Howard L. Nixon II, "Idealized functions of sport: religious and political socialization through sport," *Journal of Sport and Social Issues,* 6 (Spring/Summer 1982): 1-11.

[8]Howard L. Nixon II, *Sport and Social Organization* (Indianapolis: Bobbs-Merrill, 1976), pp. 44-45.

[9]The "New Games" have been promoted by Stewart Brand and discussed by George Leonard in *The Ultimate Athlete* (New York: Viking, 1974). See also, Stephen K. Figler, *Sport and Play in American Life* (Philadelphia: Saunders, 1981), pp. 309-312.

# Name Index

# Subject Index

National Collegiate Athletic Association (NCAA)—107, 110, 111, 113, 155
National Education Association—74, 77
National Federation of State High School Athletic Associations—74
National Junior College Athletic Association (NJCAA)—113
Nazi Olympics—145
New Games—250-251
New York Public School Athletic League (PSAL)—71, 72, 75
  Girls' Branch—72
newspapers—187

Olympic Creed—184
Olympic eligibility and Rule 26—196-197 (#10)
Olympic Games, financial costs—197-198 (#34)
Olympic sports—111
  and professionalism—144-145, 146, 147-148
  defined—197 (#11)
  organization and operation—152-156
options in professional sports contracts—170

Parental pressure—54-55, 59
"Peter Seitz Revolution"—170-172
physical education
  legislation—99 (#8)
  programs—72
play, defined—13-14
"players," defined—207
positive (and negative) addictions—230, 231, 234, 235
President's Commission on Olympic Sports—154, 155
President's Council on Youth Fitness—77
pressures from high school coaches—82, 84
professional athletes
  and career pressures—175-178
  and militance—170
  and money—166-170
  and retirement—179-183, 203 (#134)
  as heroes—172-175
professional sports
  and antitrust laws—149, 150, 151
  modern development—143-144, 148
  player strikes—152
  prize money—165, 167
professional sports club ownership
  changing patterns—157-158
  major costs—149-150
professional sports teams, financial status—158-159

# *About the Author*

Howard Nixon is an associate professor in the Department of Sociology at the University of Vermont. He has held this position for the past ten years teaching a variety of courses in sport sociology. He has authored several articles for numerous professional journals and currently is a member of the editorial boards of *The Review of Sport and Leisure* and *The Journal of Sport and Social Issues.* Dr. Nixon resides in Shelburne, Vermont, with his wife Sara and their three sons.